Life

Beginnings of Life
Animal Life
Plant Life
Evolution of Life
Behavior and Ecology of Life

Ricki Lewis

State University of New York at Albany

Contributing Authors

Animal Biology, Behavior and Ecology

Judith Goodenough
University of Massachusetts at Amherst

Plant Biology

Randall C. Moore
Wright State University

 Wm. C. Brown Publishers

Book Team

Editor *Kevin Kane*
Developmental Editor *Margaret J. Manders*
Production Editor *Sherry Padden*
Visuals/Design Consultant *Marilyn Phelps*
Designer *Mark Elliot Christianson*
Art Editor *Janice M. Roerig*
Photo Editor *Carol Smith*
Permissions Editor *Vicki Krug*
Visuals Processor *Joseph P. O'Connell*

 Wm. C. Brown Publishers

President *G. Franklin Lewis*
Vice President, Publisher *George Wm. Bergquist*
Vice President, Operations and Production *Beverly Kolz*
National Sales Manager *Virginia S. Moffat*
Group Sales Manager *Vince DiBlasi*
Vice President, Editor in Chief *Edward G. Jaffe*
Marketing Manager *Craig S. Marty*
Managing Editor, Production *Colleen A. Yonda*
Manager of Visuals and Design *Faye M. Schilling*
Production Editoral Manager *Julie A. Kennedy*
Production Editoral Manager *Ann Fuerste*
Publishing Services Manager *Karen J. Slaght*

WCB Group

President and Chief Executive Officer *Mark C. Falb*
Chairman of the Board *Wm. C. Brown*

Life
Front cover photo by © Robert Hernandez/Allstock

Part 1: Beginnings of Life
Front cover illustration by Mark Elliot Christianson based on photographs
by © Lloyd M. Beidler/Science Photo Library/Photo researcher, Inc.

Part 2: Animal Life
Front cover photo by © Erwin & Peggy Bauer

Part 3: Plant Life
Front cover photo by © Michael Fogden/Oxford Scientific Films

Part 4: Evolution of Life
Front cover photo by © Henry Ausloos/Animals Animals

Part 5: Behavior and Ecology of Life
Front cover photo by © Larry Lefever/Grant Heilman Photography

Photo Research by Toni Michaels

The credits section for this book begins on page C-1, and is considered
an extension of the copyright page.

Library of Congress Catalog Card Number: **Life:** 91-70426

ISBN **Life** Casebound, recycled interior stock: 0-697-05392-X
ISBN **Life** Paper binding, recycled interior stock: 0-697-14187-X
ISBN **Part 1: Beginnings of Life** Paper binding, recycled interior stock: 0-697-14193-4
ISBN **Part 2: Animal Life** Paper binding, recycled interior stock: 0-697-14195-0
ISBN **Part 3: Plant Life** Paper binding, recycled interior stock: 0-697-14197-7
ISBN **Part 4: Evolution of Life** Paper binding, recycled interior stock: 0-697-14199-3
ISBN **Part 5: Behavior and Ecology of Life** Paper binding, recycled interior stock: 0-697-14201-9
ISBN **Life** Boxed set, recycled interior stock: 0-697-14189-6

Printed in the United States of America by Wm. C. Brown Publishers,
2460 Kerper Boulevard, Dubuque, IA 52001

10 9 8 7 6 5 4 3 2 1

Brief Contents

Publisher's Note to
the Instructor

Recycled Paper

Life—in all its numerous binding options (listed here)—is printed on **recycled paper stock.** All of its ancillaries, as well as all advertising pieces for *Life*, will also be printed on recycled paper, subject to market availability.

Our goal in offering the text and its ancillary package on **recycled paper** is to take an important first step toward minimizing the environmental impact of our products. If you have any questions about recycled paper use, *Life*, its package, any of its binding options, or any of our other biology texts, feel free to call us at 1-800-331-2111. Thank you.

Kevin Kane
Senior Editor
Biology

Binding Option	Description	ISBN
Life, casebound	The full-length text (chapters 1-40), with hardcover binding.	0-697-05392-X
Life, paperbound	The full-length text, paperback covered and available at a significantly reduced price, when compared with the casebound version.	0-697-14187-X
Part 1 *Beginnings of Life*, paperbound	Part 1 features the first 4 units or 15 chapters of the text, covering the scientific method, the unity and diversity of life, basic chemistry, cell biology, reproduction and development, and genetics. This paperback option is available at a significantly reduced price when compared with both the full-length casebound and paperbound versions.	0-697-14193-4
Part 2 *Animal Life*	Part 2 features chapters 16-27 on the anatomy and physiology of animals—invertebrate, vertebrate, and human. This paperback is also available at a significantly reduced price when compared with the full-length versions of the text.	0-697-14195-0
Part 3 *Plant Life*	Part 3 features chapters 28-32 on plant form and function, with popular applications chapters on "Plants Through History" (28) and Plant Biotechnology (32). Paperback bound, it is available for a fraction of the full-length casebound or paperbound prices.	0-697-14197-7
Part 4 *Evolution of Life*	Part 4 features chapters 33-35 on evolution. Paperback bound, it is also available for a fraction of the full-length casebound or paperbound prices.	0-697-14199-3
Part 5 *Behavior and Ecology of Life*	Part 5 features chapters 36-40 on behavior and ecology. Paperback bound, it also sells for a fraction of the full-length book price.	0-697-14201-9
Life, the Boxed Set	The entire text, offered in an attractive, boxed set of all five paperback "splits." It is available at the same price as the full-length casebound text.	0-697-14189-6

Contents

The *Life* Learning System

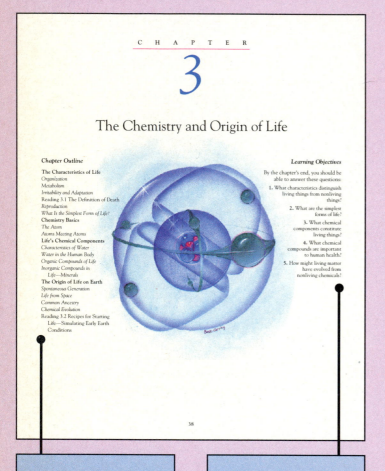

Key Concepts

At the ends of major sections within each chapter, summaries briefly highlight key concepts in the section, helping students focus their study efforts on the basics.

Dramatic Visuals Program

Colorful, informative photographs and illustrations enhance the learning program of the text as well as spark interest and discussion of important topics.

Chapter Outlines

Each chapter begins with an outline. These will allow students to tell at a glance how the chapter is organized and what major topics have been included in the chapter. The outlines include the first and second level heads for the chapter.

Learning Objectives

Each chapter begins with a list of concepts stressed in the chapter. This listing introduces the student to the chapter by organizing its content into a few meaningful sentences. The concepts provide a framework for the content of each chapter.

Content shown in the sample chapter-opener page:

C H A P T E R

3

The Chemistry and Origin of Life

Chapter Outline

The Characteristics of Life
Organization
Metabolism
Irritability and Adaptation
Reading 3.1 The Definition of Death
Reproduction
What Is the Simplest Form of Life?
Chemistry Basics
The Atom
Atoms Meeting Atoms
Life's Chemical Components
Characteristics of Water
Water in the Human Body
Organic Compounds of Life
Inorganic Compounds in Life—Minerals
The Origin of Life on Earth
Spontaneous Generation
Life from Space
Common Ancestry
Chemical Evolution
Reading 3.2 Recipes for Starting Life—Simulating Early Earth Conditions

Learning Objectives

By the chapter's end, you should be able to answer these questions:
1. What characteristics distinguish living things from nonliving things?
2. What are the simplest forms of life?
3. What chemical components constitute living things?
4. What chemical compounds are important to human health?
5. How might living matter have evolved from nonliving chemicals?

38

Content shown in the sample text page:

68   Cell Biology

Viruses—Simpler Than Cells

The simplest form of life is a unicellular organism with no organelles, such as a bacterium. However, in chapter 3 we encountered several types of "infectious agents" that appear to be living while they are infecting cells but otherwise seem to be nonliving chemicals. Before describing how we examine cells and their contents, it is interesting to take a comparative look at the viruses, both to point out their noncellular organization and because they exert very noticeable effects on human health, causing such minor ills as colds and influenza and such deadly ones as AIDS. Reading 4.1 describes effects of the herpes simplex virus.

A virus consists of a nucleic acid (DNA or RNA) surrounded by protein. Figure 4.2 illustrates the human immunodeficiency virus (HIV), which causes AIDS. A virus must be within a cell to reproduce, and hence it is called an obligate parasite. Many viruses, such as HIV, cannot survive outside of a living cell. Some other viruses are afforded protection from the physical environment by their protein coverings. A virus reproduces by injecting its DNA or RNA into the host cell, where it situates itself within the host's DNA. In fact, viral DNA sequences can probably be found within your own chromosomes. (An RNA virus, such as HIV, is called a retrovirus and must first make a replica of its RNA in DNA form.)

Once viral DNA integrates into the host's DNA, it can either remain there and be replicated along with the host's DNA whenever the cell divides, but not cause harm, or the viral DNA can actively take over the cell, leading eventually to the cell's death. To do this, some of the virus's genes direct the host cell to replicate viral DNA rather than the host DNA. As viral DNA accumulates in the cell, some of it is used to manufacture proteins. (Recall from chapter 3 that the function of DNA is to provide information from which the cell constructs proteins.) Within hours or days, the infected cell fills with viral DNA and protein. Some of the proteins wrap around the DNA to form new viral particles. Finally, a viral enzyme is produced that cuts through the host cell's outer membrane. The cell bursts, releasing new viruses.

Viruses are known to infect all kinds of organisms, including animals, plants, and bacteria. A particular type of virus, however, infects only certain species, which constitute its *host range*. (Refer back to figure 3.6 for an illustration of a tomato infected by the tomato bunchy top virus.) Figure 4.3 illustrates what happens to a moth infected by a type of virus called a baculovirus.

Figure 4.2
A virus is a nucleic acid coated with protein. The human immunodeficiency virus (HIV), which causes AIDS, consists of RNA surrounded by several layers of proteins. Once inside a human cell (usually a T cell, part of the immune system), the virus uses an enzyme to convert its RNA to DNA, which then inserts into the host DNA. HIV damages the human body's protection against disease by killing T cells and by using these cells to make more of itself.
From "AIDS viron" (January 1987 cover painting), copyright © 1987, by Scientific American, Inc., George V. Kelvin, all rights reserved.

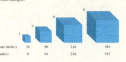

Readings

Throughout *Life*, selected readings both elaborate and entertain. Some describe experiments, some provide health information, and others are closer looks at specific topics. All readings are written by the author.

Tables

Numerous strategically-placed tables list and summarize important information, making it readily accessible for efficient study.

To Think About

Located at the end of each chapter, these questions are springboards for class discussions and term paper topics.

Boldfaced Words

New terms appear in boldface print as they are introduced within the text and are immediately defined in context. If any of these terms are reintroduced in later chapters, they are italicized. Key terms are defined in the text glossary with appropriate page reference.

Chapter Summaries

At the end of each chapter is a summary. This should help students more easily identify important concepts and better facilitate their learning of chapter concepts

Questions

The end-of-chapter questions often continue the storytelling style of the chapter, using anecdotes and experiments from the chapter to illustrate and apply concepts.

Suggested Readings

A list of readings at the end of each chapter suggests references that can be used for further study of topics covered in the chapter. The items listed in this section were carefully chosen for readability and accessibility.

Preface

Life was written with the nonbiology major in mind, but contains enough information to be suitable for a majors' course too.

Diversity in Action

While human examples and applications are emphasized, *Life*'s diversity is treated early in a separate chapter, later in an appendix on taxonomy, and is logically integrated into all chapters. The animal biology chapters, for example, explore a deep-sea shrimp's vision, an insect's exoskeleton, a cow's digestion, and much more. The behavior and ecology chapters are filled with glimpses into the lives of a variety of organisms, from aardwolves to fire ants to naked mole rats. The reader of *Life* will learn many new things, but also encounter familiar territory. The science of biology will not seem foreign— it will be fun and make sense.

Discovery and Evolution

Two conceptual threads weave their way through *Life*. The book opens with the first theme, discovery. The story of how the sweetener aspartame was discovered takes the student through the scientific method and experimental design, yet points out how the initial detection of the food additive was very much a surprise.

In chapter 2, "The Diversity of Life," taxonomy is alive and vibrant in the treetops of a Peruvian wildlife preserve, where biologists catalog the abundance of insect life; and in such an unlikely place as an urban fish market. A pair of children playing with spectacles led to the development of the compound microscope, as described in chapter 4. In chapter 6, "Biological Energy," the student can be the discoverer by using the reactions of photosynthesis to develop a photograph on a leaf. The inborn errors of

metabolism, PKU (chapter 15, "Genetic Disease: Diagnosis and Treatment") was discovered thanks to a mother's alertness of her infant's odd-smelling diapers. And a simple treatment for newborn jaundice (chapter 24, "The Digestive System") was discovered by an observant English nurse changing "nappies" in the sunlight. Chapter 15 also tells the story of how a seemingly drunken sailor and his 5,000 living descendants helped provide the first genetic marker.

Not all discovery is accidental. The look at "Molecular Genetics" in chapter 13 is liberally sprinkled with descriptions of the most elegant experiments ever performed. The scientific method is reviewed in chapter 36, "The Behavior of Individuals," as students at the University of Miami track singing birds, and in chapter 38 "Populations," through ecologists conducting wildlife surveys. The creation of an artificial mini-biosphere, described in chapter 39 "Ecosystems," is an exciting view of scientific investigation—whether it works or not.

The second conceptual thread, evolution, accustoms the reader to continually wonder, "How did all of this happen?" How did a duo of protein and nucleic acid join forces long ago to form the first cell? How could random mutations in those early cells build the metabolic pathways of today? How did eukaryotic cells come by their highly successful "bags within a bag" organization? How do species arise, change, become extinct? How have our ideas about evolution themselves evolved?

Humor, History, and Human Values

An occasional foray into humor can help students learn. Consider the example of epistasis in chapter 11, borrowed from the soap opera "Gen-

eral Hospital," or the opening to chapter 34 "The Forces of Evolutionary Change," a love story between a moose and a dairy cow.

Historical references add interest and chronicle the evolution of ideas. The confusing multiple phenotypes of the blood disorder porphyria, for example, may have led the "mad king" George III to provoke the American Revolution. The study of genetics begins with early agricultural efforts nearly 10,000 years ago. How different were Edward Jenner's problems with how best to test his smallpox vaccine (chapter 28, "Plants Through History") from today's scientists' attempts to test AIDS vaccines? The state of the American temperate forest today reflects pioneer activity over the past centuries. Recent history brings the ecology chapters alive, from Mt. St. Helens to the Yellowstone fires to the nuclear explosion at Chernobyl.

Examining human values teaches the student to develop informed opinions and judgments about biologically relevant issues—a skill that will last long after the steps of glycolysis or the parts of the cell are forgotten. Should a pregnant woman who smokes or drinks alcohol be responsible for the health effects on her fetus? Should an employer be told the results of an employee's genetic marker test for Alzheimer's disease? Should we take extraordinary measures to save extremely premature babies if they will be handicapped after (or by) the treatment? Should we even attempt to clean animals drenched in oil from tanker spills? Should we limit reproduction? These disturbing queries are most often found in the "To Think About" sections at the chapters' ends, both so that they will not distract from learning major facts and concepts and so that the student is left thinking.

Integrating Technology

Technology has given new, exciting meaning to some difficult subjects. Discussing the development of extraembryonic structures segues into a peek at chorionic villus sampling. Liposomes are but an extension of cell membrane structure and function. Teaching DNA replication is no longer a hurdle, now that we have the polymerase chain reaction to demonstrate elegantly the power of the process. Filling in the details of food webs no longer requires being on the scene of a meal, thanks to stable isotope tracing (chapter 39, "Ecosystems").

The chapters on plant anatomy and physiology are bracketed by two unique applications chapters—chapter 28, "Plants Through History," chronicles our harvesting of the major crop plants, and chapter 32, "Plant Biotechnology," looks at how molecular and cellular techniques are likely to continue that harvest, via the genetic alteration of plant life.

Finally, Appendix A, "Microscopy", provides a closer look at the technology that really breathed life into biology, from the first crude lenses to today's powerful confocal microscopes. Yet the very technology that has taught us so much and made our lives so comfortable can get out of control, upsetting the delicate balance of life. Chapter 40 "Environmental Concerns," describes these problems, but emphasizes natural resiliency, leaving the reader, ultimately, with a sense of hope and purpose:

"This book has shown you the wonder that is life, from its constituent chemicals, to its cells, tissues, and organs, and all the way up to the biosphere. Do nothing to harm life—and do whatever you can to preserve its precious diversity. For in diversity lies resiliency, and the future of life on earth."

Pedagogy

A great deal of creative energy has gone into the pedagogical aids, and some are quite different from those in the run-of-the-mill textbook. (For a visual walkthrough of these aids, examine the *Life* Learning System preview in this book's frontmatter.) The end-of-chapter "Questions" often continue the storytelling style of the chapter, using anecdotes and experiments from the literature to illustrate and apply concepts. The "To Think About" questions are springboards for class discussions and term paper topics. "Suggested Readings" go far beyond *Scientific American* and other textbooks, including sources such as *Science News, FDA Consumer* and the *New York Times*—sources that students are more likely to read, understand, and appreciate.

"Learning Objectives," which open the chapters, "Key Concepts" following major sections, and end-of-chapter summaries reinforce main points.

"Readings" throughout the chapters both elaborate and entertain. Some describe experiments: "Enticing Cells to Divide in the Laboratory," "Recipes for Starting Life—Simulating Early Earth Conditions," "Tracking Development in Different Organisms;" some provide health information, "Cardiovascular Spare Parts," "Jon and Linda—The Plight of an Infertile Couple," "Our Overdrugged Elderly," "Steroids and Athletes—An Unhealthy Combination," "The War on Cancer;" others are closer looks, "A Closer Look at an Organelle—The Lysosome," "Tumor Necrosis Factor," "Odd Human Traits," or "The Herpes Simplex Virus." Some are practical, "Nutrition and the Athlete," "Food Inhalation and the Heimlich Maneuver" and many highlight diversity "Falling Felines," "Rumbles, Roars, Screeches, and Squeals—Animal Communication," or "Sexual Seasons."

Ancillaries

Instructor's Manual/Test Item File

Prepared by Heather McKean and James Hanegan of Eastern Washington University, the instructor's manual offers helpful suggestions for course outlines and developing daily lectures. Each chapter provides key concepts, key terms, chapter outlines, learning objectives, answers to the text's end-of-chapter questions, and suggested audiovisual materials. There are also 25 to 50 objective questions in a *Test Item File* in the back of the manual. (ISBN 0-697-10181-9)

Laboratory Manual

Written by Alice Jacklet, a colleague of mine at SUNY-Albany, the *Laboratory Manual* strongly emphasizes and guides students through *the process of scientific inquiry*. Beautifully illustrated in full-color, it features 20 self-contained exercises that can easily be reorganized to suit individual course needs. (ISBN 0-697-05637-6)

Laboratory Resource Guide

This helpful prep guide offers instructions for assembling lab materials and preparing reagents, as well as suggestions for using the Lab Manual in different kinds of lab settings. (ISBN 0-697-10178-9)

Customized Laboratory Manual

Inexpensive, one-color separates of each lab in the Laboratory Manual are available for individual use, for combination with labs of local origination, or for combination with labs from other Wm. C. Brown manuals. All materials will be custom, spiral-bound for your convenience. Contact your local Wm. C. Brown sales representative for more details.

Readings in Biology

A compilation of original journal and magazine articles by Ricki Lewis is also available to students at a nominal price. The readings, which correlate closely with the sequence of topics in the text, present additional high-interest information on cell biology, genetics, reproduction, and animal biology. (ISBN-0-697-12059-7)

Student Study Guide

Also written by Heather McKean and James Hanegan, the study guide offers students a variety of exercises and keys for testing their comprehension of basic as well as difficult concepts. (ISBN 0-697-05636-8)

TestPak

This computerized classroom management system/service includes a data base of objective test questions, copyable student self-quizzes, and a grade-recording program. Disks are available for IBM, Apple, and MacIntosh PC computers and require no programming experience. If a computer is not available, instructors can choose questions from the *Test Item File* and phone or FAX in their request for a printed exam, which will be returned within 48 hours.

Transparencies and Slides

More than 200 overhead *transparencies* or a comparable *slide set* is available for free to all adopters, on request. The acetates and slides feature key illustrations from the text that, in most cases, have images and labels that have been significantly enlarged for more effective classroom display. (Transparencies: 0-697-10179-7; Slides: ISBN 0-697-10167-3)

Customized Transparency Service

For those adopters interested in receiving acetates of text figures not included in the standard transparency package, a select number of acetates will be custom-made upon request. Contact your local Wm. C. Brown sales representative for more details.

Extended Lecture Outline Software

This instructor software features extensive outlines of each text chapter with a brief synopsis of each subtopic to assist in lecture preparation. Written in ASCII files for maximum utility, it is available in IBM, Apple, or Mac formats. It is free to all adopters, upon request.

You Can Make a Difference
by Judith Getis

This short, inexpensive supplement offers students practical guidelines for recycling, conserving energy, disposing of hazardous wastes, and other pollution controls. It can be shrink wrapped with the text, at minimal additional cost. (ISBN 0-697-13923-9)

How to Study Science
by Fred Drewes, Suffolk County Community College

This excellent new workbook offers students helpful suggestions for meeting the considerable challenges of a science course. It offers tips on how to take notes; how to get the most out of laboratories; as well as on how to overcome science anxiety. The book's unique design helps to stir critical thinking skills, while facilitating careful note-taking on the part of the student. (ISBN 0-697-14474-7)

The Life Science Lexicon
by William N. Marchuk, Red Deer College

This portable, inexpensive reference helps introductory-level students quickly master the vocabulary of the life sciences. Not a dictionary, it carefully explains the rules of word construction and derivation, while giving complete definitions of all important terms. (ISBN 0-697-12133-X)

Biology Study Cards
by Kent Van De Graaff, R. Ward Rhees, and Christopher H. Creek, Brigham Young University

This boxed set of 300, two-sided study cards provides a quick, yet thorough visual synopsis of all key biological terms and concepts in the general biology curriculum. Each card features a masterful illustration, pronunciation guide, definition and description in context. (ISBN 0-697-03069-5)

Special Software and Multi-Media Ancillaries

Life on Earth Videotapes

This critically acclaimed, twin-cassette package by David Attenborough, features thirteen programs, each about 25 minutes in duration, on Life's Diversity. Each cassette also features "Chapter Search," an on-screen numerical code for quick-scan access to each of the cassettes' thirteen programs and subtopics. The Life on Earth videotapes are available for free to all adopters of the text, upon request. (ISBN 0-697-14631-6)

Program Summary

1. THE INFINITE VARIETY
   Nature's secrets found in ancient places.
2. BUILDING BODIES
   First signs of life in the seas.
3. THE FIRST FORESTS
   The world of plants, primitive and grand.
4. THE SWARMING HORDES
   The ingenious adaptability of insects.
5. CONQUEST OF THE WATERS
   Complexities of the great groups of fish.
6. INVASION OF THE LAND
   The emergence of amphibian creatures.
7. VICTORS OF THE DRY LAND
   Reptiles and the dinosaur dynasty.
8. LORDS OF THE AIR
   Feathers, wings and birds in flight.
9. THE RISE OF THE MAMMALS
   Where dinosaurs failed, mammals succeeded.
10. THEME AND VARIATIONS
    The extremes of mammal evolution.
11. THE HUNTS AND THE HUNTED
    Patterns of behavior in the animal kingdom.
12. LIFE IN THE TREES
    Spotlighting monkeys and their relatives.
13. THE COMPULSIVE COMMUNICATORS
    The development and achievements of humans.

Bio Sci II Videodisk

This critically acclaimed laser disk, produced by Videodiscovery for Wm. C. Brown, features more than 12,000 still and moving images, with a complete, bar-coded directory. Contact your Wm. C. Brown sales representative for more details. (ISBN 0-697-12121-6)

Mac-Hypercard and IBM Linkway Biostacks

These easy-to-use MacIntosh and IBM disks allow instructors to access the Bio Sci II laserdisk through a series of programmed lecture sequences. Contact your Wm. C. Brown representative for more details. (Mac Hypercard: 0-697-13273-1; IBM Linkway Biostacks, 3.5: 0-697-13275-7; IBM Linkway Biostacks, 5.2: 0-697-13274-9)

The Gundy-Weber Knowledge Map of the Human Body
by G. Craig Gundy, Weber State University

This thirteen disk, Mac-Hypercard program is for use by instructors and students alike. It features masterfully prepared computer graphics, animations, labeling exercises, self-tests and practice questions to help students examine the systems of the human body. Contact your local Wm. C. Brown representative or call 1-800-351-7671.

The Knowledge Map Diagrams

1. Introduction, Tissues, Integument System (0-697-13255-2)
2. Viruses, Bacteria, Eukaryotic Cells (0-697-13257-9)
3. Skeletal System (0-697-13258-7)
4. Muscle System (0-697-13259-5)
5. Nervous System (0-697-13260-9)
6. Special Senses (0-697-13261-7)
7. Endocrine System (0-697-13262-5)
8. Blood and the Lymphatic System (0-697-13263-3)
9. Cardiovascular System (0-697-13264-1)
10. Respiratory System (0-697-13265-X)
11. Digestive System (0-697-13266-8)
12. Urinary System (0-697-13267-6)
13. Reproductive System (0-697-13268-4)

Demo - (0-697-13256-0)
Complete Package - (0-697-13269-2)

GenPak: A Computer Assisted Guide to Genetics
by Tully Turney, Hampden-Sydney College

This Mac-Hypercard program features numerous, interactive/tutorial (problem-solving) exercises in Mendelian, molecular, and population genetics at the introductory level. (ISBN 0-697-13760-0)

Acknowledgments

Most of the credit for this book goes to the stories of life themselves. But thanks must also go to the scores of magazine editors who have shown me how to explain concepts clearly and concisely, yet retain a distinctive style; to the manuscript reviewers who corrected my errors and contributed so many valuable insights; to Gail Marsella, Randy Moore, Tom Gregg, Tom Wissing, and Judy Goodenough for assistance with selected chapters; to a fantastic bookteam; to my editor, Kevin Kane, and my developmental editor, Marge Manders, at Wm. C. Brown, who managed to keep me going at those times when the automatic pilot faltered; to my parents, who encouraged a little girl who brought home all sorts of creatures and to my parents-in-law who never lost faith; to my three daughters, whom I gestated along with this book; and most of all to my husband, Larry, who faithfully photocopied zillions of pages, listened to countless reviews, and never tired of hearing, yet one more time, "I've only got one more sentence left!" This really is the last sentence.

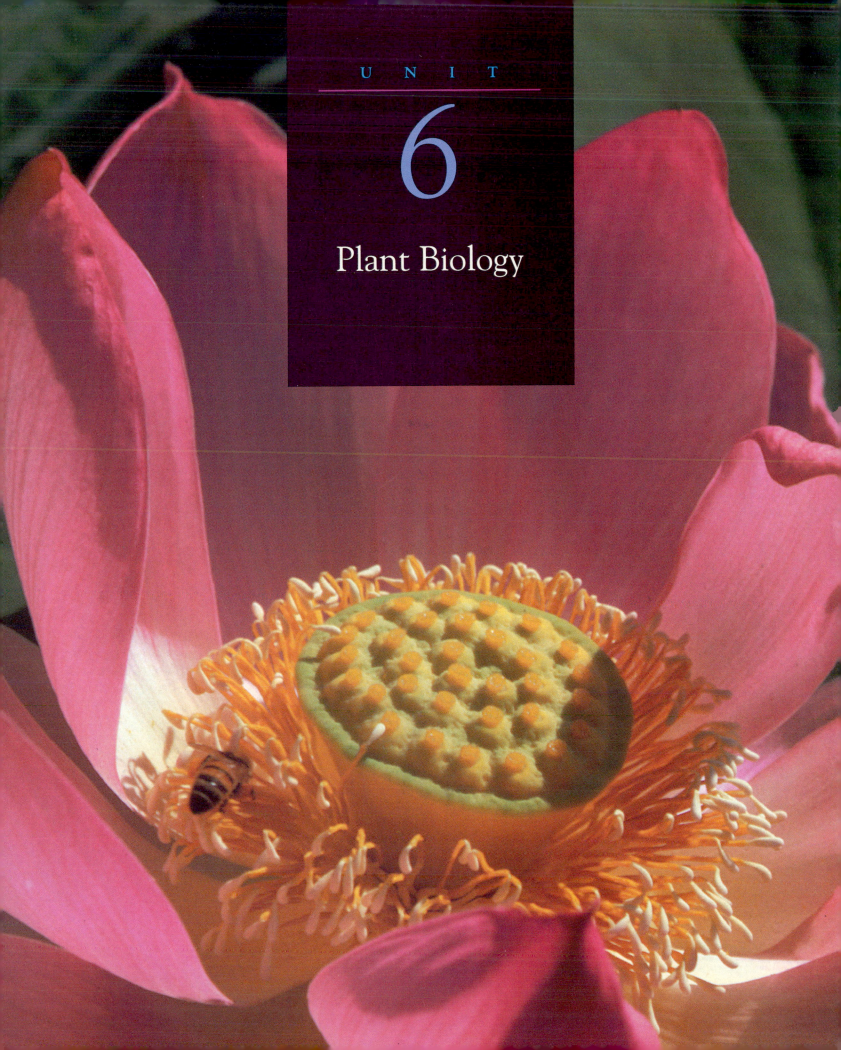

28

Plants Through History

Learning Objectives

By the chapter's end, you should be able to answer these questions:

1. In what ways do we use and depend upon plants?

2. How might agriculture have arisen? Where and when did it arise?

3. What are the major parts of a grain, and how are they used in the human diet?

4. From what types of plants is it thought that the modern bread wheats and modern corn evolved?

5. In what major way does the history of rice differ from that of wheat and corn?

6. How might we use the plant amaranth?

7. What are some examples of plant biochemicals used as medicines?

8. How have plants helped to spread malaria, as well as to treat it?

I t is difficult to name an area of human existence in which plants are not important or even vital. Grains, fruits, and vegetables feed us. Fibrous stems and leaves clothe us. Plants generate the oxygen we breathe. Trees provide us with building materials, paper to write on, and welcome shade on hot days. Many plants manufacture chemicals that have important medicinal properties or synthesize brilliant dyes, industrial chemicals, or useful oils (see table 2.6). The colors and fragrances of flowers and foliage satisfy our aesthetic senses. Plant-derived spices enhance our enjoyment of food. Yet plants are not entirely beneficial to people. Plants produce some of the most potent poisons known. Overgrowth of some plants clogs streams and water pipes. Weeds harm crops, and some plants can cause severe allergic reactions in people.

For many centuries, perhaps even longer, humans have learned to recognize those plants that help us and those that harm us. As a result, plants have become an integral part of human civilization (fig. 28.1).

Plants as Food

Obtaining a wide variety of plant foods today is as simple as a trip to the supermarket or a visit to the garden or farm stand. But for our ancestors living 12,000 years ago, finding a meal was quite a challenge. Tribes of people were constantly on the move in search of food. In what is now the United States, some of our forebearers hunted the large plant-eating mammals that roamed the great plains, while others collected seeds, nuts, edible roots, fruits, and grasses. In this **hunter-gatherer** lifestyle, people were at the mercy of the environment. If there was no food in a given area, they had no choice but to move on or starve (fig. 28.2).

From Hunter-Gatherers to Farmers—The Dawn of Agriculture

The dependence upon the environment for food changed dramatically between 12,000 and 10,000 years ago. Several factors contributed to this first spark of civilization. The last ice age was ending. As the

a.
b.

Figure 28.1
The banana and the coconut—staples of the tropics. *a*. The banana has been cultivated in tropical Africa for the past 2,000 years. The starchy bananas called plantains are a major part of the human diet in this part of the world. Sweeter varieties are popular in the United States. *b*. The 50 to 100 coconuts that grow on a palm tree each year provide proteins, oils, and carbohydrates, while the trunks, leaves, and coconut shells make excellent building materials.

a.
b.

Figure 28.2
Coffee and tea. *a*. Coffee was originally cultivated in the mountains of Ethiopia and was spread elsewhere by Arab traders. Today, *Coffee arabica* is grown for export in 50 nations. *b*. Tea comes from *Camellia sinensis* and originated in the mountains of subtropical Asia. *c*. Both coffee and tea contain caffeine, which has a stimulating effect on the human central nervous system.

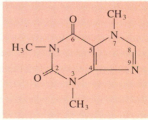

c.

great ice sheets receded, the land that was revealed became inhabited by a vast assemblage of animals and flowering plants. Humans no longer had to follow herds or gather berries to eat, because food could be found in more areas. The people could stay in one place, eating readily available small game, fish, and wild plants. By about 10,000 years ago, humans learned to take care of certain animals, such as wild sheep and goats, so that they could rely on a continual supply of milk and meat. The wild weeds that sustained many tribes also became subject to human interference. The transition from weed to crop may have happened almost by accident, perhaps as follows: A wandering band of humans found some tasty grain growing in a sparsely vegetated area. They stopped, set up camp, and ate the grain. The next day they moved on, leaving some of the grain on the ground where they had eaten it. A few months or even years later, the same people came back to the campsite, and, to their initial surprise, found the same type of grain growing in abundance. Eventually, the connection between the discarded grain of one season and the bountiful crop of the next was discovered. The people learned to leave seeds in the ground intentionally to ensure a future food supply.

Gradually, these early farmers discovered more about plant reproduction and used their knowledge to improve their food supply. They deduced by trial and error how to plant the correct seeds in the right soil and to see that they got enough water to sprout. They learned to recognize when the plants had developed sufficiently to harvest. The people regularly saved the seeds from one season's most useful plants to sow the next year's crop, thereby encouraging certain combinations of traits (a practice called **artificial selection**) that might not have predominated in the wild (fig. 28.3).

Later on, people learned to preserve their harvested food by drying it, reducing even further their dependence on the unpredictable weather and climate. The domestication of animals and the intentional planting and cultivation of crops marked the birth of **agriculture.** Farming probably arose independently in many places around the world. Archaeological evidence indicates domestication of sheep and goats and cultivation of grassy wheats and barley in the Fertile Crescent region of what is now

Figure 28.3

Jojoba—an old plant finds new uses. The earliest farmers fashioned crops by taking robust specimens and using them for the next season's crop. This technique also works well today. Before 1980, the jojoba plant was an obscure grayish green bush growing in the southwest United States. Then some innovative people realized the potential for the light golden oil from jojoba's seeds as a lubricant, a cosmetic ingredient, and even as a no-cholesterol cooking oil. In 1980, seeds from wild-growing jojoba were collected and used to start the first cultivated plantings. The next season, researchers took cuttings from the healthiest bushes and used them to start the next crop. Today, the United States' jojoba yield grows by at least 50% a year.

the Middle East about 11,000 years ago. Gradually, agriculture spread to Eastern Europe around 8,000 years ago, to the Western Mediterranean and Central Europe about 7,000 years ago, and to the British empire about 4,000 years ago. Egyptian and Assyrian tombs, mummy wrappings, paintings, and hieroglyphics from 4,000 years ago depict a rich agricultural society, which cultivated pomegranates, olives, grapes, figs, dates, and cereals. A similar spread of agriculture occurred in the Americas, based upon native corn, tomatoes, and chili peppers. Yams and cassava were early crops in Africa.

With the growth of towns and then cities, the human influence on cultivated plants spread. The distribution of crops across the planet today indicates that in many cases, when humans colonized new lands, they brought their native plants with them and likewise carried new plant varieties from the new land back to the old. Tracing the origins of crop plants is difficult because archaeological evidence is often destroyed over time. The available evidence, however, suggests that very different crop plants were domesticated in the Old and New Worlds. Today, thanks to efficient transportation, many different kinds of plants are grown quite far from where they originated (table 28.1).

Today, more than 80% of the total kilocalories consumed by humans comes from crop plants, mostly from wheat, rice, corn, potatoes, sweet potatoes, and manioc (the source of tapioca). The cereals provide much dietary carbohydrate, and the seeds of legumes (beans, lentils, peas, peanuts, and soybeans) are rich in protein. Cereals have different types of amino acids than legumes, so eating these two foods together provides a good protein balance. The best plant-derived nutrition combines a cereal (a rich carbohydrate source) with a legume (a protein source) with a green leafy vegetable (rich in vitamins and minerals) and perhaps small amounts of sunflower oil, avocado, or olives (which provide fats). Plants also yield spices, which have been used to flavor food since at least the time of the Roman Empire. Spices can also preserve foods, which made possible the colonization of the New World. The biochemicals that we use as spices offer a defense against herbivores to the plant.

Table 28.1
Agricultural Origins

Time (years ago)	Location	Crops
15,000	Yellow River, China	Millet, rice
12,000	Nile Valley, Egypt	Barley, wheat, lentils, chickpeas
	Thailand	Rice
10,000	Fertile Crescent: Iran, Iraq, Syria, Lebanon	Barley, wheat, lentils, broad beans, olives, dates, grapes, pomegranates
9,000–8,000	Mexico, Peru	Corn, kidney beans, lima beans, peanuts, chili peppers, tomatoes, tobacco, cocoa, pumpkins, avocados, squashes
5,000	Africa	Sorghum, millet, okra, coffee, cotton
4,000	Andes (South America)	Potatoes
3,000	India	Cotton

KEY CONCEPTS

About 12,000 years ago, humans were hunter-gatherers, moving to find food. As the ice age ended, ample food was revealed, so gradually people stayed in one place and raised animals and crops for food. Agriculture dawned as people artificially selected crops and learned to store and preserve plant foods and domesticate animals. Agriculture began at different times in different parts of the world. Agriculture changed as people moved to start new settlements and took their crops and animals with them. Today 80% of kilocalories consumed by humans comes from plant foods.

Cereals—Staples of the Human Diet

In the Orient, the principal food is rice. Corn is a major part of the human diet in South America. In the United States, many of our foods are based on wheat. Rice, corn, and wheat, along with oats, rye, barley, and a few others, are all **cereals,** defined as members of the grass family (Poaceae), which have seeds that can be stored for long periods of time. The seed is the kernel or grain, and it consists of the embryo, a large starch supply called the **endosperm,** and outer protective layers called the **aleurone** and the **pericarp,** which are rich in protein, lipid, and vitamins. Figure 28.4 shows the parts of a wheat grain and their dietary uses. Although wheat, corn, and rice feed much of the human population, other edible cereals await discovery.

Wheat

Modern wheat comes in thousands of varieties. It grows in a range of climates, from the Arctic to the equator, from below sea level to 10,000 feet (3,048 meters) above it, and from areas with less than 2 inches (5 centimeters) of annual rainfall to places with more than 70 inches (178 centimeters) of rain per year. Most wheat is used for food. The grain of the "hard" bread wheats contains 11% to 15% protein, mostly of a type called gluten, and when ground and mixed with water it forms an elastic dough that is excellent for making bread. The grain of the "soft" bread wheats contains 8% to 10% protein and is best for making cakes, cookies, crackers, and pastries.

Today's wheats fall into three categories, based upon their number of chromosomes—14 (diploid), 28 (tetraploid), or 42 (hexaploid) (table 28.2). The bread wheats are hexaploid; durum wheat used to make macaroni is tetraploid. Geneticists study the number of chromosomes in modern wheats to reconstruct the evolution of these important crop plants. It is a fascinating and complex story. Wheat as we know it apparently evolved from an accidental merger between a distant

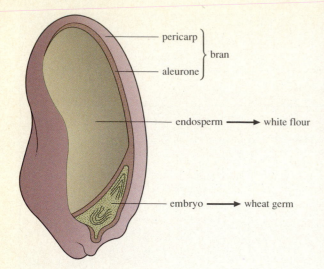

Figure 28.4
Anatomy of a wheat grain. Different components of a wheat grain give us different food products. The endosperm comprises 80% of the grain, and when separated and mashed, it yields a white flour. If the embryo, or wheat germ, is included along with the endosperm, the resulting flour is more nutritious than pure white flour because of vitamins in the germ, but it does not last as long, because of the high fat content of the germ. Bran, also vitamin-rich, consists of the pericarp and aleurone layers, which surround the endosperm. Flour made from ground whole wheat grains is called graham.

wheat ancestor and a weedy grass. It may have happened as follows: About 10,000 years ago, wandering peoples in what is now Jericho, in Israel, came upon a rich oasis, a spring in the desert ringed by hills covered with wild grass. In looking about for food, the people discovered that the grain held in the grass, when ground, made a fine flour. For many years, they did not know how to encourage the grass's growth intentionally, so each season they would simply forage for whatever nature provided.

Then about 8,000 years ago, something happened that was to have profound effects on agriculture and human civilization. The grass that the people had grown fond of, really an ancient wheat called Einkorn, crossbred with another type of grass that was not very good to eat (fig. 28.5). The hybrid grass then underwent a genetic accident (nondisjunction) that prevented the separation of chromosomes

Table 28.2 Types of Wheat			
Type	**Number of Chromosomes**	**Location**	**Uses**
Einkorn	14 (diploid)	Hills of southeast Europe, southwest Asia	Cattle and horse feed
Emmer	28 (tetraploid)	Europe, United States	Stock feed, macaroni
Bread wheat	42 (hexaploid)	Throughout the world	Bread

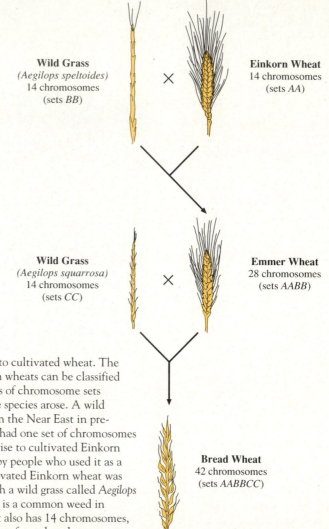

Figure 28.5
From wild grass to cultivated wheat. The fact that modern wheats can be classified by their numbers of chromosome sets suggests how the species arose. A wild wheat growing in the Near East in pre-Neolithic times had one set of chromosomes (AA) and gave rise to cultivated Einkorn wheat, perhaps by people who used it as a cereal. The cultivated Einkorn wheat was then crossed with a wild grass called *Aegilops speltoides*, which is a common weed in wheat fields that also has 14 chromosomes, but 7 of the A type from the wheat parent and 7 of the B type from the grass parent. An "accident" in which the chromosome number doubled then led to the appearance of Emmer wheat, which has 28 chromosomes (AABB). The bread wheats arose in the Bronze Age, when Emmer wheat crossed with another grassy weed, *Aegilops squarrosa*, a pest also known as goat grass, which had 14 chromosomes of yet a third type, CC. The initial hybrid of Emmer wheat with goat grass had 21 chromosomes (7 A, 7 B, and 7 C), which accidentally doubled to yield a wheat with 42 chromosomes (AABBCC), which is modern bread wheat.

Figure 28.6
A popular grain hybrid is triticale, which is a combination of wheat (genus *Triticum*) and rye (genus *Secale*). The cells of triticale are polyploid, containing a complete set of chromosomes from wheat as well as a set from rye. The plant has the high yield of wheat and the ability to cope with harsh environments of rye.

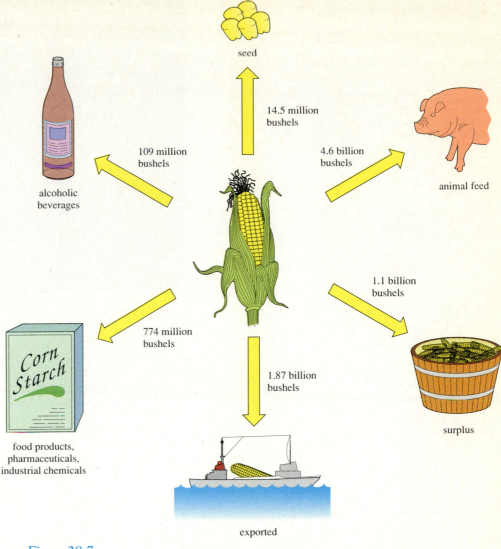

seed

14.5 million bushels

109 million bushels

4.6 billion bushels

alcoholic beverages

animal feed

1.1 billion bushels

774 million bushels

Corn Starch

food products, pharmaceuticals, industrial chemicals

1.87 billion bushels

surplus

exported

Figure 28.7
The corn crop in the United States in 1982 hit a then all-time high of 8.4 billion bushels.

in some of the developing germ cells. The result was a new type of plant that had twice the number of chromosomes as either parent plant, or 28 chromosomes total. This plant was called Emmer wheat, and it was a far better source of food than the parent wheat whose grains had become a staple. The doubled number of chromosomes in each cell resulted in a plant with larger grains. Plus, the grains were attached to the plant in such a way that they could be easily loosened and spread by the wind, so that the new wheat was soon plentiful. It was probably about this time that early farmers learned to select seed from the most robust plants to start the crops of the next season.

Then about 6,000 years ago, another mistake of nature further improved the quality of wheat. Emmer wheat crossed with another weed, goat grass, and after another fortuitous "accident" of chromosome doubling, led to bread wheat, which has 42 chromosomes. Bread wheat has even larger grains that the Emmer wheat that gave rise to it, but at a cost. Its ears are so compact that, on its own, the grain cannot be released. However, with the help of farmers the rich seed was collected each season for food, and a certain percentage held to be planted the next season. The interdependence of humans and crops that is the basis of modern agriculture was thus

born. Today, interesting hybrids add variety to our diets, such as triticale, a combination of wheat and rye (fig. 28.6).

Corn

The tasty, sweet, or starchy kernels of the corn plant *Zea mays* have sustained the Incas, Aztecs, and Mayan Indians of South America and the pilgrims of colonial Massachusetts, and today they continue to be a dietary staple from Chile to Canada. The corn crop in the United States presently exceeds 9 billion bushels a year and is used to manufacture food products, drugs, and industrial chemicals, as well as to feed humans and animals directly (fig. 28.7).

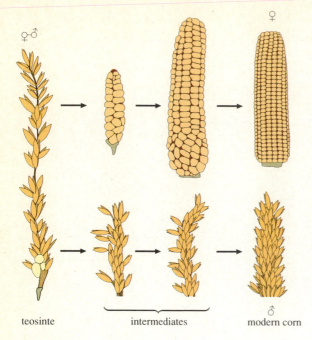

teosinte   intermediates   modern corn

Figure 28.8

Corn from teosinte. The wild grass teosinte (*Zea mexicana*) bears structures that may have given rise to modern corn (*Zea mays*). The small hard seeds of teosinte evolved into corn kernels, and the tassels eventually became the familiar tassels of corn.

Figure 28.9

The making of a cornflake. The invention of flaked cereals took place accidentally at the Battle Creek Sanitarium for the Seventh Day Adventist Church in 1894. The sanitarium was run by a physician, Dr. John Harvey Kellogg, and his business manager brother, Keith. The Kellogg brothers were health-food advocates somewhat ahead of their time, and they regularly put wheat dough through rollers to form wheat sheets, which when ground up, became a sort of cereal.

At first, the patients didn't like the consistency, so the brothers worked to perfect their invention. One night, the brothers were called away on an emergency and left some wheat soaking for many hours longer than usual. When they tried to make their wheat sheets the next day, they found instead that the moisture had equalized in each wheat berry. When run through the rollers, each wheat berry formed its own flake. The sanitarium had a new food favorite, wheat flakes.

Four years later, the Kellogg brothers tried their approach with corn, added some malt flavoring, and the cornflake was born. One of their patients paid particularly close attention to the flaking process. His name was C. W. Post, and he would become one of the Kellogg brothers' chief competitors.

Like wheat, modern corn probably arose from a naturally occurring wild grass that initially produced a grasslike type of corn with small ears. Fossil evidence exists of such a primitive corn. A clue to the origin of modern corn comes from a grass called **teosinte** (*Zea mexicana*), which grows in Mexico today and probably has for many thousands of years. The Indians call teosinte "madre de maize," which means "mother of corn." Corn and teosinte have a few interesting similarities. Teosinte is more grasslike than corn, but it does have small ears that each bear a single row of small, hard seeds. Both species have 20 chromosomes and produce very fertile hybrids when they are crossed. Sometimes wild teosinte grows on the outskirts of cultivated corn fields.

Evolutionary biologists have constructed a scenario of corn's origins, based upon the similarities between modern-day corn and teosinte (fig. 28.8). About 7,500 years ago, a population of wild teosinte faced an environmental stress that was overcome only by individual plants whose tassels included some female structures. Farmers noticed that the unusually hardy plants had larger and better-tasting kernels, and they chose those plants to cultivate. Part of the teosinte tassel might have enlarged to evolve into the corn tassel. Over the centuries, modern corn, with female ears and male tassels, was artificially selected by farmers seeking plants with plump and tasty kernels.

Charles Darwin, the father of evolution, was interested in the origin of corn, and in the late nineteenth century, he bred the plants in greenhouses. He found that corn plants that were continually self-fertilized produced increasingly weaker offspring—that is, inbred plants were more prone to disease and produced ears with fewer rows of kernels. Darwin noted, however, that when he crossed unrelated corn plants to each other, the offspring were strong and healthy, with many rows of plump kernels. Although Darwin knew little about the genetic discoveries of his contemporary Gregor Mendel, what he had demonstrated was the genetic phenomenon of hybrid vigor. Plants with unrelated parents were more vigorous than self-fertilized plants because they had inherited new combinations of genes.

In the first decade of the twentieth century, George Shull, at the Station for Experimental Evolution in Cold Spring Harbor, New York, carried Darwin's greenhouse experiments one step farther, thanks to the additional insight provided by the rediscovery of Mendel's laws of inheritance. Shull continually bred plants from the same ears of corn, artificially selecting highly inbred lines. The inbred corn plants were sickly looking, with very small ears. But when Shull crossed two

Figure 28.10
Planting several varieties of rice encourages success. This rice paddy is planted with several varieties of rice. Should disease strike, some may survive.

Figure 28.11
Banking plant genes. At the cryogenic gene bank at the University of California at Irvine, pollen is frozen in small plastic ampules.

different inbred lines to one another, the offspring—hybrids—were exceptionally vigorous. Shull had developed hybrid corn, which revolutionized corn output worldwide. United States production of corn has jumped from 21.9 bushels per acre in 1930 to 95.1 bushels per acre in 1979 and well beyond that today, thanks largely to hybrid corn. Many of us start our days with this tasty grain (fig. 28.9).

Rice

In Taiwan, a hungry person is not asked, "Are you hungry?" or "What would like to eat?" but "Would you like some rice?" In much of the world, like in Taiwan, rice is so much a dietary staple that it is synonymous with "food." For 2 billion people in Asia, rice provides 80% of their calories. The 400 million metric tons of rice produced each year there are grown in many types of environments, ranging from 53° north latitude to 40° south latitude.

Today's rices include 20 wild species plus 2 cultivars, which are domesticated species produced by agriculture rather than by the evolutionary forces of natural selection. Cultivars do not grow in the wild. The oldest species of rice for which we have fossil evidence, *Oryza sativa*, originated about 130 million years ago in parts of

South America, Africa, India, and Australia, which were then joined into one landmass. So unlike wheat and corn, rice is a very ancient plant that evolved in a tropical, semiaquatic environment.

Human cultivation of rice began about 15,000 years ago in the area bordering China, Burma, and India. By 7,000 years ago, efforts to control rice growth had spread to China and India; by 2,300 years ago, the crop was growing in the high altitudes of Japan. By 300 B.C., rice was a staple throughout Asia. It has only been over the past six centuries that rice has been eaten in West Africa, Australia, and North America.

As migrating peoples took their native rices with them to new lands, the plants adapted to a wide range of environments, from deep salty water to the driest of drylands. From the 1930s to the 1950s many nations collected hundreds of native rice varieties, growing small amounts of each type every season just to keep the collections going (fig. 28.10).

In the 1960s, highly productive newcomers, the **semidwarf rices,** became very popular with farmers and soon accounted for nearly all of China's crop and almost half of the rices of many other Asian nations. To offset a potential disaster due to reliance on

a few types of rice, the International Rice Research Institute (IRRI) was founded in 1961 in the Philippines. It soon became a clearinghouse for the world's rice varieties, cold storing the seeds of 12,000 natural variants by 1970 and of more than 70,000 by 1983. Representatives of other important crops are being banked as well. Potato cells are stored at the International Potato Center in Sturgeon Bay, Wisconsin, and wheat cells are banked at the Kansas Agricultural Experimental Station. Pollen and seeds from 250 endangered species of flowering plants have been frozen at a plant gene bank at the University of California at Irvine (fig. 28.11).

Plant banks offer three priceless services to humanity: a source of variants in case a major crop is felled by disease or an environmental disaster; the return of endangered or extinct varieties to their native lands; and, perhaps most important, a supply of genetic material from which researchers can fashion useful plants in the years to come, even after the species represented in the bank have become extinct.

Establishing a seed or pollen bank is one solution to a growing problem in traditional plant agriculture—the decrease in genetic diversity that makes a crop vulnerable to disease or a natural disaster because it does not have resistant variants. Farmers felt

Figure 28.12
The sunflower—a native American plant. The sunflower was first cultivated in what is now the United States by Mexican Indians. Today it remains a favorite among home gardeners but it is also an important cash crop because of its oil. The Soviet Union produces more than one-half of the world's sunflower crop, and the plant is being grown for its oil in the Mediterranean nations and Spain as well.

Figure 28.13
Amaranth—a "new" grain food. This regal-looking plant is amaranth, which may one day be a major food source in the United States, as it was in years past to many Central and South American peoples.

this short-sightedness painfully in 1970, when the southern corn leaf blight fungus destroyed 15% of the United States corn crop, at a cost of a billion dollars. Genetic uniformity of the potato crop in Ireland contributed to the extent of the famine suffered from 1846 to 1848, when the mold *Phytophthora infestans* decimated the crop. Two million people died and an equal number left the country. Today in Ireland, more than 60 species of potatoes are actively farmed to prevent crop vulnerability.

Another strategy to increase our supply of plant foods is to look for new crops among the many naturally occurring plants. Fewer than 30 of the 240,000 species of flowering plants provide more than 90% of plant-based foods eaten by people (fig. 28.12).

Amaranth

A plant with great promise as a food source is the majestic-looking **amaranth,** which stands 8 feet (2.4 meters) tall and has broad purplish green leaves and massive seed heads (fig. 28.13). Each plant harbors a half million of the mild, nutty-tasting seeds, which are each

the size of a grain of sand. The flowers are a vivid purple, orange, red, or gold. Amaranth was cultivated extensively in Mexico and Central America until the arrival of the Spanish conquistadors in the early 1500s, who banned the plant from use as a crop because of its importance in the Aztec religion.

Amaranth is being grown experimentally at the Rodale Research Center in Kutztown, Pennsylvania, and is available from commercial seed catalogs for home garden use. It grows fast, adapts to a wide range of environmental conditions (high salt, high acid, high alkalinity), yields many seeds, and comes in many varieties. Problems with cultivating amaranth include combating weeds and pests and difficulty in harvesting the tiny seeds.

Nutritionally, amaranth is superb. Its seeds contain 18% protein, compared to 14% or less for wheat, corn, and rice. Amaranth is rich in amino acids that are poorly represented in the other major cereals. The seeds can be used as a cereal, a popcornlike snack, and a flour to make graham crackers,

pasta, cookies, and bread. The germ and bran together are 50% protein, making them ideal to add to prepared foods and animal feeds. The broad leaves of amaranth are rich in vitamins A and C and the B vitamins riboflavin and folic acid. They can be cooked like spinach or eaten raw in salad.

KEY CONCEPTS

Most human diets are rich in cereals. Seeds of these grasses consist of the embryo, the starchy endosperm, and the surrounding aleurone and pericarp. Wheats are classified by their chromosome numbers, which provide evolutionary clues. Polyploid edible wheats evolved from hybridization of wheats with fewer chromosome sets. Modern corn probably evolved from a similar wild grass, teosinte. Charles Darwin and later George Shull discovered that hybrid corn varieties were more vigorous than pure strains. Rice is much more ancient than wheat or corn. Overreliance on a few very productive species is dangerous. Pollen and seed banks help to preserve species. We can also use less common grains, such as amaranth.

Nature's Botanical Medicine Cabinet

Several years ago, I was on a plant collecting trip near Serengeti National Park in East Africa. I was searching for the rare medicinal plant Kigeria africana. After 3 days of combing the Serengeti plain, I came upon an outcrop of K. africana trees. Feeling very lucky indeed, I climbed up onto one of the tree's branches to collect the sausage-shaped fruit.

But as I busily went about my collecting, I realized I was being watched. Two menacing eyes from an adjacent tree stared at me through the branches. Those eyes belonged to a rather large leopard. I tried with all my might to keep from falling from my perch as my knees knocked and sweat poured from my body. This brief encounter ended abruptly, however, when the leopard decided I was not a suitable meal and disappeared into the bushes. Well, I thought, another day in the life of a natural products chemist.

Isao Kubo, Professor of Natural Products Chemistry, University of California at Berkeley, *From Medicine Men to Natural Products Chemists* (1985)

Figure 28.14

The lemon—a multipurpose plant to humans. The tart fruit of the lemon has had various uses in human health care. The juice promotes urination and perspiration and has been used to stimulate these body functions in the treatment of conditions as commonplace as the common cold and as serious as malaria. The astringent nature (skin pore closing) of lemon juice makes it a soothing treatment for sunburn, an effective gargle for a sore throat, and, it has been claimed, a cure for hiccups. Lemon juice kills bacteria on teeth and gums, and chewing the rind can reduce tartar buildup. The high vitamin C content of the fruit makes it an excellent defense against scurvy, a condition characterized by weakness, anemia, and hemorrhage caused by severe vitamin C deficiency. The leaf of the lemon plant is useful too—it makes a soothing, sleep-promoting tea.

Natural products chemists search through the bounty of chemicals manufactured by organisms for substances that may treat illness in people. A chemical that oozes from a tree's bark to discourage hungry caterpillars from eating it may also be an effective drug. For example, a chemical in the bark of the Indian neem tree keeps desert locusts off the tree. The people of Serengeti National Park in east Africa chew the twigs of the Indian neem tree to prevent tooth decay. Other, more familiar plants have healing properties as well (fig. 28.14). Few natural products chemists are as adventurous as Isao Kubo. Most work in laboratories, trying to imitate nature by synthesizing compounds that plants normally make.

Today's natural products chemist is a modern version of the "medicine man" (or woman) who traditionally explored the healing powers of plants. Herbal medical practices may have begun in prehistoric times, when some individuals became botanical experts by sampling plants themselves. Clay tablets carved 4,000 years ago

in Sumaria list several plant-based medicines, as do records from ancient Egypt and China. Roman philosopher Pliny the Elder wrote in the first century A.D., "If remedies were sought in the kitchen garden, none of the arts would become cheaper than the art of medicine." Modern-day medicine men called the Bwana mgana practice herbal medicine in the region of East Africa explored by Isao Kubo.

A good example of medicines derived from plants used today are the chemicals called **alkaloids,** which come from the periwinkle plant and other species. Alkaloids have helped revolutionize the treatment of some leukemias (blood cancers), and alkaloid narcotics derived from the opium poppy, including morphine, are excellent painkillers. Today, nearly half of all prescription drugs contain chemicals manufactured by plants or bacteria, and many other drugs contain compounds that were synthesized in a laboratory but were modeled after plant-derived substances. The many medicines "borrowed" from the

plant kingdom provide one compelling reason why we must halt the present rapid destruction of the world's tropical rain forests. Here, plant life is so abundant and diverse that all of the species have not even been cataloged by taxonomists.

One disease whose spread has been greatly influenced by plants is malaria, which kills more people worldwide each year than any other disease. Malaria starts with chills and violent trembling and progresses to an extremely high fever accompanied by delirium. Finally, the person sweats profusely, is completely exhausted, and has a dangerously enlarged spleen. The disease strikes in a relentless cycle, with symptoms returning every 2 to 4 days. Within weeks, the sufferer either dies of circulatory system collapse or manages to marshall the body's immune defenses against the invading parasite that causes the disease.

Malaria is an interesting example of the relationship between plants and human disease, because plants both contribute to

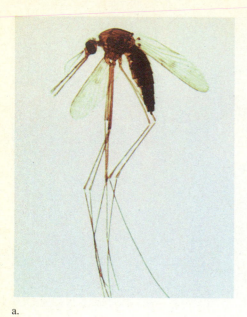

a.

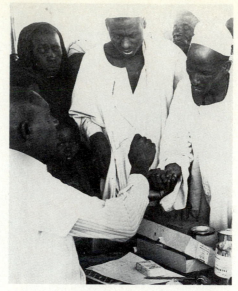

b.

c.

Figure 28.15

Plants and malaria. In an estuary community near the Demerava River in Guyana, malaria was almost unheard of before the 1960s, when the natural vegetation was destroyed and replaced with the "cash crop" rice. *a.* The *Anopheles aquasalis* mosquito thrived in the new, damp environment. *b.* So did malarial parasites within the mosquitoes, and soon the people were ill with the fever. Here, malaria sufferers receive a drug treatment. *c.* A potent antimalarial drug called artemisinin, new to the Western world but a folklore treatment in China for centuries, is derived from the dried leaves and flowers of *Artemisia annua*, which grows near Washington, D.C.

the disease's spread and to its cure. Like many parasitic diseases, the malaria parasite (*Plasmodium falciparum, vivax, malariae,* or *ovale*) must spend part of its life cycle within an intermediate host organism—mosquitoes of the genus *Anopheles*. This insect must bite humans for the disease to be spread. The type of vegetation in an area determines whether or not the mosquito, and the parasite it carries, will thrive. Unfortunately, agriculture often ushers in malaria by replacing dense forests with damp rice fields that are a haven for the mosquitoes.

However, some plant products can kill the malaria parasite. In the sixteenth century, natives of Peru gave Jesuit missionaries who were on their way to Europe their secret malaria remedy—the bark of the cinchona tree. It was not until 1834, though, that French chemist Pierre Joseph Pelletier extracted the active ingredient from cinchona bark, which was called quinine. This substance reigned as the standard treatment for malaria until the 1930s, when chemists began to synthesize substitutes because the malaria parasites

were developing resistance to the bark-derived treatment. Malaria spread through the developing nations as more and more land was cleared for farming. New natural antimalarial drugs were sought, and one very promising one has come from ancient Chinese folk medicine.

In 1967, researchers in the People's Republic of China began a systematic study of all plants known to have medicinal properties in search of a new drug to fight malaria. In a document entitled "Recipes for 52 Kinds of Diseases" unearthed from a Mawangdui Han dynasty tomb from 168 B.C., a plant called qinghao was described as a treatment for hemorrhoids. A reference from A.D. 340 cited the same plants (also known as *Artemisia annua* or sweet wormwood, a relative of tarragon and sagebrush) as a treatment for fever. In 1596, a Chinese herbalist prescribed qinghao to combat malaria.

In the 1970s, chemists isolated the active ingredient from sweet wormwood and called it artemisinin (fig. 28.15). By 1979 it had been tested on more than 2,000

malaria patients, in whom it cured the fever in 72 hours and rid the blood of parasites within 120 hours. The drug is more than 90% effective in treating cerebral malaria, the most severe form of the disease. In animal tests, artemisinin is proving effective against other parasitic diseases as well, including the worm infection schistosomiasis.

Plants are essential to our comforts and to our very existence. Nature has certainly provided a bountiful harvest from which we can choose. The following chapters probe into the structures and functions of plants and conclude with new types of plants made possible by biotechnology.

KEY CONCEPTS

Natural products chemists explore biochemicals with healing properties, many of which come from plants. This is an ancient art as well as a modern science. Many drugs are derived from plant chemicals or intentionally resemble them. Plants both contribute to the spread of malaria and provide a treatment.

SUMMARY

Plants help provide us with food, clothing, shelter, and medicine. About 12,000 to 10,000 years ago, groups of people gradually changed from a *hunter-gatherer* life-style to an *agricultural* way of life, intentionally saving and planting seeds from the strongest individual plants of crops that could be used as food. Encouraging the propagation of certain individuals *artificially selected* particular traits, and in this way, humans have influenced plant evolution.

Cereals are members of the grass family, whose edible seeds (grains) can be stored for long periods. The *endosperm* is the starchy food supply in the seed, the *germ* is the embryo, and outer protective layers are the *aleurone* and *pericarp*. Modern wheats contain two, four, or six sets of chromosomes, and they probably evolved from a natural cross between ancient Einkorn wheat (a diploid) and a wild grass (also a diploid), followed by chromosome doubling in some germ cells (nondisjunction), about 8,000

years ago. This event yielded tetraploid Emmer wheat. Emmer wheat too crossed with a wild grass to produce the first hexaploid wheats, which today are used to manufacture bread and other baked goods.

Corn probably evolved from an ancient grass relative, *teosinte*. Corn and teosinte each have 20 chromosomes, they sometimes grow in the same fields, and they can crossbreed. About 7,500 years ago, an environmental stress may have selected teosinte plants with large kernels, and early farmers may then have cultivated these individual plants. Breeding experiments by Charles Darwin and later by George Shull led to the development of *hybrid corn*, which results from crosses between separate inbred lines to yield bountiful crops.

Rice is perhaps the most widely consumed modern cereal crop, and fossils of the plants date back some 130 million years. Today, rice grows in a wide range of

environments. In 1961, a rice *seed bank* was started in the Philippines to preserve different varieties and prevent reliance on a few types. Seed and pollen banks have since been founded for many other valuable plant species. Amaranth is a new crop. Its abundant seeds are highly nutritious.

Plants have been used for their medicinal properties probably since the beginning of human existence. Today, *natural product chemists* use a combination of laboratory techniques and information from folklore and herbal medicine to synthesize compounds with similar activities to plant-derived compounds, in the search for new and more effective drugs. Malaria is one disease whose spread has been greatly influenced by plants. The clearing of land for agricultural purposes in many tropical regions has encouraged the spread of the malaria-carrying *Anopheles* mosquito. On the other hand, several plant products have been used to treat the fever of malaria.

QUESTIONS

1. What is a cereal?

2. What is agriculture?

3. How might agriculture have arisen?

4. Describe the ways in which scientists hypothesize that modern varieties of wheat, corn, and rice arose.

5. Why is reliance on only a few varieties of a crop plant dangerous? Cite two examples of when such reliance led to devastation.

6. In what two ways can biochemicals from plants help treat human disease?

TO THINK ABOUT

1. Artificial selection has sculpted a modern corn plant that has tasty, nutritious kernels. However, modern corn cannot reproduce successfully without the help of people. The kernels are so tightly protected within the ears that a human or animal must disperse the kernels to start the next year's crop. Do you think that this intervention with a natural process is justified? Why or why not?

2. Devise an experiment to demonstrate that the scenario for the evolution of bread wheat from tetraploid and diploid relatives breeding with wild grasses is possible.

3. Devise an experiment to demonstrate that the scenario of corn evolving from teosinte is possible.

4. Would you eat, or attempt to grow, amaranth? Why or why not?

5. You are planning your vegetable garden and intend to purchase five packets of carrot seeds. The seed catalog describes a new variety of carrot that is resistant to nearly every known garden pest and produces long, highly nutritious carrots in a variety of climates. It sounds too good to be true, but the company that publishes the catalog has had a lot of experience in plant breeding. If you want to obtain as many carrots as possible, would you be better off buying five packets of the new variety or five different types of carrot seeds? Give a reason for your answer.

6. In an effort to conserve and perhaps increase genetic diversity of crop plants, many nations are cooperating by donating seeds to plant gene banks. Sometimes, however, a developing nation will donate

to a bank and that genetic material is then used in more industrialized countries to breed or engineer new plant varieties. The new plants—based on the genetic material from the poor nation but the technology of the more wealthy nation—are then sold to the developing nation. Can you think of a more equitable way for nations to cooperate in the development of new plant varieties?

7. Many people claim that certain herbs have specific healing powers. How would you design a scientifically sound experiment to test whether or not a particular plant product alleviates symptoms of a specific human ailment?

SUGGESTED READINGS

Brown, William L. November 1984. Hybrid corn. *Science 84*. The invention of hybrid corn revolutionized the crop worldwide.

Boucher, Douglas H. February 1991. Cocaine and the coca plant. *BioScience*. The coca plants *Erythroxylon coca* and *E. novograratense* are rich in alkaloids, which have been used, medicinally and recreationally, for centuries.

Doebley, John. June 1990. Molecular evidence for gene flow among *Zea mays*. *BioScience*. Corn evolved from teosinte: now genes engineered into corn are being transferred to teosinte.

Feldman, Moshe and Ernest R. Sears. February 1981. The wild gene resources of wheat. *Scientific American*. Modern crops arose from wild plants. we may have to return to wild varieties to regain vigor.

Kubo, Isao. April 1985. The sometimes dangerous search for plant chemicals. *Industrial Chemical News*. Natural product chemists can sometimes be found in the laboratory and are called modern-day "medicine men."

Plucknett, Donald L., and Nigel J.H. Smith. January 1989. Quarantine and the exchange of crop genetic diseases. *BioScience*. Saving seeds today may be vital to our future.

Shulman, Seth. November 1986. Seeds of controversy. *BioScience*. Who owns and should have access to stored plant genetic material?

Tucker, Jonathan B. January 1986. Amaranth: The once and future crop. *BioScience*. Amaranth is an ancient crop with much future promise.

Vaughan, Duncan A. and Lesley A. Sitch. January 1991. Gene flow from the jungle to farmers. *BioScience*. How can we best use wild rice genes?

29

Plant Form and Function

Learning Objectives

By the chapter's end, you should be able
to answer these questions:

1. What are the main tissues and
   structures of the plant body?

2. What functions are provided by
   a plant's tissues and structures?

3. How does a plant transport water
   and nutrients?

4. How does a plant elongate?

5. How does a plant increase in girth?

A summer garden offers a spectacular display of plant life. Towering and flowering green bean plants curl about each other, as the tiniest tomatoes peek out from where vibrant yellow flowers stood a few days earlier. Melon and cucumber vines snake along the ground, and cabbages are just starting to build their tight knots of leaves. Feathery green tufts in one corner herald growing carrots beneath the surface, as robust leafy plants indicate potatoes forming below. In the evergreens that ring the garden, birds gather, eager to attack the succulent ears of corn wrapped in their tight leafy jackets.

Although these plants look very different from one another, each is built of similar cells, tissues, and organs. These structural building blocks, like those of other types of organisms, are evolutionary adaptations that provide such basic requirements as protection, structural support, transport and storage of water and nutrients, and waste removal. This chapter explores how plant cells and tissues interact to carry out the activities of life.

Primary Tissues

The **primary body** of a plant is an axis consisting of a root (usually below ground) and a shoot (above ground). Shoot and root systems are extensive in many plants and increase available surface area on which the chemical reactions of life can occur. Shoots and roots support one another. Shoots, through photosynthesis, provide carbohydrate nourishment to the roots below. Roots gather water and minerals, which are sent to the shoots.

The **primary tissues** of the plant body, like tissues in general, are groups of cells with a common function. Four tissues comprise the primary plant body: meristems, ground tissue, dermal tissue, and vascular tissue (fig. 29.1). Each of these is made of distinctive cell types and provides a specific function.

Meristems

Meristems are localized regions of cell division, consisting of undifferentiated plant tissue from which new cells arise. They are the ultimate source of all the cells of a plant, although some cell types descended from meristems can themselves divide. The cells

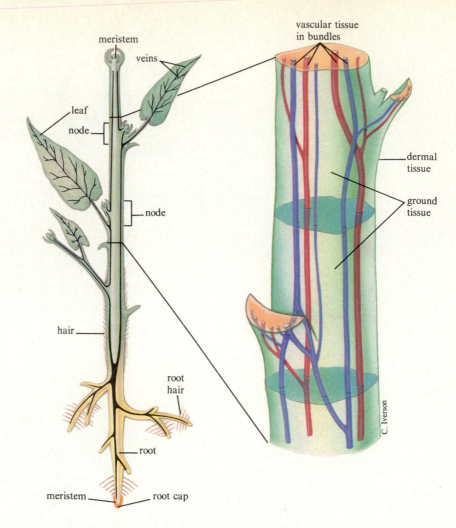

Figure 29.1
Parts and tissues of higher plants.

farthest away from meristems are the most mature and differentiated, and they may be many times larger than the meristematic cells from which they arose. Meristems function throughout a plant's life, and because of them, plants never stop growing.

Apical meristems are found near the tips of roots and shoots. Cells in these regions are small and unspecialized. When these meristematic cells divide and elongate, the plant lengthens. This extension is called **primary growth.** Apical meristems give rise to three primary meristems, which form the other three primary tissues.

Lateral meristems grow outward, thickening the plant, which is called **secondary growth.** Wood formation is due to secondary growth. Unlike primary growth, secondary growth does not occur in all plants.

Intercalary meristem is an unusual type of dividing tissue found in grasses between mature regions of stem. If the tip of a stem or leaf is torn off—by a lawnmower or hungry cow, for example—intercalary meristems reform the structure of the plant. This is why grass blades grow back so quickly after a lawn is mowed.

Ground Tissue

Ground tissue comprises most of the primary body of a plant, filling much of the interior of roots, stems, and leaves. Cells of ground tissue have many functions, including storage, support, and basic metabolism. Ground tissue consists of three cell types: parenchyma, collenchyma, and sclerenchyma.

Parenchyma cells are the most abundant cells in plants. They are relatively unspecialized and often lack distinctive features. More specialized cell types probably evolved from these versatile parenchyma cells. At maturity, parenchyma cells are alive and capable of dividing. This is an important characteristic, because it enables them to specialize in response to a plant's changing situation. For example, parenchyma cells can help a plant respond to wounding or adapt to a new environmental condition.

The substances that give plants their familiar edible parts, such as the carbohydrates in a potato, an ear of corn, or a coffee bean, are stored in parenchyma cells. Fragrant oils, salts, pigments, and organic acids are also stored in parenchyma cells. Oranges and lemons, for example, store citric acid, which gives them their tart taste. Parenchyma cells are also important sites of life-support functions such as photosynthesis, cellular respiration, and protein synthesis. **Chlorenchyma** are chloroplast-containing parenchyma cells that take part in photosynthesis, imparting to leaves their green color (fig. 29.2).

Collenchyma cells are elongated, living cells that differentiate from parenchyma and support the growing regions of shoots. Collenchyma cells have unevenly thickened primary (outer) cell walls that can stretch, enabling the cells to elongate. As a result, they provide support without interfering with the growth of young stems or expanding leaves. Collenchyma strands are the "strings" in celery that often lodge between your teeth.

Sclerenchyma cells are long with thick, nonstretchable secondary cell walls (a trilayered structure beneath the outer cell wall). These cells support regions of plants that are no longer growing and are usually dead at maturity. Two types of sclerenchyma form from parenchyma: sclereids and fibers.

Sclereids have many shapes and occur singly or in small groups. The gritty texture of a pear is due to small groups of sclereids. Occasionally, sclereids form hard layers, such as the hulls of peanuts. Fibers are elongated cells that usually occur in strands varying in length from a few to a few hundred millimeters. Many sclerenchyma

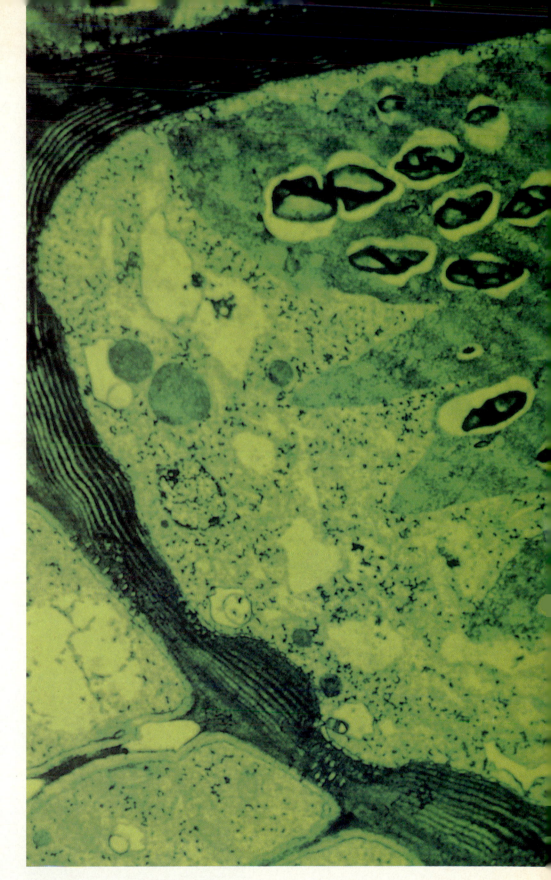

Figure 29.2
Chlorenchyma in a grass leaf.

fibers are used to produce textiles. Humans currently cultivate more than 40 families of plants for fibers and have fashioned cords from fibers since 8000 B.C. The fibers of *Agave sisalana*, commonly known as sisal or the century plant, are used to make brooms, brushes, and twines (see fig. 31.13). Linen comes from the fibers of *Linum usitassimum*, or flax. Even the notorious *Cannabis sativa*, from which marijuana comes, is used to make twine and rope.

Dermal Tissue

Dermal tissue covers the plant body. The **epidermis** covers the primary plant body and is usually only one cell thick. Epidermal cells are flat, transparent, and tightly packed. Special features of the epidermis such as the cuticle, stomata, and trichomes provide diverse functions, including protection, gas exchange, secretion, and digestion.

The **cuticle** is a covering over all but the roots of a plant that protects and keeps out water. The cuticle consists primarily of **cutin,** a fatty material produced by epidermal cells. This covering prevents desiccation by retaining water. As a result, the plant can maintain a watery internal environment—a prerequisite to survival on dry land. Also, the cuticle and underlying epidermal layer act as a plant's first line of defense against predators and infectious agents. In many plants a smooth, whitish layer of wax covers the cuticle and when thick can be seen on leaves and fruits. The layer on the undersides of wax palm leaves may be more than 5 millimeters thick. It is harvested and used to manufacture polishes, record albums, and lipstick.

Since the tightly packed epidermal cells are covered with an impermeable cuticle, how do plants exchange water and gases with the atmosphere? This problem is solved with pores called **stomata. Guard cells** control the opening and closing of the pore, regulating gas and water exchange. The movements of stomata regulates the amount of carbon dioxide diffusing into a leaf for photosynthesis, and loss of water from leaves due to evaporation (transpiration). Stomata may be very numerous. The underside of a black oak leaf, for example, has 100,000 or so stomata per square centimeter! Because stomata help plants conserve water, they are an essential adaptation for life on land (fig. 29.3).

Trichomes are outgrowths of epidermal cells found in almost all plants. Single celled or multicellular, trichomes deter predators in interesting ways. Hook-shaped trichomes may impale marauding animals. Other times, predators inadvertently break off the tips of trichomes that release a sticky substance that traps the invading animals. Trichomes of stinging nettle have spherical tips that break off and penetrate a predator's body, where the poisonous contents are injected into the wounds. Trichomes of carnivorous plants such as the Venus's-flytrap secrete enzymes to digest trapped animals. These trichomes then absorb the digested prey.

Trichomes often reflect light, which helps to prevent overheating. Since cooler plants lose less water via evaporation, trichomes prevent excessive water loss. **Root hairs** are trichomes that appear near root tips and absorb water and minerals from soil.

Many trichomes are economically important. Cotton fibers, for example, are trichomes produced by the epidermis of cotton seeds. Menthol comes from peppermint trichomes, and hashish, a powerful narcotic, is purified resin from *Cannabis* trichomes.

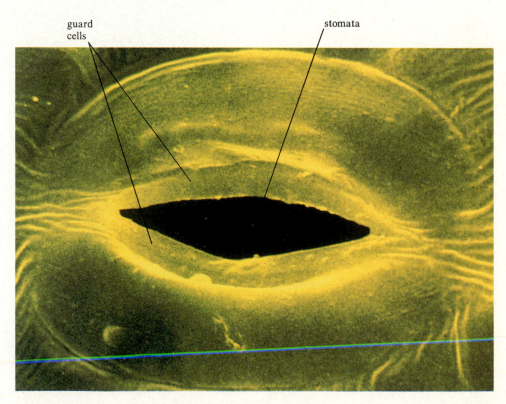

Figure 29.3
Stomata are found on leaf hairs of *Mascagnia macroptera*. Guard cells hug the stomatal pore and closely packed epidermal cells lie under the cuticle.

Vascular Tissues

Vascular tissues are specialized conducting tissues, and form the veins in leaves. Vascular tissues transport water, food, and other materials to all parts of a plant. Two kinds of vascular tissues occur in plants: xylem and phloem. Each is formed during primary and secondary growth.

Xylem forms a continuous system that transports water with dissolved nutrients from roots to all parts of a plant, only in an upward direction. The two kinds of conducting cells in xylem are called **tracheids** and **vessel elements.** Both are elongate, are dead at maturity, and have thick walls. Thick walls are essential for these conducting cells, because water is pulled through plants under negative pressure (suction). Without thick cell walls, tracheids and vessel elements might collapse.

Tracheids are the least specialized conducting cells. These cells are long and narrow, and their tapered ends overlap one another. Water moves from tracheid to tracheid through thin areas in cell walls called pits. Vessel elements are more specialized cells that evolved from tracheids. Unlike tracheids, vessel elements are short, wide cells shaped like barrels. Vessel elements are stacked end to end, and their end

walls usually dissolve, forming hollow tubules, or vessels, for efficient transport of water (fig. 29.4).

Phloem transports water and food materials, primarily dissolved sugars, throughout a plant. Unlike xylem, which transports water upward under negative pressure (suction), phloem transports substances under positive pressure, which is like blowing up a balloon. Thus, water and dissolved sugars can move through phloem in all directions. Also unlike xylem, the conducting cells of phloem are alive at maturity. Their cell walls have thin areas perforated by many **sieve pores,** through which solutes move from cell to cell. Phloem has two kinds of conducting cells: sieve cells and sieve tube members.

Sieve cells are the more primitive (that is, less specialized) conducting cells in phloem. They are elongate cells with tapered, overlapping ends. Sieve pores permeate all walls of sieve cells. **Sieve tube members** are more complex, shorter, and wider than sieve cells. Sieve tube members are arranged end to end to form long sieve tubes. The pores of individual cells are concentrated on contacting end walls, forming an area called a **sieve plate.** This organization allows faster, more efficient transport of nutrients (fig. 29.5). Mature

sieve tube members lack nuclei but contain living protoplasm—unique among plant cells. Can you think of a functioning type of animal cell that also lacks a nucleus? Table 29.1 reviews the major cell types in plants.

KEY CONCEPTS

The epidermis is a one-cell-thick layer that covers the plant and is itself covered by a cuticle. These coverings help to retain water and keep out invaders. Stomata are pores that allow exchange of water and gases with the atmosphere. Guard cells regulate the opening and closing of the pores. Trichomes are epidermal projections that provide protection, reflect light, and increase absorptive surface area. Xylem is a vascular tissue that transports water and dissolved nutrients upwards. Tracheids are less specialized xylem and vessel elements are more specialized. Tracheid cells overlap, and vessel elements form hollow tubules. Phloem transports water and nutrients in all directions. Phloem includes the more primitive sieve cells and the more complex and organized sieve tube members. Xylem and phloem form during primary and secondary growth.

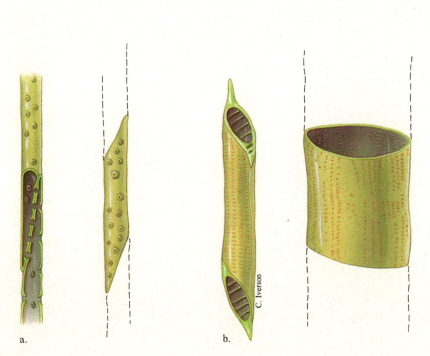

Figure 29.4
Xylem: (*a*) tracheids and (*b*) vessel elements.

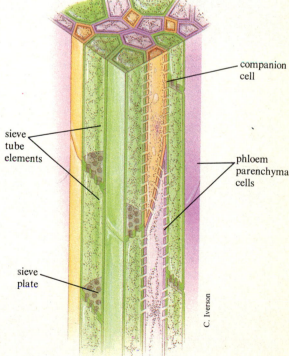

Figure 29.5
A longitudinal view of phloem in a tobacco stem.

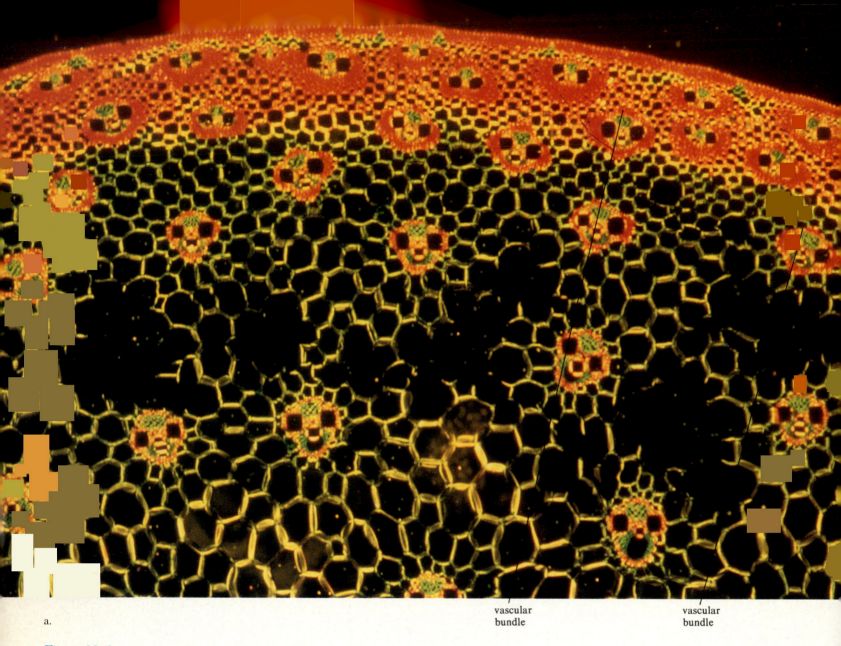

a.   vascular   vascular
                                                                                            bundle   bundle

Figure 29.6
Cross sections of (*a*) monocot (*Zea mays*) and (*b*) dicot (*Helianthus*) stems. Notice the
scattered vascular bundles in the monocot and the ring of vascular bundles in the dicot.

Table 29.1 Major Cell Types in Plants		
Cell	**Tissue Type**	**Function**
Parenchyma	Ground	Storage, division, metabolism
Collenchyma	Ground	Support
Sclerenchyma	Ground	Support
Tracheids	Vascular—xylem	Water transport
Vessel elements	Vascular—xylem	Water transport
Sieve cells	Vascular—phloem	Water and nutrient transport
Sieve tube members	Vascular—phloem	Water and nutrient transport

Parts of the Plant Body

The stems, leaves, and roots of a plant are
all built of the same meristematic, dermal,
ground, and vascular tissues. Yet plants
exhibit a wide variety of forms—contrast a
prickly cactus to a lush vine to the majestic
sunflower. The different arrangements of
plant tissues are sculpted by the forces of
evolution, because certain forms are better
adapted to particular environments than
others.

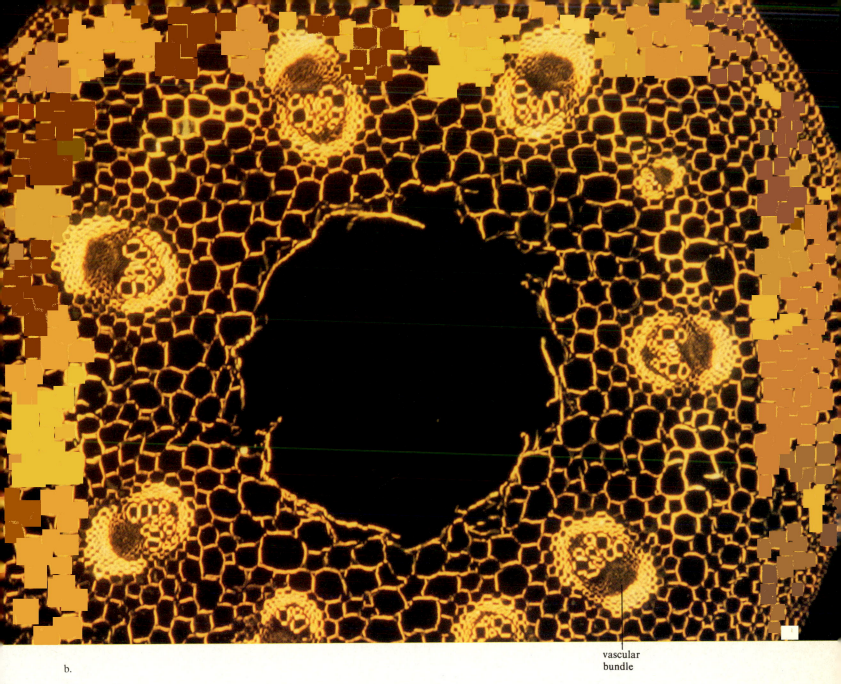

vascular
bundle

b.

Stems

The central axis of a shoot system is the stem, which is a collection of nodes and internodes. **Nodes** are areas of leaf attachment, and **internodes** are portions of stem between nodes (see fig. 29.1). The region between a leaf stalk and stem is a leaf **axil.** Axillary buds are undeveloped shoots that form in leaf axils. Although axillary buds may elongate to form a branch or flower, many remain small and dormant.

Normally, stem elongation occurs in the internodal regions. However, some plants have stems called **rosettes** that do not elongate. Rosettes have short internodes and overlapping leaves. A banana tree is a rosette—its "trunk" is made of large, tightly packed leaves.

The epidermis surrounding a stem is a transparent, unicellular layer. It contains stomata—fewer than the epidermis of a leaf, however. The epidermis of a stem also may possess protective trichomes.

Vascular tissues in stems are organized into **vascular bundles,** which branch into leaves at nodes. Food-conducting phloem forms on the outside of a bundle, whereas water-conducting xylem forms on the inside of a bundle. Often, thick-walled sclerenchyma fibers are associated with vascular bundles. These fibers strengthen the vascular tissue.

Vascular bundles are arranged differently in different types of plants. Consider the familiar flowering plants, which are divided into two classes: monocotyledons (**monocots** for short), which have one first, or "seed," leaf; and dicotyledons **(dicots),** which have two seed leaves. Monocots such as corn have vascular bundles scattered throughout their ground tissue, whereas dicots such as sunflower have a single ring of vascular bundles (fig. 29.6). In contrast to flowering plants, pines have an outer

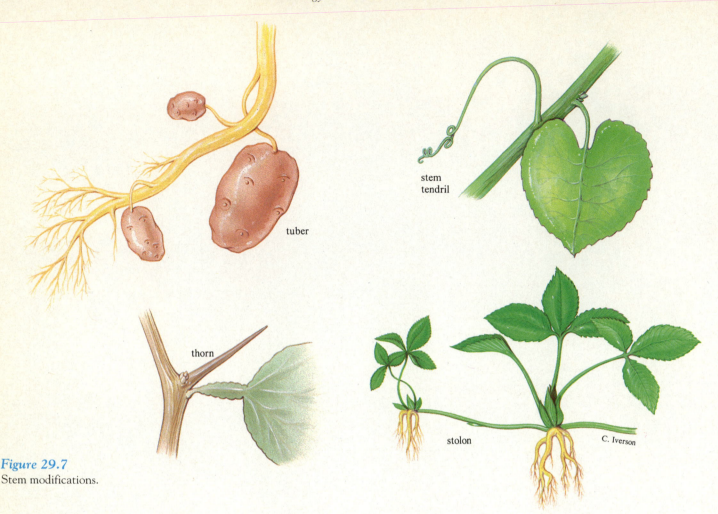

Figure 29.7
Stem modifications.

cylinder of phloem surrounding an inner cylinder of xylem. In all plants, a single layer of cells between the xylem and phloem remains meristematic. In dicots and pines, this layer becomes a lateral meristem.

The ground tissue that fills the area between the epidermis and vascular tissue in stems is called the **cortex.** Although a few collenchyma strands may help support the cortex, most cortical cells are parenchyma. Some cortical cells are green and photosynthetic and store starch. In plants having concentric cylinders of xylem and phloem—pine, for example—the ground storage tissue in the center of the stem is called **pith.**

Stems support leaves, produce and store food, and transport food and water between roots and leaves. Asparagus is an example of an edible stem. Many plants modify their stems for special functions such as reproduction, climbing, protection, and storage (fig. 29.7):

Stolons, or runners, are stems that grow along the soil surface. New plants form from their nodes. Strawberry plants have stolons after they flower, and several plants can arise from the original one.

Thorns often are stems modified for protection, such as thorns on a rosebush.

Succulent stems of plants such as cacti are fleshy and store large amounts of water.

Tendrils are shoots that support plants by coiling around objects, sometimes attaching by their adhesive tips. The stem tendrils of green bean plants readily wrap themselves around posts put in the ground by a helpful gardener. If the garden is planted too densely, the green bean plants will wrap around its neighboring plants. It can form a new anchorage in just minutes!

Tubers are swollen regions of stems that store nutrients. Potatoes are tubers produced on burrowing stolons.

KEY CONCEPTS

The stem forms the central axis of the plant body. Leaves attach at nodes. Elongation occurs at internodes. Rosettes are nonelongated stems. Stem vascular bundles have phloem on the outside and xylem on the inside. Bundles are scattered in monocots and form a ring in dicots. Between the epidermis and vascular tissue of stems lies ground tissue called the cortex. In general, stems provide support, food storage, and transport of nutrients and water, but they can be specialized for reproduction, climbing, protection, and storage.

a.

b.

c.

Figure 29.8
The diversity of leaves: (*a*) the leaves of *Costus*, on a spiral stem; (*b*) the succulent leaves of a stone plant (*Lithops*); and (*c*) *Setaria*, an African grass. Magnification, x10.

Leaves

In addition to the stem, a shoot system consists of leaves. Leaves are the primary photosynthetic organs of most plants. Like stems, leaves are made of epidermal, vascular, and ground tissues. Leaves are the most diverse of all plant organs. The fronds of tropical palms may be 65 feet (20 meters) long, whereas the leaves of *Wolffia*, an aquatic plant, are no larger than a pinhead. A mature American elm has several million leaves, whereas a desert plant called *Welwitschia mirabilis* produces only two leaves during its entire lifetime. Leaves may be needlelike, feathery, waxy, or smooth. The leaves on no two species are identical. Botanists classify leaves according to their basic forms as well as their arrangements on stems (fig. 29.8).

Most leaves consist of a flattened **blade** and a supporting, stalklike **petiole.** There are four basic kinds of leaves. *Simple* leaves have flat, undivided blades. The blades of *compound* leaves are divided into leaflets. *Pinnate* leaflets are paired along a central line, whereas *palmate* leaflets are all attached to one point at the top of the petiole.

Leaves can be arranged in different patterns on stems, which maximizes sun exposure. Plants with one leaf per node have *alternate*, or spiral, arrangements. Plants with two leaves per node have *opposite* arrangements, and plants with three or more leaves per node have *whorled* arrangements (fig. 29.9).

The leaf epidermis consists of tightly packed transparent cells. The epidermis is usually nonphotosynthetic and has many stomata—more than 11 million in a cabbage leaf, for example. Although plants use stomata for gas exchange, they also lose

a.

b.

c.

d.

e.

f.

blade

sheath

h.

g.

C. Iverson

i.

j.

k.

Figure 29.9
Botanists use a dizzying variety of terms to describe leaves: (*a*) a palmately compound leaf of
buckeye; (*b*) pinnately compound leaf of black walnut; (*c*) a tulip tree's simple alternate leaves; (*d*)
simple leaves of dogwood; (*e*) palmately veined leaf of maple; (*f*) succulent leaves of string-of-
pearls; (*g*) pinnately veined oak leaf; (*h*) leaf of grass; (*i*) whorled leaves of bedstraw; (*j*) linear
leaves of yew; (*k*) fan-shaped leaf of ginkgo.

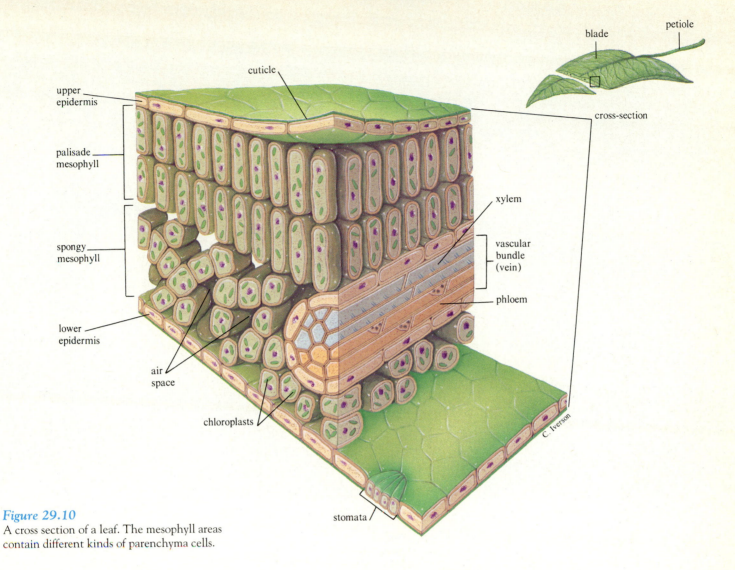

Figure 29.10
A cross section of a leaf. The mesophyll areas contain different kinds of parenchyma cells.

large amounts of water through stomata in transpiration. In fact, in Amazon rain forests, transpiration accounts for half of the moisture in rainfall. However, this water loss is minimized because stomata are concentrated on the protected lower side of leaves. How do you think stomata are distributed on vertically oriented leaves?

Vascular tissues in leaves occur in strands called **veins.** Xylem forms on the upper side of a vein, and phloem forms on the lower side. Leaf veins often are associated with thick-walled sclerenchyma fibers for support. Also, a layer of parenchyma cells surrounds and supports leaf veins. Leaf veins may be *net*, with minor veins branching off from larger, prominent midveins, or *parallel*, with several major parallel veins connected by smaller minor veins. Most dicots have netted veins, and many monocots have

parallel veins. *Vein endings* are the blind ends of minor veins, where water and solutes move into and out of veins.

The ground tissue of leaves is called mesophyll, which is parenchyma. Here chlorenchyma cells produce sugars via photosynthesis. Horizontally oriented leaves have two types of chlorenchyma. The long, columnar cells along the upper side of a leaf are called **palisade mesophyll** cells, and they are specialized for light absorption. Located below the palisade layer are **spongy mesophyll** cells, which are irregularly shaped chlorenchyma cells separated by large intercellular spaces. These cells are specialized for gas exchange. In contrast to horizontally oriented leaves, vertically oriented leaves have uniformly shaped chlorenchyma cells and are called uniform mesophyll cells (fig. 29.10).

In addition to their photosynthetic role, leaves provide support, protection, and nutrient procurement and storage with the following specializations:

Tendrils are modified leaves that wrap around nearby objects to support climbing plants. Pea plants growing in a garden will hold to a fence with leaf tendrils. (Both leaves and stems can be modified into tendrils.)

Spines of plants such as cacti are leaves modified to protect plants from predators and excessive sunlight.

Bracts are floral leaves that protect developing flowers. They are colorful in some plants, such as poinsettia.

Figure 29.11

Leaf modification for trapping insects: the leaves of the Venus's-flytrap snap shut to catch prey.
This fascinating plant is found only in North and South Carolina.

Storage leaves are fleshy and store food. Onion bulbs consist of the bases of such leaves.

Insect-trapping leaves are found in about 200 types of carnivorous plants and are adapted for attracting, capturing, and digesting prey. Some leaves have sticky "flypaper" surfaces, whereas others form water-filled chambers in which insects drown. Trigger hairs of Venus's-flytrap respond to movements of a visiting insect by stimulating the two leaves to snap together. The insect is trapped, as the leaves secrete digestive enzymes that destroy it (fig. 29.12).

Cotyledons are embryonic leaves found in flowering plants that often store energy used for germination.

Anyone who has ever raked leaves is well aware that leaves have a limited life span. **Leaf abscission** is the normal process by which a plant sheds its leaves. **Deciduous trees** shed their leaves at the end of a growing season. Evergreens have leaves throughout the year but gradually shed a few leaves at a time.

Leaves are shed from an **abscission zone,** a region at the base of the petiole. In response to environmental cues such as shortening days or climatic changes, a separation layer forms in the abscission zone, isolating the dying leaf from the stem. Eventually, wind, rain or some other disturbance, such as a scurrying squirrel, breaks the dead leaf from the stem.

Roots

Although plants are immobile, much biological activity takes place underground. Roots are so indispensable to plant growth and photosynthesis that annual production of roots often consumes more than half of a plant's energy and may account for

a.

C. Iverson

b.

c.

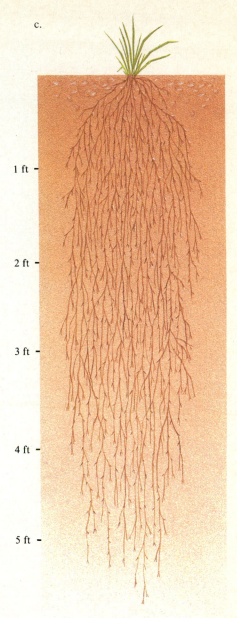

1 ft

2 ft

3 ft

4 ft

5 ft

Figure 29.12
Two main root types: (a) the fibrous root system of barley and (b) the taproot of a dandelion.
c. A mature root system may be very complex, as is this one of winter wheat.

a substantial portion of its body. Roots provide anchorage and absorb, transport, and store water and nutrients. They absorb oxygen from between soil particles. Roots pushing through very firmly packed soil may die from lack of oxygen.

The first root to emerge from a seed is the **radicle.** In a **taproot system,** the radicle enlarges to form a major root that persists throughout the life of the plant. Taproots grow fast and deep, maximizing support and enabling a plant to use material located deep in the soil. Engineers once found a mesquite root 174 feet (53 meters) below the earth's surface! Most dicots develop taproot systems.

In a **fibrous root system,** the radicle is short-lived. **Adventitious roots,** which are roots that form on stems or leaves, replace the radicle. The result is an extensive system of similarly sized roots. Fibrous root systems are relatively shallow, rapidly absorbing materials from near the soil surface and preventing soil erosion. Most monocots form fibrous root systems (fig. 29.12).

As rapidly growing roots push through the soil, as many as 10,000 cells per day are lost. Cell replacement and protection are provided by the **root cap,** a thimble-shaped structure covering the tips of roots. A root cap has a rapidly dividing meristem that continually pushes cells forward. Eventually, these cells are pushed to the outside of the root, where they are sloughed off as the root grows (fig. 29.13). The root cap also produces **mucigel,** a slimy substance that protects root tips from desiccation. Mucigel lubricates the root tips as they force their way between soil particles. Mucigel even helps roots absorb water and nutrients from the soil.

Just behind the root cap is a cluster of seemingly inactive cells called the **quiescent center.** This region functions as a reservoir to replace damaged cells of the adjacent meristem. The portion of the root above the tip anchors the plant in the ground. The region immediately behind the root cap is called the **subapical region.** It is loosely divided into three zones. The **zone of cellular division** is meristematic. Cells

here divide as rapidly as every 12 to 36 hours. The meristem of a root surrounds the quiescent center. The **zone of cellular elongation** lies behind the zone of cellular division. Cells here elongate by as much as 150-fold as their vacuoles fill with water. This action pushes the root rapidly through the soil.

Cells mature and differentiate in the **zone of cellular maturation.** This is also called the root hair zone, because it is here that tiny root hairs protrude from epidermal cells (fig. 29.14). Root hairs are plentiful, a

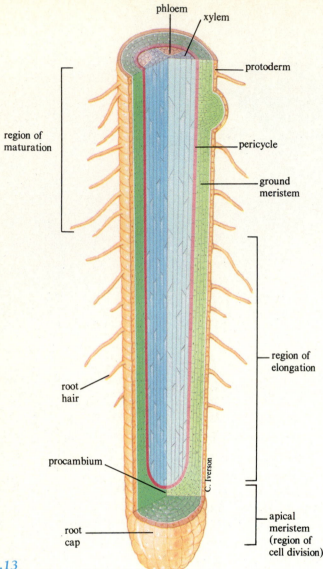

phloem — xylem

protoderm

region of maturation

pericycle

ground meristem

root hair

region of elongation

procambium

C. Iverson

root cap

apical meristem (region of cell division)

Figure 29.13
A dicot root tip has distinct regions.

ing each brick. Due to this arrangement, the endodermis can regulate the movement of nutrients and water into and out of the central vascular tissue of the root. Figure 29.15 shows a monocot root in cross section.

Inside the cortex, the **pericycle** is the ring of parenchyma cells that produces branch roots that burst through the cortex and epidermis and finally into the soil. The root's vascular tissues are interior to the pericycle, where bundles of xylem alternate with bundles of phloem. Roots absorb water and minerals from the soil and transport them to shoots via the xylem. In return, roots receive organic nutrients from shoots via the phloem. Often, these organic nutrients are stored in cortex cells for later use.

Like stems and leaves, roots are modified for special functions (fig. 29.16):

Storage is a familiar root specialization. Beet and carrot roots store starch, sweet potato roots store sugar, and desert plant roots store large amounts of water.
Pneumatophores are specialized roots of plants growing in oxygen-poor environments. These roots grow up into the air, and oxygen diffuses into the plant body.
Adventitious roots that form and grow in the air are called **aerial roots.** They are important modifications for mangroves, trees that typically grow in low-oxygen environments. Mistletoe and orchids are two familiar plants that have aerial roots.

Many roots form mutualistic associations called **mycorrhizae** with beneficial fungi. The fungi absorb nutrients from the soil, while the host plants provide the fungi with vitamins or other needed substances.

Roots of legume plants, such as peas, are often infected with bacteria of the genus *Rhizobium*. The roots form nodules in response to the infection (fig. 2.3). The bacteria function as built-in fertilizer, providing the plant with nitrogen "fixed" into compounds that it can use. Genetic engineering to bring the benefits of this nitrogen fixation to plants not normally inhabited by *Rhizobium* is discussed in chapter 32.

single plant growing several billion of them, and they greatly increase the surface area of the root through which water is absorbed. The root hairs give this portion of the root a downy, fuzzy appearance. When a garden plant is transplanted, many root hairs are destroyed. It is only after they begin to grow back that the plant regains its vigor. Can you see why root hairs grow in the zone of cellular maturation and not at the root tip?

The zone of cellular maturation is also where primary tissues such as the epidermis and cortex develop. The epidermis surrounds all of the root except the root cap. Epidermal cells either lack or have a very thin cuticle and are thus well adapted for absorbing water and minerals. Root epidermal cells usually lack stomata.

The epidermis surrounds all the cortex, which consists of three layers: hypodermis, storage parenchyma cells, and endodermis. The **hypodermis** is the outermost, protective layer of the cortex. Loosely spaced storage parenchyma cells make up most of the cortex. These cells form a vast collecting system that absorbs water and minerals moving through the epidermis and stores these nutrients for future growth.

The **endodermis** is the innermost ring of the cortex. It consists of a single layer of tightly packed cells, called a **Casparian strip,** which contains a waxy, waterproof material called **suberin.** The endodermal cells resemble bricks in a wall, and the Casparian strip is like the mortar surround-

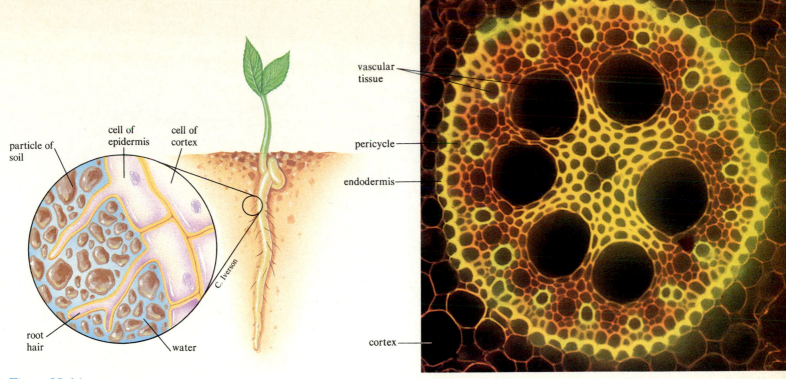

Figure 29.14
Root hairs. These outgrowths of epidermal cells extend through the soil, greatly increasing absorptive surface area.

Figure 29.15
Cross section of a monocot (corn) root.

a.

b.

c.

Figure 29.16
Root modifications. *a.* Yams are fleshy roots that store carbohydrate. *b.* The banyan tree has aerial roots growing out of its branches. *c.* This tropical fig tree has roots that are so enormous that they resemble a trunk.

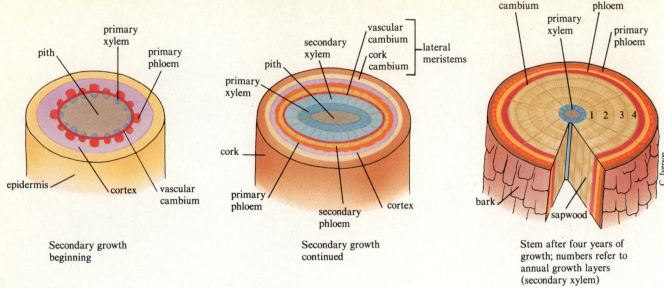

Figure 29.17

The secondary growth of a woody stem involves the activities of two lateral meristems—vascular cambium and cork cambium. Primary xylem and phloem are produced by the apical meristem, whereas secondary xylem and phloem are produced by the vascular cambium.

KEY CONCEPTS

Roots anchor plants and absorb, transport, and store nutrients. Taproots are large, deep, and fast-growing and last a lifetime. Fibrous roots are smaller, shallow, and short-lived. The root cap provides new cells and protects the root tip. The region behind the root cap includes zones of division, elongation, and maturation. In the maturation zone, numerous root hairs greatly increase absorptive surface area. Here also is found epidermis and the three-layered cortex. The hypodermis protects, parenchyma stores nutrients, and the endodermis regulates entry of substances into vascular tissue lying interior to the pericycle. Roots can be modified.

Secondary Growth

Plants must compete with each other to intercept light. One way they maximize light absorption is by growing taller than neighboring plants. Continued elongation presents a problem for plants, however, because primary tissues cannot support them very well. Thus, an improved support system has evolved: the formation of lateral meristems that increase the girth of stems and roots. These meristems, called the vascular cambium and cork cambium, produce the secondary plant body.

The results of secondary growth can be impressive. A 2,000-year-old tule tree in Oaxaca, Mexico, is 148 feet (45 meters) in circumference and only 131 feet (40 meters) tall. A 328-foot-tall (100-meter) giant Sequoia in northern California is more than 23 feet (7 meters) in diameter.

The **vascular cambium** produces most of the secondary plant body and is a thin cylinder of meristematic tissue found in roots and stems. Generally, the vascular cambium forms only in plants that exhibit secondary growth—primarily dicots and gymnosperms (conifers). Meristematic cells produce secondary xylem on the inner side of the vascular cambium and secondary phloem on the other side. Overall, the vascular cambium produces much more secondary xylem than secondary phloem. Secondary xylem is more commonly known as wood (fig. 29.17).

The vascular cambium produces wood during the spring and summer. During the moist days of spring, the vascular cambium produces *spring wood* made of large, thin-walled cells. Spring wood, also called early wood, is specialized for conduction. During the drier days of summer, the vascular cambium produces *summer*, or late, *wood*. Summer wood consists of small, thick-walled cells and is specialized for support. Because of the differences between spring and summer wood, wood often displays visible demarcations called **growth rings.** Reading 29.1 explains how growth rings can be "read" to reveal climatic conditions of years past.

Hardwoods are woods of dicots such as oak, maple, and ash. **Softwoods** are woods of gymnosperms such as pine, spruce, and fir. Recall that xylem has two kinds of conducting cells, tracheids and vessel elements. Hardwoods contain tracheids, vessels, and supportive fibers, whereas softwoods are 90% tracheids. As a result, hardwoods are stronger and denser than softwoods. In fact, hardwoods often are too hard to penetrate with nails and as a result are not used for construction.

Different regions of wood are specialized for different functions. **Heartwood,** wood in the center of a tree, collects a plant's waste products. It forms a solid,

Reading 29.1   *Tree Rings Reveal the Past*

ASK A DENDROCHRONOLOGIST WHAT THE TEMPERA-
TURE AND RAINFALL WERE IN THE AMERICAN
SOUTHWEST FROM A.D. 341 TO 832 AND HE OR SHE
MAY HAVE AN ANSWER. With the help of slices
from the interiors of trees, the tree ring special-
ist can reconstruct "weather reports" back thousands of years (fig. 1).

The pattern of secondary xylem indicates the
passage of time because the cells of wood laid
down in the spring are large, with thin walls
(appearing light colored), and wood cells laid
down in the summer are smaller, with propor-
tionately thicker walls. The contrast between
the latest wood of one season and the earliest of
the next creates the characteristic annual ring.
The most recent ring is next to the vascular
cambium, which is microscopic. On the outside
of the cambium is the phloem and then the
bark. Can you see why tropical species, which
have secondary growth all year long, do not
have rings?

Tree rings provide other information. The
larger the ring, the more plentiful was rainfall
that year. A fire leaves behind a charred "burn
scar." A season when voracious caterpillars or
locusts chomped away the early leaves is represented by two rings very close together,
because nutrients
for growth were
in short supply with
photosynthesis

inhibited. Dendrochronologists can also read
information on light availability, altitude,
temperature, and length of the growing season in the patterns of tree rings.

But not all temperate species can reveal
the climatic past. Meaningful rings have one
predominating environmental factor, such as
temperature in Alaska and precipitation in
the American Southwest, which must
change from year to year yet have similar effects on trees in a wide geographical area.
Trees growing in the best conditions—high
groundwater and low run-off—produce uniformly wide rings, despite changing rainfall
patterns. They are very healthy but provide
no information. Trees in flat areas, such as
roadsides, lakesides, and river valleys, produce these noninformative, or "complacent"
rings. In contrast, useful, or "sensitive," rings
are found on rocky hills, where drainage is
good and there is no underground water for
the roots to tap into when rainfall is low.

An occasional missing ring can
be a problem. This happens
because the tree rings are
actually cones in three
dimensions, with

uneven widths throughout the tree. By
chance, the section of the tree viewed may
be missing one ring. Dendrochronologists
date a tree by removing a slice of wood
through a tiny hole that they bore. A disin-
fectant and a bandage protects the tree.

The most revealing use of tree ring dating
is to align common ring patterns of several
trees that lived at different times but with
some overlap, including dead trees. As long
as one of the trees has a ring next to the vascular cambium so that the most recent year
is known, such series can yield a very accu-
rate "master chronology." For example, the
oldest known living tree is a bristle cone pine
(*Pinus longaeva*) growing in the White
Mountains of California. It is 4,906 years
old! Combining its tree ring information
with that from other trees in the area has
provided rainfall data going back 8,200
years!

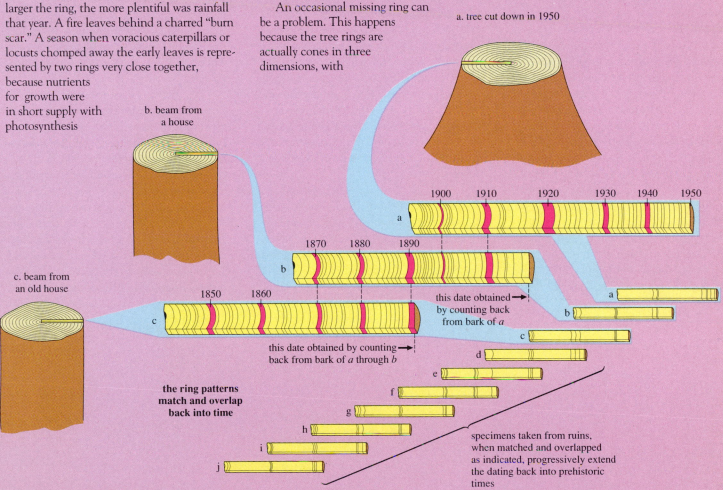

a. tree cut down in 1950

b. beam from
a house

c. beam from
an old house

the ring patterns
match and overlap
back into time

1900   1910   1920   1930   1940   1950

a

1870   1880   1890

b

1850   1860

c

this date obtained → by counting back
from bark of *a*

this date obtained by counting →
back from bark of *a* through *b*

a
b
c
d
e
f
g
h
i
j

specimens taken from ruins,
when matched and overlapped
as indicated, progressively extend
the dating back into prehistoric
times

rodlike center that adds support to the organism. **Sapwood,** wood located nearest the vascular cambium, transports water and dissolved nutrients within a plant.

Bark includes all of the tissues outside of the vascular cambium. Secondary phloem forms the inner layer of bark, but only the innermost secondary phloem functions in transport. The **periderm** portion of the bark is the outer protective covering on mature stems and roots. It forms after secondary growth breaks through the epidermis. The periderm consists of the cork cambium, cork, and phelloderm.

The **cork cambium** is the lateral meristem that produces the periderm. The cork cambium produces cork cells to the outside; it produces phelloderm to the inside. **Cork cells** are waxy, densely packed cells covering the surfaces of mature stems and roots. They are dead at maturity and form waterproof, insulating layers that protect plants. Areas of loosely packed cells penetrate cork layers and enable gas exchange to occur. **Phelloderm** consists of living parenchyma cells, which may be photosynthetic and store nutrients. A familiar example of cork is the "skin" of a potato. The cork used to stopper wine bottles comes from a cork oak tree that grows in the Mediterranean. Every 10 years, harvesters remove the cork cambium and cork, which grows back.

Ninety percent of a typical tree is secondary xylem. Secondary xylem plays important roles in our lives. United States forests produce 18.6 million cubic meters of secondary growth per day. That may not seem like so much when you consider that each year the average American uses about 500 pounds of paper! We use 250,000 tons of napkins and 2 million tons of newsprint and writing paper each year. We can thank the secondary growth of plants for such diverse products as rubber, chewing gum, turpentine, cardboard, rayon, synthetic cattle food, and ice cream fillers.

KEY CONCEPTS

Vascular cambium and cork cambium are lateral meristems that increase a plant's girth. Vascular cambium forms secondary xylem (wood) on its inner side and secondary phloem on its outer side. The cells of spring wood are large, and of summer wood small, so that rings appear. Hardwoods and softwoods have different proportions of xylem components. Bark includes secondary phloem and the outer periderm, which is produced by the cork cambium.

SUMMARY

Meristematic tissue actively divides. *Apical meristems* are located at the plant's tips, and *lateral meristems* add girth. *Ground tissue* is abundant and multifunctional. It includes *parenchyma* cells, which can divide, store substances, and carry out photosynthesis, respiration, and protein synthesis; *collenchyma* cells, which are supportive; and *sclerenchyma* cells, which support nonliving plant parts. *Dermal tissue* includes the *epidermis* and the *cuticle*. Gas and water exchange can occur through pores called *stomata*. *Trichomes* are epidermal outgrowths. Vascular tissue consists of *xylem*, which transports water upward, and *phloem*, which transports water and nutrients in all directions. Xylem cells include *tracheids* and the more specialized *vessel elements*. Phloem includes *sieve cells* and the more specialized *sieve tube members*.

A stem is the central axis of the shoot and consists of nodes, where leaves attach, and internodes. *Vascular bundles* in stems contain xylem and phloem, which are scattered in monocots and form a ring in dicots. Between a stem's epidermis and vascular tissue lies the *cortex*, made of ground tissue. *Pith* is storage ground tissue in the center of a stem. Stem modifications include stolons, thorns, tendrils, bulbs, and tubers.

Leaves are photosynthetic organs. *Simple* leaves have undivided blades, and *compound* leaves form leaflets. *Pinnate* leaves have a central axis, and *palmate* leaves extend from a common point. Leaf arrangement is *alternate*, *opposite*, or *whorled*. Leaf epidermis is tightly packed, transparent, and nonphotosynthetic. Vascular tissue is found in veins, which may be in *net* or *parallel* formation. Leaf ground tissue, *me-* sophyll, is organized into palisade and spongy layers. Leaf modifications include tendrils, spines, and bracts. Leaves are shed from an *abscission zone* in response to environmental cues.

A plant's first root is the *radicle*. *Taproot systems* have a large, persisting major root, whereas *fibrous root systems* are shallow and shorter-lived. A meristem in the *root cap* replaces cells lost during a root's rapid extension. The *subapical* region behind the root cap is divided into zones of cellular division, elongation, and maturation. This last zone includes root hairs, epidermis, and cortex, which itself has three layers. Some roots are specialized for storage or adapted to low-oxygen environments. Some roots form symbiotic relationships with fungi or bacteria. *Vascular cambium* and *cork cambium* produce secondary xylem and phloem, which increase a plant's girth.

QUESTIONS

1. Which plant tissue is responsible for the fact that plants never stop growing?

2. Which tissue is the most abundant in plants?

3. What are the functions of the following substances?
   a. Cutin
   b. Mucigel
   c. Suberin

4. Is the trunk of a banana plant a stem or leaves? How might you demonstrate which type of structure it is?

5. What are some of the ways in which leaves are classified?

6. Cite a stem and a leaf specialization that provide protection.

7. Corn is a monocot and cucumber a dicot. How do these plants differ in the following?
   a. Stem structure
   b. Leaf venation
   c. Root organization

TO THINK ABOUT

1. If some stems and leaves of a tomato plant are torn off by an overanxious tomato picker, the plant regrows these parts in a few weeks. Which tissue type is responsible for this regrowth?

2. Why are stomata necessary?

3. Why can phloem transport materials in all directions, whereas xylem can transport materials upward only?

4. How does a tree "know" when to shed its leaves?

5. How can roots grow in compact soils, such as clays?

6. How are root hairs similar to human intestinal villi?

7. What would happen (or not happen) if a plant's quiescent centers were destroyed?

SUGGESTED READINGS

Briffa, K. R. et al. August 2, 1990. A 1,400-year tree-ring record of summer temperatures in Fennoscandia. *Nature*. Tree-ring data indicate that there was a "little Ice Age" between 1570 and 1650.

Feldman, Lewis, J. October 1988. The habits of roots. *BioScience*. Roots can be meticulously separated from the soil and their complex structures revealed.

Gower, Stith T. and James H. Richards. December 1990. Larches: deciduous conifers in an evergreen world. *BioScience*. Larches shed their leaves like deciduous trees, but the leaves are shaped and water is conducted in manner similar to evergreens.

Ross, Gary N. December 1986. Night of the radishes. *Natural History*. The root of the radish provides the plant with stored nutrients. It also serves as sculpture material for Mexican families.

Stern, Kingsley R. 1991. *Introductory plant biology*. Dubuque, Iowa: William C. Brown. A more detailed yet easy-to-read look at the basic parts of the plant body.

CHAPTER

30

Plant Life Cycles

Chapter Outline

Learning Objectives

By the chapter's end, you should be able to answer these questions:

1. What are the diploid and haploid phases of the life cycle of a sexually reproducing plant?

2. What are the functions of the parts of a flower?

3. How do the gametes of flowering plants come together?

4. What events follow fertilization to form and nourish the plant embryo?

5. What is a fruit, and how does it assist a plant's reproduction?

6. What factors provoke a seed to germinate?

7. How does sexual reproduction in pines differ from that in flowering plants?

8. How do plants reproduce asexually?

N ewly emerged from his cocoon, the male wasp is already eager to locate a female. The females, though, will not emerge for another week. Meanwhile, the male wasp flies among orchid plants of the genus *Ophrys*. Suddenly he becomes intensely excited. He smells a female! The unmistakable fragrance of a sexually receptive female wasp wafts from the orchid flowers. Sexually stimulated, the male wasp approaches the blooms more closely. To his eyes, which can discern ultraviolet light that human eyes cannot, one petal of each flower looks incredibly like a female wasp, seeming to sport eyes, antennae, and wings.

The now-frantic male alights on the provocative petal, which not only looks and smells like a female but whose fuzzy surface feels like the touch of a potential mate. Completely fooled, he begins the motions of copulation wasp style, and in the process, small packets of pollen are deposited on his confused head. Despite his sexual movements, the male does not achieve sexual satisfaction, so, still highly agitated, he moves on to the next flower. He tries again to mate with a beguiling petal, and in doing so, he leaves behind some of the pollen clinging to his head from the first flower (fig. 30.1).

The behavior of the male wasp seeking a mate and finding a flower may seem to be a waste of biological energy, but it is an amazingly efficient mechanism for pollen—the male sex cells of flowering plants—to be delivered from one plant to another. The sexual reproduction of orchids and other flowering plants is tied intimately to the behavior of certain animals. Rather than being just pretty appendages of plants, flowers are sophisticated, highly evolved structures. They facilitate the recombination of genetic material that provides the genetic diversity essential to the survival and success of a species.

Plants evolved from a multicellular green alga that invaded land more than 430 million years ago. Although life on land was harsh compared with life in water, plants adapted to the terrestrial environment by developing waxy coverings to contain moisture and mechanisms to combine sex cells without relying on delivery via water. Today tracheophytes and bryophytes are the two main groups of plants. The

Figure 30.1
A male wasp finds this orchid quite enticing.

tracheophytes, or vascular plants, dominate on land. They possess vascular tissues, which transport water and dissolved nutrients throughout a plant. Bryophytes lack vascular tissue and are smaller than vascular plants.

Alternation of Generations

The life cycle of a plant differs from that of an animal. In mammals special haploid cells are set aside that combine from two individuals to form an offspring. In plants,

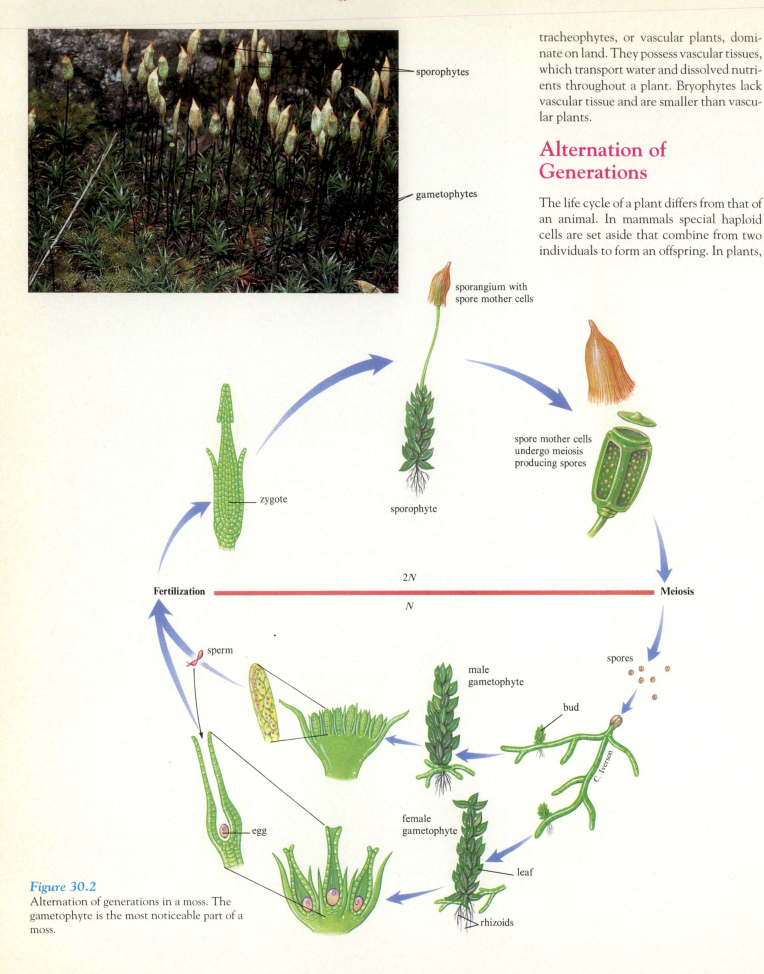

Figure 30.2
Alternation of generations in a moss. The gametophyte is the most noticeable part of a moss.

however, a complete life cycle of an individual includes both a diploid stage and a haploid stage. These stages are called **generations,** and because they alternate within a life cycle, sexually reproducing plants are said to undergo **alternation of generations.**

The diploid generation, or **sporophyte,** produces haploid spores through meiosis. Haploid spores divide mitotically to produce a multicellular haploid individual, the **gametophyte.** Eventually, the gametophyte produces haploid gametes—eggs and sperm—which fuse to form a **zygote.** The zygote grows to become a sporophyte, and the cycle begins anew.

In most vascular plants, gametophytes produce either eggs or sperm, but not both. Because often the female egg-producing gametophytes are larger than the male sperm-producing gametophytes, the female gametophytes are called **megagametophytes,** and the male gametophytes are called **microgametophytes.** Male and female gametophytes arise from two different

types of spores called **megaspores** and **microspores.** Not surprisingly, these spores form in two different types of structures, **megasporangia** and **microsporangia** ("mega" simply means "big," and "micro" means "small").

Although alternation of generations is characteristic of all plants, the gametophyte stage dominates some plant life cycles, while the sporophyte stage dominates others (figs. 30.2 and 30.3). For example, the gametophyte stage is the more obvious phase in bryophytes such as the mosses. In contrast, vascular plants have a reduced

gametophyte phase and a dominant sporophyte phase. Familiar vascular plant forms such as a fern, a tree, and grass are sporophytes.

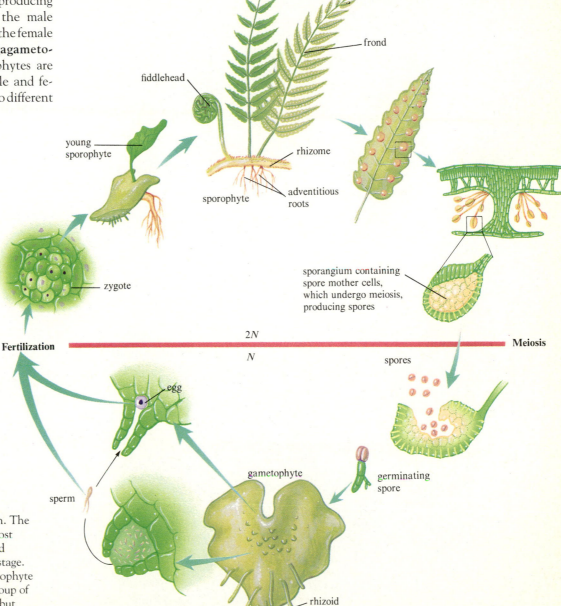

Figure 30.3
Alternation of generations in a fern. The diploid sporophyte generation is most clearly visible, although the haploid gametophyte still forms a separate stage. In many vascular plants, the gametophyte is reduced still further to a small group of cells that produces eggs and sperm but that is no longer a free-living, separate stage.

Flowering Plant Life Cycle

Flowering plants, or **angiosperms,** are the dominant group of vascular plants. The approximately 235,000 species of angiosperms include such familiar plants as shrubs, grasses, vegetables, and grains. The reproductive structures of angiosperms are **flowers.**

Structure of the Flower

Complete flowers have four types of organs, all of which are modified leaves. Each type of organ occurs in a whorl, or circle, about the end of the flower stalk (fig. 30.4). The calyx is the outermost whorl of a flower. It is made up of green, leaflike **sepals** that enclose and protect the inner floral parts. Inside the calyx is the corolla, a whorl made up of **petals.** Petals often are large and colorful, especially when they are important in attracting pollinators to the flower. The **calyx** and the **corolla** do not play a direct role in sexual reproduction and are therefore referred to as accessory parts.

The two innermost whorls of a flower, the **androecium** and the **gynoecium,** are essential for sexual reproduction. The whorl to the inside of the corolla, the androecium, consists of the male reproductive struc-

tures. These are the **stamens,** which are built of stalklike filaments bearing pollen-producing oval bodies called **anthers** at their tips. The whorl at the center of a flower, the gynoecium, consists of the female reproductive structures, or **pistil.** The gynoecium is formed from one or more **carpels,** leaflike structures enclosing the **ovules.** The carpels and their enclosed ovules are referred to as the **ovary.** The ovary gives rise to a stalklike **style** bearing a **stigma** at its tip. The stigma receives pollen.

Formation of Gametes

Microspores form in the anthers. Each anther contains four microsporangia called **pollen sacs.** Pollen sacs contain **microspore mother cells** that divide meiotically to produce four haploid microspores. Each microspore then divides mitotically, producing a haploid **generative nucleus** and a haploid **tube nucleus.** A thick, resistant wall forms around each two-celled structure, forming male microgametophytes, more familiarly known as **pollen grains.** The generative cell divides to form two sperm cells, either before or after the pollen grains are shed. Millions of pollen grains may be released when mature pollen sacs burst open.

Megaspores form in the ovary of the flower. Each ovule within the ovary is a megasporangium containing a **megaspore**

mother cell, which divides meiotically to produce four haploid cells. Three of these cells quickly disintegrate, leaving one large haploid megaspore. The megaspore undergoes three mitotic divisions, forming a female megagametophyte having eight nuclei but only seven cells—one large cell has two nuclei called **polar nuclei.** In a mature megagametophyte, also called an **embryo sac,** one of the cells with a single nucleus is the egg. The top part of figure 30.5 illustrates formation of the pollen grains and embryo sac.

KEY CONCEPTS

Flowers are reproductive structures. Accessory parts include the calyx, the outermost whorl made up of sepals, and inside it the corolla, made of petals. Inside the corolla are the male structures (stamens built of filaments and anthers) and the female structures (ovaries built of carpels and ovules). The style and stigma arise from the ovary. Microspore mother cells are in pollen sacs, and they undergo meiosis to yield four haploid microspores. Each microspore divides mitotically to yield a generative nucleus and a tube nucleus, which, surrounded by a thick wall, form a pollen grain. An ovule contains a megaspore mother cell, which yields four haploid cells, three of which disintegrate. The remaining megaspore mitotically divides three times, forming the eight cells of the embryo sac.

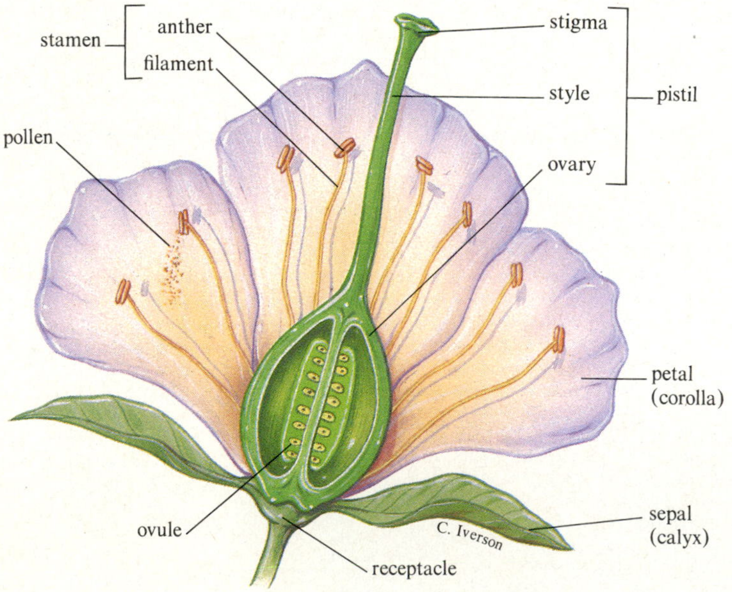

Pollination

Pollination is the transfer of pollen from an anther to a receptive stigma. Some angiosperms are self-pollinating, meaning that pollen grains are transferred from the anther of one flower to the stigma of the same flower. Other angiosperms are **outcrossing** species in which pollen grains from one flower are carried to the stigma of another flower.

Self-fertilization leads to reduced genetic variability and is common in temperate regions where environmental conditions are relatively uniform. Outcrossing is crucial in a changing environment because it produces a genetically variable population that can adapt to changing conditions. Interestingly, some angiosperms actually promote outcrossing by producing physically isolated anthers and stigmas. Others lack the androecium or gynoecium, making self-fertilization impossible. The magnolia, one of the first flowering

Figure 30.4

Flower anatomy. The stamen comprises the androecium, and the pistil comprises the gynoecium. Flowers can be diverse from one another yet still contain the same basic parts.

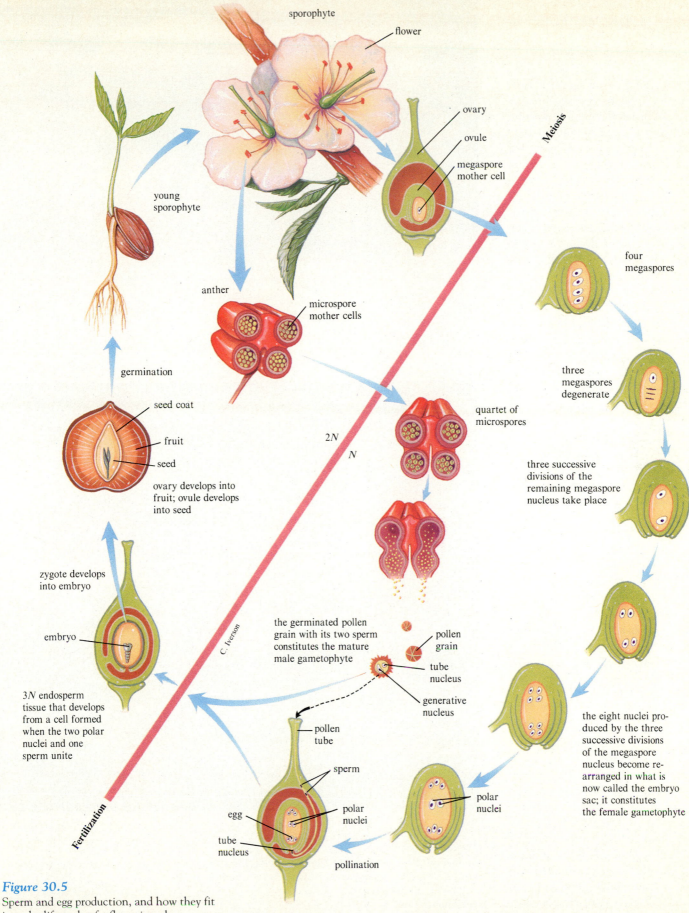

sporophyte

flower

ovary

ovule

megaspore
mother cell

Meiosis

young
sporophyte

four
megaspores

anther

microspore
mother cells

three
megaspores
degenerate

germination

seed coat

fruit

seed

2N

N

quartet of
microspores

three successive
divisions of the
remaining megaspore
nucleus take place

ovary develops into
fruit; ovule develops
into seed

C. Iverson

the germinated pollen
grain with its two sperm
constitutes the mature
male gametophyte

pollen
grain

tube
nucleus

generative
nucleus

the eight nuclei pro-
duced by the three
successive divisions
of the megaspore
nucleus become re-
arranged in what is
now called the embryo
sac; it constitutes
the female gametophyte

zygote develops
into embryo

embryo

3N endosperm
tissue that develops
from a cell formed
when the two polar
nuclei and one
sperm unite

pollen
tube

sperm

polar
nuclei

egg

tube
nucleus

polar
nuclei

pollination

Fertilization

Figure 30.5

Sperm and egg production, and how they fit
into the life cycle of a flowering plant.

plants, ensures cross pollination by releasing its pollen only after its eggs have been fertilized by pollen from other individuals.

Pollen is often assisted in traveling from plant to plant. Animals, particularly insects, play an important role in pollination (fig. 30.6). In animal-pollinated angiosperms, floral characteristics such as morphology, color, shape, and odor often attract particular animals to particular flowers, as the wasp in the orchid described in the chapter's opening illustrates. (See Reading 30.1 for further examples of orchid adaptations to attract pollinators.) Some flowers produce heat, which volatizes their aromatic molecules, releasing their characteristic fragrances. Pollinating animals visit flowers in search of food, such as sugary nectar, and end up carrying pollen from flower to flower. Nectar is a sweet-tasting substance that has no known function in the plant other than attracting pollinators. Myrtle plants take another approach to luring insects. They make two types of pollen—one to entice visiting insects, and the other type are the actual sex cells.

Bees, the most common pollinators of flowers, initially locate a food source by its fragrance and then by its color. Because ultraviolet light is highly visible to bees, bee-pollinated flowers often have conspicuous ultraviolet markings (fig. 30.7).

Different types of insects have characteristic floral preferences. In contrast to bees, which are partial to blue or yellow sweet-smelling blooms, beetles prefer spicier scents with dull-colored flowers.

Birds are attracted to red flowers, a color that insects cannot distinguish. The structure of the flower almost ensures that a visiting bird will transport pollen. A hummingbird flitting about a California fuchsia plant, for example, sticks its long, thin beak into the flower. The bird catches its bill in a network of fine threads, on which pollen grains descend. Carrying the pollen on its bill, the hummingbird ferries the cells to the next plant it visits.

Some flowers are pollinated by butterflies and moths. These flowers often are white or yellow and are heavily scented—characteristics that make them easy to locate at night, when these insects are the most active. The flowers may even have flat surfaces on which their pollinators can land. Bats are important pollinators in the tropics, where flowers are open at night.

a.

b.

Figure 30.6

Pollinators. Bumblebees (*a*) and hummingbirds (*b*) are efficient pollinators of many angiosperm species. Animal pollinators range from ants to butterflies to bats. When wind is the principal pollinator, modifications may be necessary. Corn, for example, must be planted in blocks to allow wind pollination.

Reading 30.1 *Orchids Entice Pollinators*

ORCHIDS ARE AN EXTREMELY SUCCESSFUL TYPE OF FLOWERING PLANT, WITH 35,000 SPECIES COMPRISING 10% OF KNOWN ANGIOSPERMS. The unusually large number of species, and the fact that naturally occurring orchid hybrids are very rare, reflects what is called "flower fidelity," the very specific match between what orchids display and what pollinating animals seek.

Evolution has molded traditional floral structures into traps that attract an insect and force it to transport pollen. Consider the 650 species of orchid growing in the American tropics. Their flowers release an intoxicating nectar or oil that quickly makes a visiting bee lose its coordination and stagger about. To make its way out of the labyrinth of flower parts, the tottering insect passes structures that shower it with pollen. The effects of the intoxication subside just as the insect nears an exit, and the insect flies on, carrying pollen sticking to its body to the next flower.

Orchids of genus *Epipactus* growing in marshes sport a large petal, called a labellum, that forms a runway of sorts leading to a pool of nectar at the base of the flower. But once the insect alights on the petal, the runway clamps up, trapping him. Like a circus visitor winding his way through a funhouse with only one exit, the insect wanders until it locates the only way out—past structures that trigger a pollen shower before he leaves.

Pollinating insects are very much attuned to the details of flower construction. They recognize distinctive scents, spatial relationships between the stigma and anthers, how far apart plants of its favorite species grow from one another, and the precise timing of blooming. Although the benefit to the plants of these relationships seems obvious, it is not so clear just what insects derive from them. Some insect pollinators are rewarded with a tasty treat of nectar, yet others seem attracted simply by a whiff of a fragrant oil. Whatever the subtle attractions between plant and pollinator, it is an amazingly efficient adaptation for maximizing reproductive potential.

Figure 30.7
Insects can "see" ultraviolet light, which makes these black-eyed Susans appear purple. To us they are yellow.

Not all floral scents are pleasing to the human nose. In South Africa, the "carrion flowers" of stapelia plants smell remarkably like rotting flesh, a highly attractive scent to flies. As if the stench were not sufficient to beckon the insects, stapelia's leaves are wrinkled and brown, resembling decayed meat.

Wind-pollinated angiosperms such as oaks, cottonwoods, ragweed, and grasses shed large quantities of pollen that are dispersed on breezes. The wind, however, does not carry pollen very far. This is why wind-pollinated plants grow closely together. Wind pollination is far less precise than animal pollination. Even though enormous amounts of pollen are released, the wind does not provide a mechanism to deliver it precisely to other plants of the same species, as animals do. Many people are allergic to the pollen of wind-pollinated plants such as ragweed (see fig. 27.16). The flowers of wind-pollinated angiosperms are small, greenish, and odorless. Rather than invest energy in flowers, it is more efficient for these plants to invest energy in pollen production.

Fertilization

After a pollen grain lands on a stigma (pollination), the pollen grain gives rise to a growing *pollen tube*. The pollen grain's two sperm cells enter the pollen tube as it

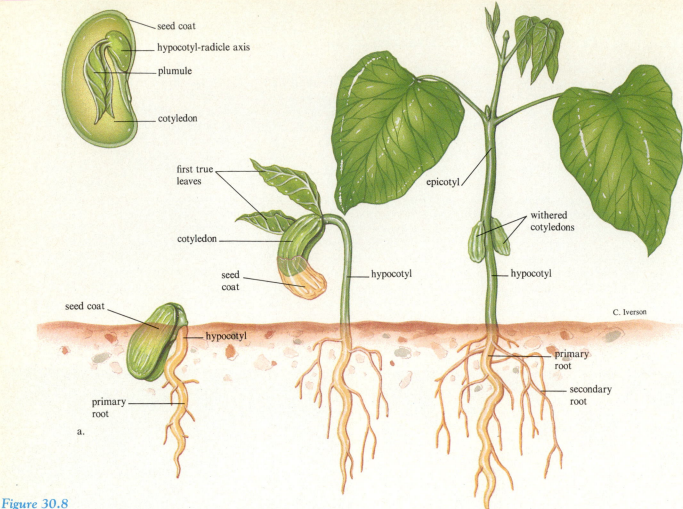

Figure 30.8
Seed structure, germination, and development in (*a*) a dicot (green bean).

Seed Development

grows down through the tissues of the stigma and the style towards the ovary. When the pollen tube reaches an ovule, it discharges its two sperm cells into the embryo sac. One sperm cell fuses with the egg, forming a diploid **zygote.** After a series of cell divisions, the zygote will become the **plant embryo.** The second sperm cell fuses with the two polar nuclei, forming a triploid nucleus that will divide to form a nutritive tissue called **endosperm.** Endosperm is stored food for the developing embryo. Familiar endosperms are coconut milk and the fleshy part of a kernel of corn. Notice that the egg and the polar nuclei both are fertilized, a process termed **double fertilization.** The bottom of figure 30.5 depicts fertilization and subsequent development of the seed and fruit.

A **seed** is a temporarily dormant sporophyte individual surrounded by a tough protective coat. Immediately after fertilization, the ovule contains an embryo sac with a diploid zygote and a triploid endosperm nucleus, both of which are surrounded by several layers of protective maternal tissue. Initially, the endosperm nucleus divides more rapidly than the zygote, forming a large mass of nutritive endosperm. The developing embryo forms **cotyledons,** or seed leaves. Angiosperms that have one cotyledon are called **monocots,** while those having two cotyledons are **dicots** (fig. 30.8).

Further development in monocot and dicot seeds differs. In many dicots, the cotyledons become thick and fleshy as they absorb the endosperm. In monocots the cotyledon does not absorb the endosperm, but absorbs and transfers food from the endosperm to the embryo.

The apical meristems form early in embryonic development. Recall that these are regions of cellular division that will remain active throughout the entire life of a plant. The **shoot apical meristem** forms at the tip of the **epicotyl,** which is the stemlike region above the cotyledons. The **root apical meristem** differentiates near the tip of the embryonic root, or **radicle.** When one or more embryonic leaves form on the epicotyl, the epicotyl plus its young leaves is called a **plumule.** The stemlike region below the cotyledons is the **hypocotyl.**

In monocots, a sheathlike structure called the **coleoptile** covers the plumule. Also, the ovary wall remains attached to a monocot seed, forming a fruit. A cereal grain such as a corn kernel actually is a hard fruit.

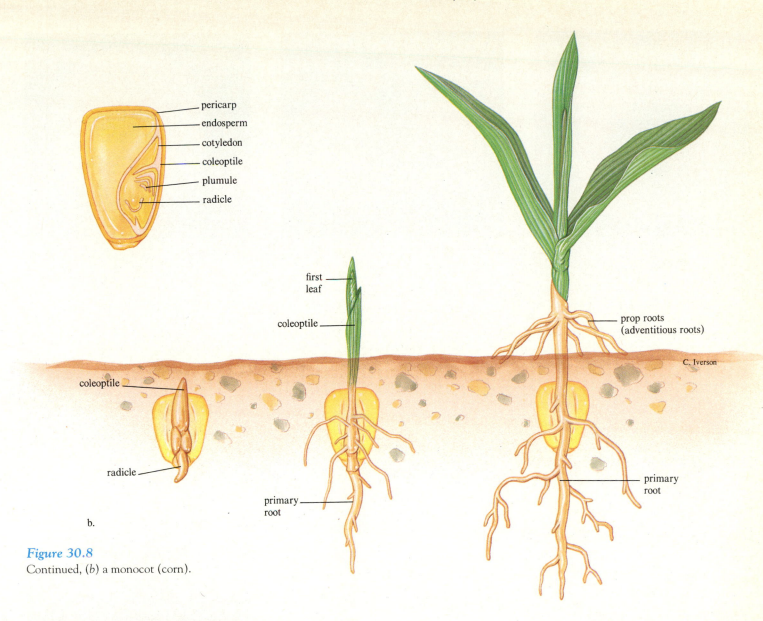

pericarp
endosperm
cotyledon
coleoptile
plumule
radicle

first
leaf

coleoptile

prop roots
(adventitious roots)

C. Iverson

coleoptile

radicle

primary
root

primary
root

b.

Figure 30.8
Continued, (*b*) a monocot (corn).

KEY CONCEPTS

Pollen is transferred from anthers to stigmas by animals or the wind. Here the pollen grain forms a pollen tube, which grows through the stigma and style to the ovary, where its two nuclei enter the embryo sac. One sperm nucleus fuses with the egg to form the zygote, and the other fuses with two polar nuclei to form the endosperm. A dicot embryo forms two seed leaves, and a monocot embryo forms one. Dicot cotyledons grow thick by absorbing endosperm, but in monocots the cotyledon transfers food from endosperm to embryo. The epicotyl develops above the cotyledons, with an apical meristem. Another meristem develops at the embryonic root, or radicle.

Seed Dormancy

At a certain point in embryonic development, cell division and growth stop, and the embryo becomes dormant. The dormant plant embryo and its food supply are protected by a tough outer layer called the **seed coat.** Together, the plant embryo, stored food, and seed coat comprise the seed.

Why should a plant embryo simply stop growing? Seed dormancy is a crucial adaptation enabling seeds to postpone development when the environment is unfavorable such as during a drought. Seeds of some plants can delay development for hundreds of years. Favorable conditions trigger growth to resume when young plants

are more likely to survive. Dormant seeds are also more likely to disperse into new environments.

Fruit Formation

A flower begins to change during seed formation. When a pollen tube begins growing, the stigma produces large amounts of **ethylene,** a simple organic molecule that is a plant hormone. (Recall that a hormone is a biochemical produced in one part of an organism that exerts a physiological effect on some other part of the organism.) Ethylene triggers senescence of the flower. Floral parts that are no longer needed—all parts except the ovary—wither and fall to the ground. Sometimes the ovary swells

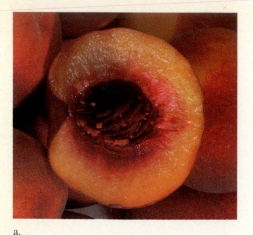

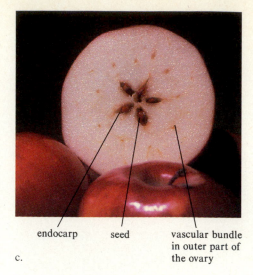

a.

b.

c.

endocarp   seed   vascular bundle in outer part of the ovary

Figure 30.9

Fruits. *a.* A drupe is a fleshy fruit with a hard pit surrounding a single seed. A peach is a drupe. *b.* A berry is fleshy and contains many seeds. Tomatoes, peppers, and eggplants are berries, although we mistakenly think of them as vegetables. Ironically, blackberries, raspberries, and strawberries are not true berries. They are termed aggregate fruits and consist of several small fruits clustered together. *c.* An apple is an example of a pome, a fleshy fruit that develops mostly from the tissues surrounding the ovary. The outermost layer feels like paper.

and develops into a **fruit,** which is a ripened ovary enclosing a seed. Different types of fruits are shown in figure 30.9.

Plant hormones continue to influence fruit development. Seeds within fruits synthesize the hormone **auxin,** which stimulates fruit growth. Ethylene hastens fruit ripening in many species, including tomatoes, apples, and pears. Fruit falls from the plant when auxin levels drop and ethylene levels rise. (Plant hormones are discussed in the next chapter.)

Fruit and Seed Dispersal

In addition to protecting vulnerable seeds from desiccation, fruits facilitate seed dispersal. Attractive fruits such as shiny berries are eaten by birds and other animals. The animals carry the ingested seeds to new locations where they are released in the animals' feces. Surprisingly, some seeds will germinate only after passing through the intestines of birds or mammals. The beginning of chapter 33 describes the relationship between the now-extinct dodo bird and the hard fruits of the calvaria tree. The plant could not germinate unless the hard coats of its fruits were dismantled in the digestive tracts of the large birds.

Mammals spread seeds from place to place when fruits bearing hooked spines become attached to their fur. The fruit of

the burdock plant, for example, has barbed hooks that cling to a passing deer or the jeans of a hiker. The inspiration for velcro, a fuzzy fabric that sticks to other fabrics, came from the annoyingly strong attachment of burdock fruits (fig. 30.10).

Wind-dispersed fruits such as those of dandelions and maples have wings or other structures that enable them to ride far from their places of origin on air currents. Coconuts are water-dispersed fruits that travel long distances before colonizing distant islands.

Seed Germination

Germination, the resumption of growth and development, is a sort of reawakening for a seed. Germination usually requires water, oxygen, and a source of energy. The first step is **imbibition,** which is the absorption of water by a seed (fig. 30.11). In some seeds imbibition causes the embryo to release hormones that stimulate the breakdown of the endosperm or stored food reserves. Starch is converted to sugar that the embryo uses for energy. Imbibition also swells a seed, eventually rupturing the seed coat, and exposing the plant embryo to oxygen. At this point a seed may resume growth. However, seeds of many plants normally germinate only after some addi-

tional requirement is met—exposure to light of a certain intensity or a series of cold days, for example.

Plant Development

After the growing embryo bursts out of the seed coat, further growth and development depend upon the root and shoot apical meristems. The hypocotyl, with its attached radicle, emerges first from the seed. In response to gravity, the radicle grows downward and anchors the plant in the soil. Root systems develop rapidly because plants require a constant water supply for continued growth.

The ways in which the shoot emerges from the soil differ from species to species. In most dicots, the elongating hypocotyl forms an arch that breaks through the soil and straightens in response to light, pulling the cotyledons and epicotyl out of the soil. In most monocots the epicotyl begins growing upward shortly after the initiation of root growth, protected by its coleoptile as it pushes through the soil. The single cotyledon remains underground.

A plant is producing its first chloroplasts by the time its shoot emerges from the soil. When embryonic food reserves are exhausted, plants can produce their own food photosynthetically.

a.

b.

c.

d.

e.

Figure 30.10
Seed dispersal. *a.* Velcro resembles the burdock fruit. *b.* This tree sparrow helps disperse the seeds of winterberry, a type of holly. *c.* These tumbleweed plants look calm and firmly rooted, but if a brisk wind comes along, an entire plant can blow away. *d.* Seeds of the dandelion have fluff that enables them to float on a breeze. *e.* Some seed pods have their own explosive methods of scattering seeds. Beans pop out of this garbanzo bean pod.

Figure 30.11
Seed germination. The imbibition of water is necessary for a seed to germinate. Notice that as the percentage of water increases, the oxygen uptake increases too, signaling the onset of cellular respiration.

KEY CONCEPTS

Plant embryos become dormant, as seeds, enabling them to avoid environmental extremes and to be dispersed. When seeds form, most parts of the flower fall off, but the ovary enlarges to become a fruit. The fruit protects the seed and disperses it. Germination begins with imbibition of water. Oxygen and energy and sometimes environmental cues must also be present. Nutrient stores are broken down to yield energy. The embryo bursts from the seed coat and primary growth ensues. As the shoot emerges, photosynthesis begins.

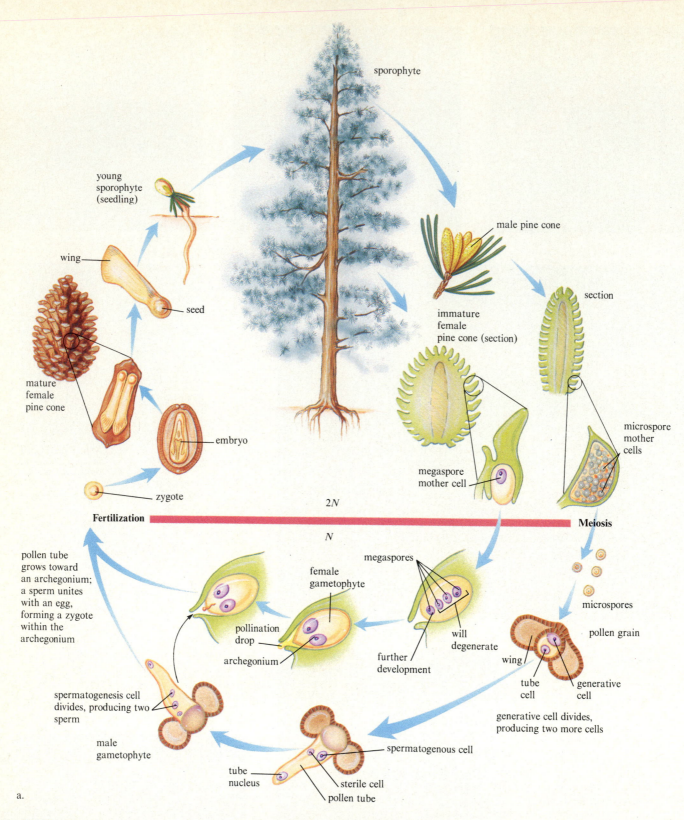

sporophyte

young sporophyte (seedling)

male pine cone

wing

seed

immature female pine cone (section)

section

mature female pine cone

microspore mother cells

embryo

megaspore mother cell

zygote

2N

Fertilization   **Meiosis**

N

pollen tube grows toward an archegonium; a sperm unites with an egg, forming a zygote within the archegonium

megaspores

female gametophyte

microspores

pollination drop

will degenerate

pollen grain

archegonium

further development

wing

tube cell

generative cell

spermatogenesis cell divides, producing two sperm

generative cell divides, producing two more cells

male gametophyte

spermatogenous cell

tube nucleus

sterile cell

pollen tube

a.

Figure 30.12

a. Pine life cycle. Notice once again the alternation of generations. Pines have no flowers, but they do possess male and female cones, which produce pollen and eggs. Notice also that the sporophyte stage is entirely dominant, and the gametophyte consists of only a few cells. *b.* Pollen can be seen blowing from the male cones of this tree.

b.

Pollination occurs when airborne pollen grains drift down between the scales of female cones and adhere to drops of a sticky secretion. Afterwards the cone scales grow together, and the pollen tube begins growing through the ovule toward the egg. But the pollen is not yet mature—before the pollen tube reaches the egg, the pollen grain must undergo two more cell divisions to become a mature, six-celled microgametophyte. Two of six cells become active sperm cells, one of which fertilizes the egg cell. The whole process happens so slowly that fertilization occurs about 15 months after pollination!

Within the ovule, the developing embryo is nourished by the haploid tissue of the megagametophyte. Following a period of metabolic activity, the embryo becomes dormant and the ovule develops a tough, protective seed coat. It may remain in this state for another year. Eventually, the ovule is shed as a seed. If conditions are favorable, the seed germinates, giving rise to a new tree.

The gymnosperm life cycle differs from the angiosperm life cycle in several ways:

The reproductive structures are cones instead of flowers.
Ovules lie bare on female reproductive structures rather than embedded in their tissues.
Gymnosperms have no fruit.
Gymnosperms have single fertilization rather than double fertilization.
The haploid tissue of the female gametophyte rather than a triploid endosperm nourishes the gymnosperm embryo.

The Pine Life Cycle

Angiosperms are the only vascular plants that bear seeds in protective structures. Vascular plants whose seeds are not protected are the gymnosperms, a term that literally means "naked seed." Conifers are the best-known group of gymnosperms, including such familiar species as pines, spruces, firs, and redwoods.

Cones are the reproductive structures of pines. Large, female cones bear two ovules (megasporangia) on the upper surface of each **scale.** Through meiosis, each ovule produces four haploid megaspores, three of which degenerate and one of which continues to develop into a female gameto-phyte. Over many months the female gametophyte undergoes mitosis (fig. 30.12*a*). Finally, two to six structures called archegonia form, each housing an egg that is ready to be fertilized.

Small male cones have pairs of microsporangia borne on thin, delicate scales. Microsporangia produce microspores through meiosis, and each microspore eventually becomes a four-celled pollen grain (microgametophytes). Millions of winged pollen grains are released when microsporangia burst. If you tap a male cone in the spring, you can see a halo of pollen released (fig. 30.12*b*). Most pollen grains, however, never reach a female cone.

a.

b.

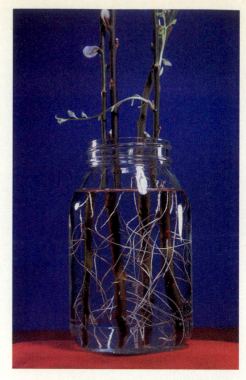
c.

Figure 30.13

Vegetative propagation comes in many forms. New shoots can come from underground, as in bamboo (*a*), or new plantlets can form on leaves, as in a fern (*b*). In the laboratory, greenhouse, or home kitchen window, cuttings from many plants can be coaxed to grow roots and even flower in water or in a growth medium, like this pussy willow in water (*c*).

Asexual Reproduction

Many plants reproduce by asexually forming new individuals by mitotic cell division. Compared with sexual reproduction, it is a simple process—there is no meiosis, no gamete production, and no fertilization. Instead, a parent simply gives rise to genetically identical individuals called **clones.**

Asexual reproduction is particularly advantageous when environmental conditions are stable and plants are well-adapted to their surroundings. Recall that sexual reproduction introduces genetic variation into a population. Why risk losing a favorable combination of genes when asexual reproduction will produce clones well suited to the environment?

Plants often reproduce or propagate, vegetatively (asexually) by forming new plants from portions of their roots, stems, or leaves (fig. 30.13). For example, adventitious buds form on roots of cherry, pear, apple, and black locust plants, and when they sprout, aerial shoots grow upward. These shoots are called "suckers" because they draw on materials from the parent plant. If separated from the parent plant, suckers become new individuals.

A few plants use their leaves to reproduce asexually. When the leaves of walking fern or maternity plant lie on a moist surface, roots and shoots develop at their edges. These plantlets become new individuals when they are shed from the parents' leaves.

Asexual reproduction also occurs from modified stems. Stolons, also called runners, grow along the soil surface. Roots and shoots form at intermittent nodes and eventually form new plants some distance from the parent plant. Stolons are common in plants such as strawberry, Boston fern, spider plant, and crabgrass.

Tubers are swollen regions of stems that grow below ground. They produce nodes that can grow roots and shoots. A potato is a swollen stem, and the eyes are buds from which new potato plants arise asexually.

The reproductive structures of plants add a great deal of joy to our lives. Imagine a celebration without flowers! How wonderful that these beautiful and fragrant biological structures also provide an efficient mechanism for the mixing of genetic material, which is the backbone of evolutionary success in these organisms.

KEY CONCEPTS

Asexual reproduction in plants is much simpler than sexual reproduction. Vegetative propagation occurs from adventitious buds, leaves, and modified stems.

SUMMARY

Sexually reproducing plants exhibit *alternation of generations,* in which the diploid *sporophyte* generation produces spores through meiosis. The spores divide mitotically to produce the haploid *gametophyte,* which in turn produces haploid gametes. In different species, either the sporophyte or gametophyte generation dominates.

Flowers are reproductive structures of angiosperms. The *calyx,* made of *sepals,* and the *corolla,* made of *petals,* are accessory structures. Inside the corolla is the *androecium,* which consists of the male *stamens* and their pollen-containing *anthers.* At the center of the flower is the *gynoecium,* enclosing the *ovary.* The *stigma* extends from the ovary and captures pollen.

In the anther, four *pollen sacs* contain *microspore mother cells,* each of which divides by meiosis to yield four haploid *microspores,* which divide mitotically to yield a haploid *generative nucleus* and a haploid *tube nucleus.* These two cells and their covering constitute a *pollen grain.* Sperm cells arise from the generative cells. In the ovary, *megaspore mother cells* divide meiotically to yield four haploid cells, one of which persists as a haploid *megaspore,* which then divides mitotically three times. The resulting megagametophyte, or *embryo sac,* contains several cells, one of which is the egg.

Pollen is transferred from an anther to a stigma, either within the same flower or plant or between plants. Flower structures and odors have evolved to appeal to pollinators or to utilize wind dispersal. Once on a stigma, a pollen grain grows a *pollen tube,* in which the sperm approaches the ovary. In the embryo sac, one sperm fertilizes the egg to form the zygote, and the second sperm fertilizes the *polar nuclei,* forming the *endosperm,* which nourishes the embryo. *Cotyledons* develop, absorbing the endosperm in dicots and transferring nutrients in monocots. Apical meristems promote growth of the shoot and root ends of the embryo.

After fertilization, no longer needed floral parts fall off, and the ovary may develop into a fruit, under the influence of hormones. A seed germinates in response to an environmental cue, and it requires oxygen, energy, and water. When the embryo bursts from the seed coat, primary growth ensues.

In pines, large female cones bear two ovules per scale, which yield three haploid degenerate cells and one haploid megaspore through meiosis. Microsporangia grow on the small scales of males cones. Through meiosis, microspores are produced, which become pollen grains. Pollen lands on sticky material on female cones, and the pollen tube grows towards the egg. Here the pollen matures by dividing twice. Two of the resulting cells are sperm, one of which fertilizes the egg. The embryo is nourished by the megagametophyte and enters dormancy, protected by a tough seed coat.

In asexual reproduction, a parent plant gives rise to clones, which can develop from roots, stems, or leaves.

QUESTIONS

1. Describe the steps in alternation of generations.

2. What is the function of flowers? Which floral structures participate directly in this function? Which structures participate indirectly?

3. What floral structures might a male wasp encounter when pollinating orchids?

4. What are three adaptations that have evolved in plants to encourage outcrossing?

5. What type of pollinator might be attracted to a plant with the following:
   a. Red, sweet-smelling flowers
   b. Dull-colored, spicy-smelling flowers
   c. Yellow, heavily scented flowers

6. Why do wind-pollinated species produce more pollen than animal-pollinated plants?

7. Name a tissue or cell in an angiosperm that is haploid, diploid, and triploid.

8. Gardeners know to plant many more seeds than should suffice for the number of plants desired, because not all of them will germinate. What are some reasons why seeds might fail to germinate?

9. How is the life cycle of a corn plant and a spruce pine similar and different?

TO THINK ABOUT

1. Chefs consider a plant food a fruit or a vegetable according to when it is eaten and how sweet it tastes. How does this differ from the biological definition of a fruit?

2. Why is it important for a particular insect species to pollinate only one species of flowering plant?

3. How could you tell if a portion of a plant is part of the sporophyte generation or the gametophyte generation?

4. Under what type of environmental condition might asexual reproduction be of most benefit to a species, and when would sexual reproduction be the most beneficial?

5. Humans and plants each have diploid as well as haploid cells. How do the life cycles of humans and flowering plants differ?

6. How are petals, which are considered accessory structures, nevertheless necessary for reproduction?

7. In the Midwest, children can get summer jobs "detasselling" corn, which is removing the male parts. Why might a farmer want this done to the crop?

8. Why might a flower smell like putrefied meat?

SUGGESTED READINGS

Beattie, Andrew J. February 1990. Ant plantation. *Natural History*. Ants help disperse seeds.

Darwin, Charles. 1862. *On the various contrivances by which British and foreign orchids are fertilized*. The father of evolution was particularly fascinated by the adaptations of flowers to their pollinators' tastes.

Goldberg, Robert B. June 10, 1988. Plants: Novel developmental processes. *Science*, vol. 240. Structurally plants are simpler than animals, but on the molecular level they too are complex.

Huntly, Brian, and I. Colin Prentice. August 5, 1988. July temperatures in Europe from pollen data, 6,000 years before present. *Science*, vol. 241. The structures of fossilized pollen hold clues to long-ago environments.

Pennisi, Elizabeth. April-May 1990. Planting the seeds of a nation. *National Wildlife*. Native wildflowers make spectacular garden displays.

Raab, Mandy M., and Ross E. Konig. November 1988. How is floral expansion regulated? *BioScience*, vol. 38, no. 10. For successful pollination, a flower must unfold rapidly in a specific way.

Robackes, David C., et al. June 1988. Floral aroma. *BioScience*, vol. 38, no. 6. The fragrances of flowers are closely tied to the olfactory preferences of their pollinators.

31

Plant Responses to Stimuli

Learning Objectives

By the chapter's end, you should be able to answer these questions:

1. How do hormones regulate a plant's growth and development?

2. What is the mechanism behind a plant's growth towards or away from a particular stimulus?

3. How do carnivorous plants trap insects?

4. How are plants affected by the length of daylight?

5. How do plants respond to seasonal changes?

6. How do plants synchronize their activities?

To a human observer, the sundew plant is a magnificent member of a swamp community. To an insect, however, its beckoning club-shaped leaves, bearing nectar-covered tiny tentacles, are treacherous. Once the insect alights on the plant and begins to enjoy its sweet, sticky meal, the surrounding hairlike tentacles begin to move. Gradually they fold inward, entrapping the helpless visitor, forcing it down toward the leaf's center. Here, powerful digestive enzymes go to work, dismantling the insect's body, releasing its component nutrients. After 18 hours, the leaves open. All that remains of the previous day's six-legged guest is a few bits of indigestible matter (fig. 31.1).

The response of the sundew plant to an insect touching structures on its leaves dramatically illustrates a plant's response to its immediate environment. Other plant responses may not appear as exciting but are also the culmination of a complex interplay of biochemicals and little-understood biological activities.

Unlike animals, most plants cannot escape unfavorable conditions by moving away. Plants adapt to the environment by growing, which is influenced by both internal and external factors. A plant's DNA contains the blueprints for organizing specialized cells into tissues and organs, and these genetic instructions can supply several options. External factors, such as light intensity or temperature, may determine which option is expressed. The result can be a finely tuned growth response that enables the organism to adapt to its surroundings and survive.

Plant Hormones

Many aspects of plant growth are regulated by hormones, which are biochemicals produced in small quantities. Like animal hormones, plant hormones are synthesized in one part of the organism and are transported to another part, where they stimulate or inhibit growth. Yet unlike animal hormones, plant hormones are not produced in tissues specialized for hormone production, and they do not have definite target areas.

Five major classes of plant hormones are known: **auxins, gibberellins, cytokinins, ethylene,** and **abscisic acid** (table 31.1

Figure 31.1
This sundew plant (*Drosera rotundifolia*) grows in the swamps of upstate New York. Its attractive leaves are actually insect traps.

Table 31.1
Major Classes of Plant Hormones

Class	Principal Actions
Auxins	Cell elongation in seedlings, shoot tips, embryos, leaves
Gibberellins	Cell elongation and division in seeds, roots, shoots, young leaves
Cytokinins	Stimulate cytokinesis in seeds, roots, young leaves, fruits
Ethylene	Hastens fruit ripening
Abscisic acid	Inhibits growth

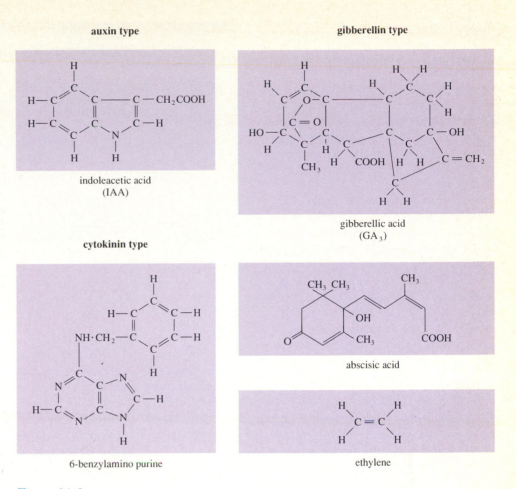

auxin type

indoleacetic acid
(IAA)

gibberellin type

gibberellic acid
(GA_3)

cytokinin type

6-benzylamino purine

abscisic acid

ethylene

Figure 31.2
The major groups of plant hormones. All hormones produce varying effects when the plant uses them in combination.

and fig. 31.2). Plant hormones have both characteristic and unpredictable effects. Their influences depend upon which other hormones are present, and the sensitivity of the tissue to the hormones. As a result, a single hormone can elicit numerous responses.

Auxins

Auxin was the first plant hormone to be described. In the late 1870s, decades before the chemical identification of plant hormones, Charles Darwin and his son Francis learned that a plant-produced "influence" caused growth towards light (fig. 31.3). They were describing auxin, a plant hormone that stimulates cell elongation in grass seedlings and herbs. Auxin apparently coaxes cells to elongate by stretching their cell walls. Auxin acts rapidly, spurring noticeable growth in a grass seedling in minutes.

Three naturally occurring auxins in plants are known. The most active auxin is **indoleacetic acid,** or **IAA.** It is produced in shoot tips, embryos, young leaves, flowers, fruits, and pollen. Synthetic compounds having auxin-like effects are important commercially, such as 2,4-D (2,4-dichlorophenoxyacetic acid), which is used extensively as an herbicide. When applied in concentrations higher than auxin would normally be present, 2,4-D causes weeds to elongate rapidly and literally grow to death.

Figure 31.3
Effects of auxin. The pea plants on the left were not treated with auxin; those on the right were.

Gibberellins

In the late 1920s, Japanese botanists studying "foolish seedling disease" in rice discovered gibberellin, another plant hormone involved in shoot elongation. Plants suffering from foolish seedling disease grow rapidly because they are infected by a fungus that produces gibberellin. The infected plants become so spindly that they fall over and die (fig. 31.4).

Gibberellin, abbreviated GA, stimulates shoot elongation in mature regions of trees, shrubs, and a few grasses and is also found in immature seeds, apices of roots and shoots, and young leaves of flowering plants. GA induces both cell division and elongation. GA-induced elongation occurs after about a 1-hour delay, which is much slower than auxin-induced growth. More than 65 naturally occurring gibberellins are known.

Cytokinins

As early as 1913, scientists knew that some compound stimulates cell division in plants. It was not until 1964 that the first naturally occurring cytokinin was discovered in corn kernels. Since then, researchers have isolated other cytokinins and have synthesized several artificial ones.

Cytokinins are so-called because they stimulate cytokinesis (the division of the cell after the genetic material has replicated and separated) by pushing cells into mitosis. Cytokinins do not work alone—auxin must be present before mitosis begins. The effects of cytokinins are similar to some of the effects of auxin and gibberellin—they promote cell division and growth and participate in development, differentiation, and senescence.

In flowering plants, most cytokinins are found in roots and actively developing organs such as seeds, fruits, and young leaves. Synthetic cytokinin-like compounds have a variety of uses, including keeping wheat stalks short so they are not blown over; shortening shrubs to a manageable level; and extending the shelf-life of lettuce and mushrooms.

Ethylene

The effects of ethylene were known long before its discovery. In 1910, scientists in Japan observed that bananas ripened prematurely when stored with oranges. Appar-

Figure 31.4
Effects of gibberellin. Note the size difference between these two California poppy plants. Can you tell which one was treated with gibberellin?

ently, the oranges produced something that induced rapid ripening. By 1934, scientists realized it was the simple gas ethylene that hastened ripening.

Ethylene ripens fruit in many species. Ripening is a complex process involving pigment synthesis, fruit softening, and breakdown of starches to sugars. A tomato picked from the garden when it is hard and green with streaks of pale orange will turn, aided by ethylene, into a soft, red, succulent tomato.

Ethylene also helps ensure that a plant will survive injury or infection. The hormone is produced when the plant is damaged, and it hastens aging of the affected part so that it can be shed before the problem spreads to other regions of the plant.

Ethylene is synthesized in all parts of flowering plants, but large amounts form in roots, the shoot apical meristem, nodes, and ripening fruits. The dark spots on a ripening banana peel are concentrated pockets of ethylene. Because ethylene is a gas, its effects can be contagious. The expression "one bad apple spoils the batch" refers to the ability of the ethylene released from one apple to hasten the ripening, and spoiling, of others nearby (fig. 31.5).

Although the chemical structure of ethylene is simple, its production by a plant is actually the culmination of several biochemical steps. Genetic engineers have cloned the gene that specifies the enzyme necessary for the very last step in ethylene production. By blocking this gene, they

can therefore block ethylene production. What commercial benefit might blocking a plant's ethylene production serve?

Abscisic Acid

Could plants manufacture growth-inhibiting substances too? By the 1940s, botanists thought so. Twenty years later, researchers isolated such a compound.

Abscisic acid, or ABA, inhibits the growth-stimulating effects of many other hormones. ABA is used commercially to inhibit growth of nursery plants so that they are less likely to be damaged during shipping.

Hormonal Interactions

Plant hormones seldom function alone. Several plant hormones, for example, influence abscission, which is the shedding of leaves or fruit. Abscission is preceded by senescence, the aging and death of a plant or plant part. Recall from chapter 29 that during senescence, an abscission zone forms at the base of the organ that will be shed. Eventually, the leaf or fruit separates from the plant at this abscission zone.

Senescence is normally retarded by auxin produced by actively growing leaves and fruit, along with cytokinin and gibberellin produced by roots. Senescence begins when auxin production drops in response to environmental stimuli, such as injury or the shorter days of autumn. During senescence, cells in the abscission zone begin producing

Figure 31.5
As ethylene accumulates, these tomatoes ripen.

ethylene, which swells the cells and prompts them to produce biochemicals that digest cell walls. As a result, the cells separate and the leaf or fruit drops.

If decreasing levels of auxin lead to abscission, then the application of synthetic auxins should prevent abscission. Indeed, synthetic auxins often are used to prevent preharvest fruit drop in orchards, to hold berries on holly, and to coordinate abscission of fruits at harvest time.

The coordinated production of several hormones permits a plant to survive the changing seasons as well as extreme weather conditions. This enables the plant to develop its reproductive organs and structures, ensuring the perpetuation of the species.

KEY CONCEPTS

Plant hormones coordinate growth and development. Auxins provoke rapid cell elongation in various growing plant parts. Gibberellins promote cell division and elongation in roots, shoots, leaves, and immature seeds of flowering plants and in mature parts of trees and shrubs. Cytokinins stimulate cells to enter mitosis and are found in rapidly dividing plant parts. Ethylene is a gaseous hormone that hastens ripening. Abscisic acid inhibits the growth-stimulating effects of other hormones.

Tropisms

Despite their obvious immobility plants are acutely responsive to some environmental signals. The glorious heads of sunflowers turn towards the sun, and roots grow downwards in response to gravity. Some plant responses are rather short-term. A Venus's-flytrap closes in less than a second, and the curving of a stem towards light usually takes only a few hours. Other behaviors, such as flowering, are long-term responses associated with changing seasons. All of these responses to environmental stimuli are a result of growth.

The term **tropism** refers to plant growth toward or away from environmental stimuli, such as light or gravity. Each of the many types of tropisms is named for the stimulus eliciting the response. Phototropism, for example, is a growth response to unidirectional light, and geotropism is a growth response to gravity.

Tropisms result from differential growth, in which one side of the responding organ grows faster than the other, bending the part. Curving of an organ towards the stimulus is called a *positive tropism*, such as stems growing toward light. Curvature of an organ away from a stimulus is a *negative tropism*. Roots are negatively phototropic.

Phototropism—A Response to Unidirectional Light

During **phototropism,** cells on the shaded side of a stem elongate faster than cells on the lighted side of the stem. The rapid elongation of cells along the shaded side of coleoptiles is controlled by auxin coming from the apex.

Precisely how auxin controls phototropism was discovered in the 1950s by Winslow Briggs and his colleagues. First, they determined that the amount of auxin produced by coleoptiles grown in the light is the same as that of coleoptiles grown in the dark—that is, light does not destroy auxin. They then discovered that more auxin could be collected from the shaded side of coleoptiles than from the lighted side, suggesting that light causes auxin to migrate to the shaded side of the stem. More recent experiments support this finding. Auxin labeled with radioactive carbon (^{14}C) and exposed to unidirectional light moves to the shaded side of coleoptiles. Cells in the shade elongate more rapidly than cells in the light, which curves the coleoptile towards the light (fig. 31.6).

How does a plant sense unidirectional light? Only blue light with a wavelength less than 500 nanometers effectively induces phototropism. The yellow pigment **flavin** is probably the photoreceptor molecule for phototropism. Flavin alters transport of auxin to the shaded side of the stem or coleoptile.

Geotropism—A Response to Gravity

Charles Darwin and his son Francis also studied **geotropism,** which is a growth response to gravity. How would roots grow if their caps were removed, they wondered. They found that decapped roots grew, but not downwards, in response to gravity. Therefore, the root cap is necessary for

Figure 31.6
Positive phototropism. This kidney bean was grown under a hood (shown on the right) for 5 days. Note how it has grown toward the light.

geotropism. It is interesting to examine root growth in the absence of gravity, which is possible by growing plants aboard orbiting spacecraft, where gravity is minimal (Reading 31.1). The nation's schoolchildren are evaluating the growth of tomatoes that spent 5 1/2 years in space as seeds. NASA has supplied "space" seeds and earthbound controls to interested classes, and the students record the growth and conduct other experiments.

A plant's shoot is negatively geotropic, because it grows upwards, and roots are positively geotropic, extending downward along with the gravitational force. Curiously, accumulation of auxin seems to provoke each of these opposite responses. In a horizontal stem or shoot, auxin accumulates on the lower side, stimulating differential growth there. As a result, the structure bends upward (fig. 31.7). However, if a root is held horizontally, accumulating auxin in the lower regions causes downward growth. How can this be? One hypothesis is that root tissue is far more sensitive to auxin than shoot tissue, and the amount of auxin accumulating is so great that it actually inhibits cell elongation. With cells in the upper portion of a horizontal root growing faster, the root bends downward.

Figure 31.7
Formerly horizontal branches of this fallen tree now grow upward, due to geotropism.

Thigmotropism—A Response to Touch

The coiling tendrils of twining plants such as morning glory and bindweed display **thigmotropism,** a response to touch. When hanging free, tendrils often grow in a spiral fashion, which increases their chances of contacting an object to which they can cling (fig. 31.8). Contact with an object is detected by specialized epidermal cells, which induce differential growth of the tendril. The tendril completely encircles the object in only 5 or 10 minutes. Thigmotropism is often long-lasting. Stroking a

Reading 31.1 *Plants in Space*

PLANTS WILL BE A KEY PART OF SPACE COLONIZATION, PROVIDING FOOD AND OXYGEN. But how will organisms that have evolved under constant gravity function in its near-absence beyond the earth?

Researchers are studying the effects of microgravity on a variety of species by sending them on space shuttle voyages. Such experiments can more realistically assess plant growth and development in space than previous earthbound simulations, which used a rotating device called a clinostat to diminish gravitational force.

So far, it appears that plants are profoundly affected by a lack of gravity, from subcellular structural organization to whole organismal functioning. These responses will present interesting challenges to space farmers of the future.

Subcellular Responses to Microgravity

Plant cells grown in space have fewer starch grains and more abundant lipid-containing bodies, indicating a change in energy balance. This may mean that space farmers may have plenty of vegetable oil but no french fries to cook in it.

Organelle organization is grossly altered in the absence of gravity. Endoplasmic reticula are bunched together and arranged randomly, and mitochondria swell when freed from the constraints of gravity. Nuclei enlarge, and chromosomes break, perhaps due to greater exposure to cosmic radiation. Chloroplasts have enlarged thylakoid membranes and small grana. Most interesting are amyloplasts, which are starch-containing granules in specialized gravity-sensing cells in roots. On earth, amyloplasts aggregate at the bottoms of these cells, but in space, they randomly float about the cell. As a result, a root tip cannot elongate downward in response to gravity (fig. 1).

Cell Division

Mitosis is halted by microgravity, usually at telophase, resulting in some cells with more than one nucleus. Oat seedlings germinated in space had only 1/10 as many dividing cells as seedlings germinated on earth. The spindle apparatus also seems to be disrupted by microgravity. Cell walls formed in space are considerably thinner than their terrestrial counterparts, with less cellulose and lignin. Regeneration is also inhibited in space. A decapped root will regenerate in 2 to 3 days on earth, but it will not do so at all in space. Distribution of dividing cells is altered. Lettuce roots, for example, have a shortened elongating zone when grown in space.

Growth and Development

Germination is less likely to occur in space than on earth because of chromosome damage, but it does happen. Early growth success seems to depend upon the particular species—bean, oat, and pine seedlings grow more slowly than on earth, and lettuce, garden cress, and cucumbers grow faster. Many species, including wheat and peas, cease growing and die before they flower. However, in 1982 Arabidopsis plants (mustard weed) successfully completed a life cycle in space—indicating that human space colonies with plant companions may indeed be possible (see fig. 32.2).

a.

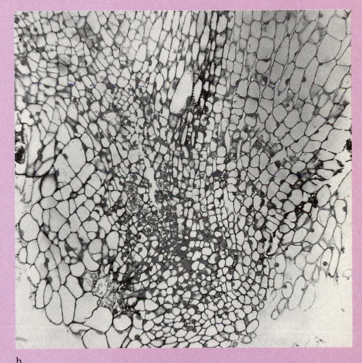

b.

Figure 1
a. On earth, a root whose cap has been removed regenerates an organized, functional root cap.
b. In the microgravity of space, however, regrowth of a decapped root is disorganized. Clearly, gravitational cues are needed to direct normal regeneration.

Figure 31.8
Thigmotropism. The twining of tendrils is a rapid response to touch. This tendril of a passion vine is wrapped around a blackberry stem.

tendril of garden pea for only a couple of minutes can induce a curling response that lasts for several days. Auxin and ethylene control thigmotropism.

Interestingly, tendrils seem to remember touch. Tendrils growing and touched in the dark do not respond until they are illuminated. It seems that sensory information is stored by tendrils in the dark, but a response does not occur until light is present.

KEY CONCEPTS

Plant growth toward or away from a stimulus is called a positive or negative tropism. Tropisms result from differential growth, which is controlled by hormone distributions. Phototropism is response to light; geotropism is response to gravity; thigmotropism is a coiling response to touch.

Table 31.2
Plant Responses

Stimulus	Tropism	Nastic Movement
Light	Phototropism	Photonasty
Dark		Nyctinasty
Gravity	Geotropism	
Touch	Thigmotropism	Thigmonasty
Temperature	Thermotropism	Thermonasty
Chemical	Chemotropism	Chemonasty
Water	Hydrotropism	Hydronasty

Nastic Movements

Nondirectional plant motions, called **nastic movements,** include some of the most fascinating responses seen in the plant kingdom (table 31.2).

Seismonasty

A nastic movement resulting from contact or mechanical disturbance is **seismonasty.** Seismonastic movements depend upon a plant's ability to transmit rapidly a stimulus from touch-sensitive cells in one part of the plant to responding cells located elsewhere. Consider leaf movement in the "sensitive plant" mimosa. When leaves of this plant are touched, the leaflets fold and the petiole droops. Touching the leaf elicits a reaction that causes the cell membrane of motor cells at the base of the leaflet to become more permeable to K^+ and other ions. As ions move out of the motor cells, the osmotic potential in the surrounding area decreases, moving water out of the motor cells by osmosis. This loss of water shrinks the motor cells and seismonastic movement occurs. Reversal of this process causes the leaves to unfold in approximately 15 to 30 minutes (fig. 31.9).

What is the adaptive significance of seismonastic movements in plants? Seismonastic movements probably decrease a leaf's chances of being eaten, because folded leaves are more difficult for an animal to see. These movements may defend sensitive plants in other ways as well. For example, sharp prickles located along a leaf axis are exposed when the leaflets close and motor cells secrete noxious substances called tannins, both of which discourage hungry animals.

The Venus's-flytrap is famous for its dramatic seismonastic response (see fig. 29.11). Unlike the sensitive plant in which seismonastic movements result from reversible changes in turgor pressure, movements of the Venus's-flytrap result from irreversible increases in cellular size, which can be initiated by acidifying the cell walls to pH 4.5 and below.

The leafy traps are built of two lobes, each of which has three sensitive "trigger" hairs overlying motor cells. When a meandering animal touches these hairs, signals are sent to the plant's motor cells, which then initiate transport of H^+ to the walls of epidermal cells along the outer surface of the trap. The resulting acidification of these cell walls expands the outer epidermal cells along the central portion of the leaf. Since epidermal cells along the inner surface of the leaf do not change volume, the flytrap snaps shut.

Closure of the Venus's-flytrap takes 1 to 2 seconds and requires a large expenditure of ATP—motor cells use almost one-third of their ATP to pump the H^+ that acidifies the cell walls and closes the trap. The trapping mechanism is quite sophisticated. A trap will not close unless two of its trigger hairs are touched in succession or one hair is touched twice. By responding to two stimuli instead of one, the plant can distinguish potential prey from other objects, such as falling leaves.

Figure 31.9
The mimosa (sensitive) plant on the top has not been touched; the one on the bottom has. This response illustrates seismonasty.

Figure 31.10
The prayer plant exhibits nyctinasty. When the sun goes down, the prayer plant's leaves turn inward.

When the trap closes, the captive animal is pressed against glands located on the inner surface of the trap that secrete digestive enzymes. Digestion of the unlucky animal may take 1 or 2 days. Opening of empty traps usually requires 8 to 12 hours and results from expansion of epidermal cells along the midrib of the inner surface of the leaf. The sundew in figure 31.1 is another carnivorous plant, like the Venus's-flytrap.

Nyctinasty

The nastic response caused by daily rhythms of light and dark is known as **nyctinasty** (from the Greek nyktos, meaning "night," and nastos, meaning "pressed together"), or "sleep movement." The prayer plant maranta is an ornamental houseplant exhibiting nyctinastic responses. Leaves of prayer plants orient themselves horizontally during the day, which maximizes their in-terception of sunlight. At night, the leaves fold vertically into a configuration resembling a pair of hands in prayer (fig. 31.10).

The movement of the prayer plant's leaves in response to light and dark occurs by changes in turgor pressure of motor cells at the base of each leaf. In the dark, K^+ moves out of cells along the upper side and into cells along the lower side of a leaf base. This ion flux moves water, via osmosis, into cells along the lower side of the leaf base, swelling them. Meanwhile, cells along the upper side lose water and shrink.

Overall, the leaf stands vertically due to the changes in cellular volume. At sunrise, the process is reversed and the leaf again lies horizontally. Changes in leaf position can decrease loss of water and heat.

Sorrel and legumes such as beans have similar sleep movements occurring at the same time each day. A clever use of these regular movements was made by Carl Linnaeus, a famous Swedish botanist. Linnaeus filled wedge-shaped portions of a circular garden with plants having sleep movements occurring at different times.

By seeing which plants of his so-called horologium florae (flower clock) were "asleep," Linnaeus could then tell the time of day.

Thigmomorphogenesis

Plants are extremely sensitive to mechanical disturbances such as rain, hail, wind, animals, and falling objects. In response, plants typically inhibit cellular elongation, remaining short and stocky, and produce large amounts of thick-walled supportive tissue (collenchyma and sclerenchyma fibers). For example, spraying tomato plants with water for only 10 seconds per day reduces their growth by 40%. This response to mechanical disturbances is called **thigmomorphogenesis,** and it is controlled by ethylene.

KEY CONCEPTS

Nondirectional plant movements are called nastic movements. Nastic response to contact is seismonasty; to daily patterns of light and dark is nyctinasty; to touch is thigmomorphogenesis.

Seasonal Responses of Plants to the Environment

Seasonal changes affect plant responses. Autumn brings cooler nights and shorter days, which produce beautifully colored leaves, dormant buds, and decreased growth in preparation for winter. In the spring, buds resume growth and rapidly transform a barren forest into a dynamic, photosynthetic community.

Flowering—A Response to Photoperiod

Flowering reflects seasonal change. Many plants flower only during certain times of the year. Clover and iris flower during the long days of summer, and poinsettias and asters bloom in the short days of early spring or fall.

Studies of how flowering is controlled by seasonal changes began in the early 1900s. W.W. Garner and H.A. Allard at a United States Department of Agriculture research center in Maryland were studying tobacco, which flowers during late summer in Maryland. One group of tobacco mutants did not flower as did the rest of the crop but continued to grow vegetatively into autumn. They became quite large, leading Garner and Allard to name them Maryland Mammoth. Since these oversized mutants had the potential for increasing yield of tobacco crops, Garner and Allard moved their Mammoth plants into the greenhouse to protect them from winter's cold and continued to observe their growth. To their surprise, the mutants finally flowered in December!

Could the plants somehow measure day length? To test this hypothesis, Garner and Allard set up several experimental plots of soybeans, each planted approximately a week apart. All of the plants flowered at the same time, despite the fact that the different planting times resulted in plants of different ages and sizes. From these experiments, Garner and Allard established the term **photoperiodism,** which is a plant's ability to measure seasonal changes by the length of day and night.

The adaptive significance of the ability of plants to anticipate and plan for seasonal changes in climate is obvious. But why would plants measure and respond to day length rather than other climatic factors such as rainfall or temperature? The answer is that weather is unpredictable, whereas day length is consistent due to the position of the earth as it travels around the sun.

Plants are classified into one of four groups, depending upon their responses to photoperiod (duration of daylight). **Day-neutral plants** do not rely on photoperiod to stimulate flowering, and include roses, snapdragons, cotton, carnations, dandelions, sunflowers, tomatoes, cucumbers, and many weeds. **Short-day plants** require light periods that are shorter than some critical length. These plants usually flower in late summer or fall. For example, ragweed plants flower only when exposed to 14 hours or less of light per day. Asters, strawberries, poinsettias, potatoes, soybeans, and goldenrods are short-day plants.

Long-day plants flower when light periods are longer than a critical length, usually 9 to 16 hours. These plants usually bloom in the spring or early summer and include lettuce, spinach, beets, clover, corn, and iris. **Intermediate-day plants** flower only when exposed to days of intermediate length, growing vegetatively at other times. They include sugarcane and purple nutsedge (fig. 31.11).

During which season a plant flowers depends upon whether the photoperiod is longer or shorter than some species-specific critical length. For example, ragweed and spinach both flower if exposed to 14 hours of daylight, yet ragweed is a short-day plant while spinach is a long-day plant. Thus, spinach flowers in the long days of summer, while ragweed blooms in the short days of fall.

Geographical distribution of plants is greatly influenced by their flowering response to photoperiod. For example, many short-day plants do not grow in the tropics where daylight is always too long to induce flowering. The measuring system in many plants is remarkably sensitive. Henbane, a long-day plant, flowers when exposed to light periods of 10.3 hours but not when the light period is 10.0 hours. Photoperiod is sensed by leaves; plants whose leaves are removed do not respond to photoperiod changes.

Some plants will not bloom unless they are exposed to the correct photoperiod and are said to exhibit **obligate photoperiodism.** For plants such as soybeans, the requirement for an inductive photoperiod is absolute—these short-day plants will not flower unless exposed to long nights. Conversely, other plants, including marijuana and Christmas cactus, will eventually flower even without an inductive photoperiod. For them, an inductive photoperiod merely hastens flowering. This response is called **facultative photoperiodism.** In some plants, the photoperiodic requirement for flowering can be influenced by other factors. For example, poinsettias are short-day plants at high temperatures and long-day plants at low temperatures.

Do Plants Measure Day or Night?

Plant physiologists Karl Hamner and James Bonner continued Garner's and Allard's work by studying the photoperiodism of the cocklebur, a short-day plant requiring 15 or fewer hours of light to flower. Controlled-environment growth chambers were used to manipulate photoperiods. The researchers were startled to discover that plants responded to the length of the dark period rather than the light period. The cocklebur plants flowered only when the dark period exceeded 9 hours.

Hamner and Bonner also discovered that flowering did not occur if the dark period was interrupted by a 1-minute flash of light, even if the regular light period remained less than 15 hours. Similar experiments in which the light period was interrupted with darkness had no effect on flowering. Furthermore, a long-day plant flowering on a photoperiod of 16 hours light to 8 hours dark will also flower on a photoperiod of 8 hours light to 16 hours dark if the dark period is interrupted by a 1-minute exposure to light. Other experiments with long- and short-day plants confirmed that flowering requires a specific period of uninterrupted dark rather than uninterrupted light. Thus, short-day plants are more accurately described as long-night plants, because they flower only if their uninterrupted dark period exceeds a critical length. Similarly, long-day plants are more accurately termed short-night plants.

> ### KEY CONCEPTS
>
> *Plants flower in response to a certain ratio of light to dark in a day, which reflects the season. This response is species-specific and is called photoperiodism. Day-neutral plants do not show photoperiodism; short-day plants require light shorter than a certain duration; long-day plants require light longer than a certain duration; intermediate-day plants require daylight of intermediate length. Photoperiod requirements can be quite specific. Plants may respond to the duration of darkness rather than to the duration of light.*

Phytochrome—A Pigment Controlling Photoperiodism

Because photoperiodism is a response to light, botanists suspected that it might be carried out by a pigment molecule whose structure is altered by absorbing light of a particular wavelength. The existence of such a pigment was suggested by the observation that red light inhibits flowering when it is used to interrupt the dark period. This inhibition can be reversed if the interruption of red light is immediately followed by far-red light, a form of red light corresponding to a wavelength at the edge of the electromagnetic spectrum (fig. 6.6). From these observations, botanists concluded that the pigment existed in two forms, one of which absorbed red light and the other far-red light.

In 1959, a pale blue pigment was isolated and identified as **phytochrome.** As hypothesized, phytochrome exists in two interconvertible forms, P_r and P_{fr}. The inactive form of phytochrome is synthesized as P_r. When P_r absorbs red light, it is converted to P_{fr}, which is the active form of phytochrome in flowering. P_{fr} promotes flowering of long-day plants and inhibits flowering of short-day plants. P_{fr} is converted to P_r when it absorbs far-red light (fig. 31.12).

How does the ratio of P_r to P_{fr} provide information on photoperiod? Sunlight has proportionally more red light than far-red light. Therefore, during the day, P_r is converted to P_{fr}. This abundance of P_{fr} could

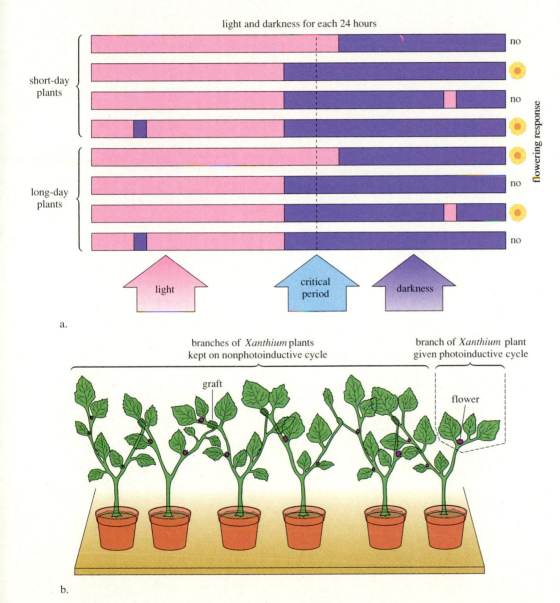

Figure 31.11

Photoperiod. *a.* Flowering response in plants requires not only the proper amount of light but also a critical length of darkness. If either period is interrupted, even for a short time, the plant will not flower. *b.* That the induction of flowering requires some chemical substance can be shown by this experiment. All the plants flowered, even though only one branch of one plant had the right amount of light and darkness, because all the plants were grafted together and could exchange sap.

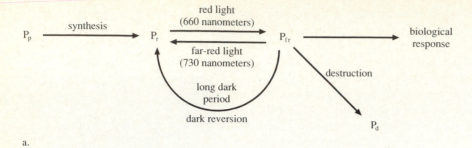

a.

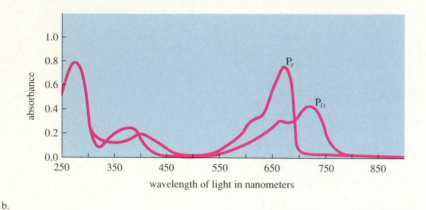

b.

Figure 31.12

Two forms of phytochrome are P_r and P_{fr}. *a.* P_{fr} stimulates biological responses, whereas P_r does not. *b.* The two different forms of phytochrome absorb light at different wavelengths.

Figure 31.13

The century plant. These plants flower only once in several decades and then die.

signal the plant that it is in light. When the plant is placed in darkness, P_{fr} is slowly converted to P_r. This dark conversion of phytochrome to P_r was originally believed to initiate a set of reactions enabling the plant to measure the length of darkness relative to the length of light. Indeed, this reasoning would explain why an uninterrupted period of dark (rather than light) controls photoperiodism. However, the dark reversion of P_r to P_{fr} requires only 3 to 4 hours, and thus it cannot fully explain the light-dark sensing mechanism that controls flowering. Some internal clocklike mechanism probably also influences flowering.

A plant can respond to a photoperiodic initiation of flowering only if it is reproductively mature. Reaching reproductive maturity can take only a few days (as in the Japanese morning glory) or weeks (as in annuals) to several years. Some species of the century plant require decades before flowering (fig. 31.13). The giant bamboo of Asia flowers only about every 33 or 66 years! The delay in flowering until repro-

ductive maturity ensures that the plant has stored enough food to completely form and maintain its flowers. Moisture, soil conditions, nearby plants and temperature may also influence flowering.

Other Responses Influenced by Photoperiod and Phytochrome

Seed germination is also affected by phytochrome. In seeds of lettuce and many weeds, red light stimulates germination, and far-red light inhibits germination. Seeds alternately exposed to red and far-red light are affected only by the last exposure. Thus, germination occurs after exposure to red/far-red/red/far-red/red light as it does after a single exposure to red light. Treatments with far-red and red/far-red/red/far-red/red/far-red light result in no germination. Therefore, the phytochrome system can inform a seed that sunlight is nearby for photosynthesis and thus promote germination. If seeds are buried too deeply in the soil, P_{fr} is absent (due to no sunlight), and germination does not occur.

Phytochrome also controls the early growth of seedlings. Seedlings grown in the dark have abnormally elongated stems, small roots and leaves, a pale color and a spindly appearance. This condition is termed **etiolated** (fig. 31.14). Bean sprouts used in Chinese cooking are etiolated.

By rapidly elongating, etiolated plants reach the light before exhausting their food reserves. Etiolated growth is replaced by normal growth once plants are exposed to the light. Red light controls transformation from etiolated to normal growth. Etiolated plants are very sensitive to red light. Normal growth ensues after exposure to only 1 minute of red light. If red light is followed immediately by an exposure to far-red light, P_{fr} is converted to P_r, and etiolated growth continues.

Phytochrome may also help direct shoot phototropism. Light coming from one direction would presumably create a gradient of P_r and P_{fr} across the stem. P_{fr} would be most abundant on the illuminated side of the stem and P_r most abundant on the shaded side of the stem. This gradient of phytochrome could bend a shoot as P_r promotes stem elongation and P_{fr} inhibits it.

Yet another function of phytochrome is to provide information about shading by overhead plants. Chlorophyll in a plant canopy absorbs much of the red light of sunlight. By the time light reaches underlying plants, such as those on a forest floor, there is less red light, and therefore less P_r is converted to P_{fr}. Since P_r promotes stem elongation (as in etiolated plants), information provided by the phytochrome system can help a plant reach sunlight more rapidly.

Horticulturists use photoperiodism to produce flowers when they are wanted for sale. For example, chrysanthemums (a short-day plant) can be made available year-round by using shades to create an inductive, short-day photoperiod. Similarly, poinsettias can be induced to flower near Christmas if kept in darkness for at least 14 hours a day for at least a month.

Figure 31.14
Etiolated seedlings, *left*, have had insufficient light for normal growth.

KEY CONCEPTS

Photoperiodism is carried out by phytochrome, a blue pigment that interconverts between two forms. Inactive P_r absorbs red light and is converted to active P_{fr}, which absorbs far-red light. P_{fr} causes long-day plants to flower and inhibits short-day plants from doing so. The state of phytochrome imparts information about day length because sunlight has more red light than far-red light. A plant must be mature to be sensitive to photoperiod. Phytochrome and photoperiodism are also involved in early seedling growth, providing information about light conditions, and seed germination.

Senescence

Senescence, or aging, is also a seasonal response of plants. Aging occurs at different rates in different species. Flowers of plants such as wood sorrel and heron's bill shrivel and die only a few hours after being formed. Slower senescence is seen in the colorful turning of leaves in autumn.

Whatever its duration, senescence is not merely a gradual cessation of growth but an energy-requiring process brought about by new metabolic activities. Leaf senescence begins during the shortening days of summer, as nutrients are mobilized and proteins broken down. By the time a leaf is shed, most of its nutrients have long since been transported to the roots for storage. The fallen leaves that so beautifully litter the ground in autumn contain little more than cell walls and remnants of nutrient-depleted protoplasm.

The destruction of chlorophyll in leaves is part of senescence. In autumn, the yellow and orange **carotenoid pigments,** which were previously masked by chlorophyll, become visible. Senescing cells also produce pigments called **anthocyanins.** The loss of chlorophyll, the visibility of the carotenoids, and the production of anthocyanins are responsible for the spectacular colors of autumn's leaves (fig. 31.15).

Dormancy

Before the onset of harsh environmental conditions such as cold or drought, plants often become **dormant,** a state of decreased metabolism. Like leaf senescence, dormancy involves structural and chemical changes. Cells synthesize sugars and amino acids, which function as antifreeze, preventing or minimizing cold damage. Growth inhibitors accumulate in buds, transforming them into winter buds covered by thick, protective scales. These changes in preparation for winter are called **acclimation.**

Growth resumes in the spring as a response to changes in photoperiod and/or temperature. Lengthening days release dormancy in birch and red oak, whereas fruit trees such as apple and cherry resume growth only after exposure to winter's cold. Apple and cherry trees transplanted in warm climates are late bloomers in the spring. The exact mechanism by which photoperiod or cold breaks dormancy is unknown, although hormonal changes are probably involved.

In some plants, dormancy is triggered by factors other than photoperiod or temperature. In many desert plants, rainfall alone releases dormancy, while potato requires a dry period before renewing growth.

KEY CONCEPTS

Plants age at different rates. Autumn leaf colors result from destruction of chlorophyll and unmasking of carotenoids and anthocyanins. Dormancy protects plants against cold damage via such acclimation events as antifreeze synthesis and growth inhibitors. In the spring, growth resumes in response to photoperiod, temperature, or moisture.

Circadian Rhythms

Some rhythmic responses in plants are not seasonal. Consider the common four-o'clock, which opens its flowers only in late afternoon, whereas the yellow flowers of evening primrose open only at nightfall. Similarly, nyctinastic movements of prayer plants occur at the same time every day, and some dinoflagellates glow in warm ocean waters within a few minutes of midnight each evening. These regular, daily rhythms are called **circadian rhythms** (from the Latin circa, meaning "about," and dies, meaning "day"). Other plant activities that occur in daily rhythms include cell division, stomatal opening, protein synthesis, secretion of nectar, and synthesis of growth regulators. Many eukaryotic organisms, including humans, have circadian rhythms (chapter 36).

How do plants measure a day? Is the passage of a day controlled internally by a plant or externally by environmental factors? Several experiments have shown that circadian rhythms in many species do not coincide with a 24-hour day. That is, they may be a few hours longer or shorter than 24 hours. In addition, circadian rhythms often

Figure 31.15
Fall leaves. Senescent leaves lose their chlorophyll and then other pigments become visible.

continue even in constant environmental conditions. Thus, circadian rhythms are probably controlled internally, by a little-understood mechanism called a biological clock, rather than externally.

A plant's circadian rhythm may be altered by environmental factors, such as a change in photoperiod, regardless of the rhythm's internal control. This resynchronization of the biological clock by the environment is called **entrainment.** However, entrainment to a new environment is limited. If the new photoperiod is too different from a plant's biological clock, the plant reverts to its own internal rhythms. Also, a plant maintained in a modified photoperiod over a long period of time reverts to its natural rhythms when placed in constant light.

Biological clocks allow plants to synchronize their activities. In this way flowers of a particular species open when they are most likely to be visited by pollinators. For some plants this timing is quite precise. Flowers of genus *Cereus* are pollinated by bats and must therefore open at night when bats are active. Furthermore, different individuals must flower within a few days of each other, because *Cereus* flowers persist for only a week.

The next chapter describes some interesting ways in which we can alter plants to our specifications. Although these methods are part of the relatively new field of biotechnology, they are actually a continuation of the agricultural approaches discussed at the start of this unit.

KEY CONCEPTS

Circadian rhythms are internally controlled daily responses characteristic of a species that coordinate activities. The internal timing mechanism of a circadian rhythm is called a biological clock. Modification of a biological clock by the environment is called entrainment.

SUMMARY

Plants respond to the environment by growing. Plant hormones have characteristic effects on growth, yet they interact in complex ways. *Auxins* stimulate cell elongation in shoot tips, embryos, young leaves, flowers, fruits, and pollen. *Gibberellins* stimulate cell division and elongation but act slower than auxins. *Cytokinins* stimulate mitosis and are found in actively developing plant parts. *Ethylene* speeds ripening. *Abscisic acid* inhibits the growth-inducing effects of other hormones.

A *tropism* is a growth response toward (positive) or away from (negative) an environmental stimulus usually caused by different rates of growth in different parts of an organ or structure. In *phototropism*, light sends auxin to the shaded portion of the plant, causing growth there and bending the plant towards the light. Shoot growth is a *negative geotropism*, and root growth is a *positive geotropism*. Auxin accumulation can cause these opposite responses because of different sensitivities of the responding tissues. *Thigmotropism* is response to touch and is evidenced by clinging tendrils.

Nastic movements are nondirectional. *Seismonasty* is response to contact, such as a carnivorous plant's entrapping an insect in its leaves. Nastic response to light and dark is *nyctinasty* and can be caused by osmotic changes that differentially alter cell volume. *Thigmomorphogenesis* is a growth-inhibiting response to mechanical disturbance.

Plants are very sensitive to seasonal changes. *Photoperiodism* is the ability of a plant to measure length of day and night.

Flowering can depend upon photoperiodism. Short-day plants flower only when the duration of light is less than some critical length, whereas long-day plants require a light period longer than some critical length. Intermediate-day plants need days of intermediate length to flower. The type of plant determines the season during which it flowers. Plants requiring a precise photoperiod display *obligate photoperiodism*, whereas plants whose flowering is merely hastened by a certain photoperiod display *facultative photoperiodism*. Plants may actually respond to length of darkness rather than length of daylight.

A plant's response to light is controlled by a pigment called *phytochrome*. The inactive form, P_r, absorbs red light to become P_{fr}, the active form. P_{fr} promotes flowering of long-day plants and inhibits flowering of short-day plants. P_{fr} reconverts to P_r by absorbing far-red light. Relative abundances of the two forms of this molecule provide information because sunlight has more red than far-red light. Phytochrome also controls early seedling growth, provides information about shading, and directs shoot phototropism and seed germination.

Senescence is both an active and passive cessation of growth. Growth becomes dormant during cold or dry times and resumes when environmental conditions are more favorable. Daily responses are called *circadian rhythms* and are controlled by internal biological clocks. These clocks can be altered, or *entrained*, by environmental change.

QUESTIONS

1. How is plant growth different from and similar to animal growth?

2. How does the action of gibberellin differ from that of auxin?

3. A tendril's pattern of coiling can be due to thigmotropism or seismonastic coiling. What is the difference between the two responses?

4. For three plant species, describe how movement of ions influences movement of leaves.

5. Give examples of how a tropism, nastic response, and flowering response to photoperiod are adaptive.

6. What is the experimental evidence that a short-day plant is more accurately described as a long-night plant?

7. How are auxin and phytochrome involved in shoot phototropism?

TO THINK ABOUT

1. Several times in the scientific investigation of plant responses, the existence of a substance was suspected before it was actually observed. How is the scientific method used in such a situation? Provide an example of how the scientific method was used to explain a plant response.

2. How can different plant hormones, or their synthetic equivalents, be used in agriculture?

3. You want to make a fruit salad for a barbecue tomorrow, but the bananas are not ripe yet. How might you hasten their ripening? Which plant biochemical would you use?

4. Why won't rain cause the leaves of a Venus's-flytrap to close?

5. Although spinach and ragweed each requires 14 hours of sunlight to flower, spinach flowers in the summer and ragweed (as hay fever sufferers can attest) flowers in the fall. Explain the seasonal difference in flowering.

6. How is the function of phytochrome similar to that of rhodopsin, the pigment that functions in human vision?

SUGGESTED READINGS

Evans, Michael L., Randy Moore, and Karl Hasenstein. December 1986. How roots respond to gravity. *Scientific American*, pp. 112–19. A plant's roots are quite in tune to gravitational forces.

Lewis, Ricki. May 28, 1990. Scientists take to the classroom to inspire youngsters. *The Scientist*. The author is one of many teachers leading schoolchildren in observing the growth of plants from space seeds.

Marsella, Gail. November 1984. Plant assassins. *Biology Digest*. Some plants protect themselves by producing biochemicals that ward off attackers.

Moore, Randy. January 1988. How gravity affects plant growth and development. *Biology Digest*. How will plants fare when the gravity under which they have evolved is absent?

Raab, Mandy M., and Ross E. Koning. November 1988. How is floral expansion regulated? *BioScience*, vol. 38, no. 10. The timing of flowering is intimately tied to a plant's environment.

32

Plant Biotechnology

Chapter Outline

Learning Objectives

By the chapter's end, you should be able to answer these questions:

1. What is biotechnology?

2. What are the similarities and differences between plant biotechnology and traditional plant breeding?

3. How can protoplast fusion produce new plant varieties?

4. How can plant cells be grown in culture to produce identical offspring or variant offspring?

5. How can novel combinations of plant cell nuclei, cytoplasms, and organelles be developed?

6. How can recombinant DNA technology introduce new traits into plants?

7. How do dicots and monocots differ in their abilities to be manipulated by specific biotechnologies?

8. What are some of the environmental questions that must be addressed when plants altered by biotechnology are field tested?

Beck/Shoemaker

I f you were asked to design a new type of plant that would offer more to human consumers than anything available in nature, what might it be? Popcorn that tastes so buttery by itself that it does not need butter, or perhaps a plant that sprouts tomatoes above ground and potatoes below? A farmer might desire plants that "fix" nitrogen from the atmosphere into a biologically usable form without costly fertilizer or crops that manufacture their own herbicide and insecticide and resist disease. Why not mix up nutritional characteristics into healthful new combinations—corn that is rich in the amino acid tryptophan, which it normally lacks, or a hardy new rice derived from cultivated and wild strains?

All of these interesting types of plants have indeed been developed in recent years, thanks to techniques that either manipulate cells or delve into the genetic material. These new variants have been produced far faster than is possible using conventional plant breeding methods. It is estimated that by 1995, 5% of agricultural output in the United States will come from technologies that manipulate plants at the cellular and subcellular levels.

The Challenge of Agricultural Biotechnology

Biotechnology is the use of organisms or their components to provide goods or services. It includes such age-old practices as fermenting wine from grapes and "folk" medicines derived from living things (fig. 32.1); cell manipulations developed throughout the twentieth century; and the genetic alterations performed and perfected since the mid-1970s. The first products of modern biotechnology served the medical, microbiological, and veterinary markets. Another major area of biotechnology is agriculture. Biotechnology applied to crop plants may become very important in expanding food supplies to serve a growing human population. Agricultural biotechnology can introduce qualities that appeal to farmers, food processors, and consumers alike, improving such agronomic characteristics as adaptability, yield, and resistance to disease and pesticides; making anatomical alterations that ease harvesting; increasing nutritional content; and fine-tuning sweetness, acidity, texture, flavor, size, and shape to consumer preferences.

Figure 32.1
Opium, ancient product of biotechnology. The opium poppy is the source of powerful painkillers called morphine alkaloids. Evidence of medicinal use of poppy extracts dates back at least 3,500 years. Morphine comes from a green ovary capsule, which protects the growing seeds. The capsule can be seen 80 days after planting, when the flower petals fall off. The active alkaloid is contained in a whitish fluid within the capsule. This juice is collected and air dried to form a black semisolid, which is the fresh opium product from which drugs are derived.

Although agricultural biotechnology may ultimately have the greatest impact upon human existence of all the applications of biotechnology, it may be the most difficult to achieve. Manipulating the genes and cells of plants has lagged behind similar work on animals and bacteria because the arrangement of genetic material in plants is more complex than in organisms. Plant DNA, for example, often contains vast regions of repeated nucleotide sequences of unknown function. Recessive traits are difficult to study in polyploids. What plant geneticists have needed for some time has been a genetically simple plant. The mustard weed *Arabidopsis thaliana* fits the bill (fig. 32.2).

Understanding plant ecology is also important. "Engineered" plants must eventually be grown in the environment, where they can interact with other organisms. A genetically engineered vaccine or drug, in contrast, would be confined to a laboratory facility.

A first set of hurdles in plant biotechnology has already been surmounted for a few species—that is, growing a mature plant from an initial cell that has been manipulated, demonstrating the new trait in the regenerated plant, and showing that the regenerated altered plant passes on the characteristic to its progeny. A second hurdle will be to understand which combinations of individual altered traits contribute to desired characteristics. Although most of the biotechnologies manipulate one inherited trait at a time, traditional plant breeding work has shown that valuable characteristics are often the product of particular combinations of inherited traits.

Traditional Plant Breeding Versus Biotechnology

The steps in traditional breeding and biotechnology are similar. First, an interesting trait is identified and bred, or engineered, into a plant whose other characteristics comprise a valuable package. For example, larger fruit size might be desired in a plant

Figure 32.2
A model organism for unraveling plant genetics—the mustard weed. With only five chromosomes, just 1% of the DNA content of wheat, it seems to say with a few genes what other plants do with many. For example, the mustard weed codes for the protein portion of chlorophyll with 3 genes, whereas the petunia does so with 16 genes. The weed also has little repetitive DNA. It is a small plant that produces lots of seeds and is easy to grow, and its life cycle is only 5 weeks. Botanists hope to unravel molecular details in this weed and then apply what they learn to more complex plants.

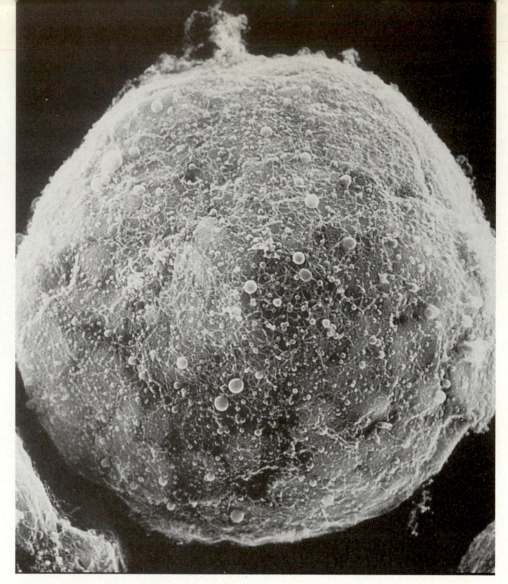

Figure 32.3
Protoplasts are denuded plant cells. Protoplasts can be fused to create hybrid cells with interesting new mixtures of traits. Magnification, x512.

that can already withstand temperature extremes and resist pests. The new variety is then tested in several different habitats and during different seasons to determine the conditions under which it grows best. Finally, seeds are distributed to growers.

Traditional plant breeding introduces new varieties by a sexual route. Pollen carrying the genes for traits in male sex cells fertilizes ovules that bear egg cells carrying a different set of traits. Because each sex cell brings with it a different combination of the parent plants' traits, offspring from a single cross are not genetically uniform. This is the reason that human siblings are not identical; similarly, some plants may be taller or more robust or produce smaller seeds than others.

Rather than beginning with sperm and egg, which have a half set of genetic instructions each, most biotechnologies begin with somatic (body) cells, which form nonsexual parts of the plant such as leaves and stems, or may come from embryos. Somatic cells have a complete set of genetic instructions. Plants that are regenerated from somatic cells do not have the unpredictable mixture of characteristics found in plants derived from sexual reproduction, because the somatic cells are usually genetic replicas, or **clones,** of each other. Biotechnology, then, offers a degree of precision, plus it can assure consistency in crop quality from season to season.

Biotechnology can alter plant structure or function at any of several levels of cellular organization: the individual cell, its organelles, and the genes within its nucleus.

Protoplast Fusion—The Best of Two Cells

In **protoplast fusion,** new types of plants are created by combining cells from different species and then regenerating a mature plant hybrid from the fused cell. A protoplast is simply a plant cell whose cell wall has been removed by treatment with digestive enzymes. Two protoplasts may join on their own, or they can be stimulated to do so

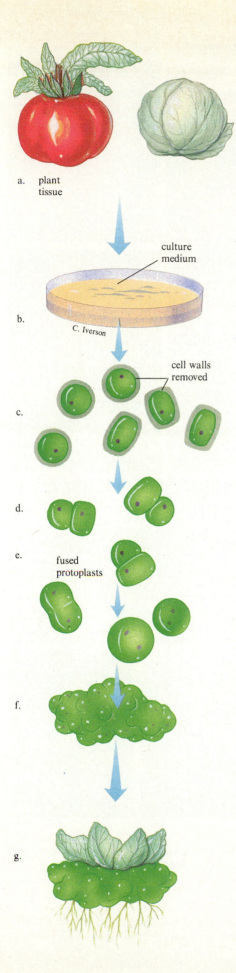

a. plant tissue

culture medium

C. Iverson

cell walls removed

b.

c.

d.

e. fused protoplasts

f.

g.

by exposure to polyethylene glycol (an anti-freeze), a brief jolt of electricity, or being hit by a laser beam (figs. 32.3 and 32.4).

A single gram (about 1/28 of an ounce) of plant tissue can yield as many as 4 million protoplasts, each of which is a potential new plant, either by itself or when fused with another protoplast. If the protoplasts from two different species look different or can be distinguished biochemically, then hybrids can be separated. A plant regenerated from a protoplast fusion of two plant types is called a **somatic hybrid.**

Not all protoplast fusions yield mature plants, and of those that do, not all are useful. Consider the "pomato" plant, which is the result of a tomato protoplast fused with a potato protoplast. The regenerated plant produces both types of vegetables in the proper part of the plant, but the tomatoes and potatoes are small and seed quality is poor. The interesting hybrid cannot be propagated. A plant derived from a protoplast fusion between parsley and carrot also produces the desirable parts—carrot roots and parsley leaves—but they are small, and the plant has tiny seeds. Even less useful is a fusion of radish and cabbage. The not-very-tasty plant grows radish leaves and cabbage roots! Protoplast fusion is more successful when the parent cells come from closely related species. For example, when a protoplast from a potato plant that is normally killed by the herbi-cide triazine is fused with a protoplast from the wild black nightshade, a relative that is naturally resistant to the herbicide, the resulting potato hybrid grows well in soil treated with triazine to control weeds.

Protoplast fusion has limitations. Bringing together quantities of two cell types gives mixed and unpredictable results: single cells, fused cells of the same species, and the

Figure 32.4

Protoplast fusion—one cell from two. Protoplast fusion can yield plants with traits from two species. Tissues from different plants (*a*) are placed in tissue culture (*b*), and the cell walls are dissolved with enzymes or pierced by electricity or a laser (*c*). The resulting protoplasts are mixed and encour-aged to fuse (*d*). Among the fusion products may be hybrid protoplasts (*e*), which are selected and grown into undifferentiated tissue called callus (*f*). Sometimes, plants can be regenerated from the callus, yielding interesting new combinations of traits (*g*).

sought-after fused cells of two different types. Not all species form protoplasts that can be coaxed to fuse. Of those that do, only some of the fusion products go on to divide and develop into plants. Of these, there is no guarantee that they will have useful traits. Many dicots can be regenerated from proto-plasts taken from leaf mesophyll tissue, but monocots such as corn, rice, and sugarcane grow best from protoplasts derived from less specialized embryonic cells (fig. 32.5). Monocot somatic hybrids have been con-structed between pearl millet and Einkorn wheat, between pearl millet and sugarcane, and between cultivated and wild rice.

KEY CONCEPTS

Agricultural biotechnology can ease harvesting, improve nutritional content, and alter taste. Plants are more difficult to manipulate genetically than are animals, and altered plants will ultimately have to grow among other species. Many plant biotechnologies use somatic cells. In pro-toplast fusion, plant cells that have had their cell walls removed are fused, and a hybrid plant can develop. Such hybrids, however, have unpredictable combinations of traits and may be difficult to propagate.

Cell Culture

A fascinating thing happens when proto-plasts or tiny pieces of plant tissue, called **explants,** are nurtured in a dish with nutri-ents and plant hormones. After a few days, the cells lose the special characteristics of the tissues from which they were taken and form a white lump called a **callus.** The lump grows, its cells dividing, for a few weeks. Then certain cells of the callus grow into either a tiny plantlet with shoots and roots or a tiny embryo. An embryo grown from callus is called a **somatic embryo** because it derives from somatic, rather than sexual, tissue.

Researchers are not sure how or why calli of some species give rise to somatic embryos, some give rise to plantlets, and others never develop beyond a lump of tissue (fig. 32.6). Callus growth of calli is apparently a phenomenon unique to plants. In humans, it would be the equivalent of a cultured skin cell, for example, multiplying into a blob of unspecialized tissue and then sprouting tiny humans or human embryos!

Callus cells are unspecialized, even though they derive from differentiated tissue in which only some genes are expressed. All of the genes of a callus cell are capable of expression, much like those of a fertilized egg. Most of the time, embryos or plantlets grown from a single callus are genetically identical to each other. Sometimes, however, the embryos or plantlets differ from each other because certain of the callus cells undergo genetic change (mutation). Biotechnologists can to some extent control whether or not growths from a callus are identical by altering the nutrients and hormones in the callus culture. This ability to control callus growth is valuable, because under some circumstances agriculture may benefit from a uniform crop, and at other times, new varieties may be sought.

Cell Culture for Uniformity

Somatic Embryos as Artificial Seeds

A natural seed is a plant embryo and its food supply, packaged in a protective shell. An **artificial seed** can be fashioned by suspending a somatic embryo in a transparent polysaccharide gel containing nutrients and hormones and providing protection and shape with an outer biodegradable polymer coat. For example, alfalfa embryos are encapsulated in a calcium alginate gel to form artificial seeds (fig. 32.7). To develop artificial seeds, the callus culture is manipulated so that the somatic embryos that they yield are genetically identical. Biotechnologists can actually improve upon nature by packaging somatic embryos with pesticides, fertilizer, nitrogen-fixing bacteria, and even microscopic parasite-destroying worms.

The advantage of artificial seeds for the farmer is their guarantee of a uniform crop because they are genetically identical. Plants that mature at the same rate, for example, can make harvesting simpler and cheaper. In contrast, the embryos of seeds obtained from sexual reproduction contain unpredictable mixtures of parental traits.

Artificial seed technology so far has been most successful for dicots such as celery, lettuce, cotton, and alfalfa, but embryos of the monocots corn, rice, and sugarcane can grow from calli if certain synthetic plant hormones and herbicides are added. Again monocot embryos grow only from calli derived

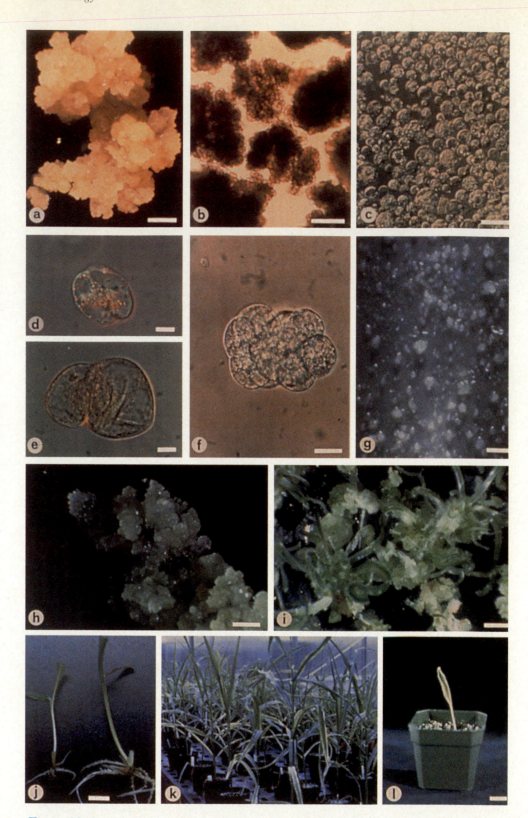

Figure 32.5
Regenerating corn plants from protoplasts, a long-sought goal of biotechnologists, was accomplished in 1988. The process begins with a corn callus developed from embryo tissue (*a*). The callus cells are gently suspended in culture (*b*) and then purified (*c*). The protoplast cells divide (*d* and *e*). After 2 weeks, a colony has formed (*f*), which gives rise to calli (*g* and *h*). When certain nutrients and hormones are added, tiny plantlets form (*i*). After some growth, the plantlets are ready to be placed in soil (*j*) and then are raised in a greenhouse (*k*). These plants grow to maturity and give rise to their own offspring (*l*). In 1990, wheat was successfully grown from protoplasts.

from embryonic or unspecialized cells. Artificial seed technology for the cereals is not economically feasible, however, because these plants provide abundant seed in their natural form. In addition, growing calli takes up a great deal of laboratory space.

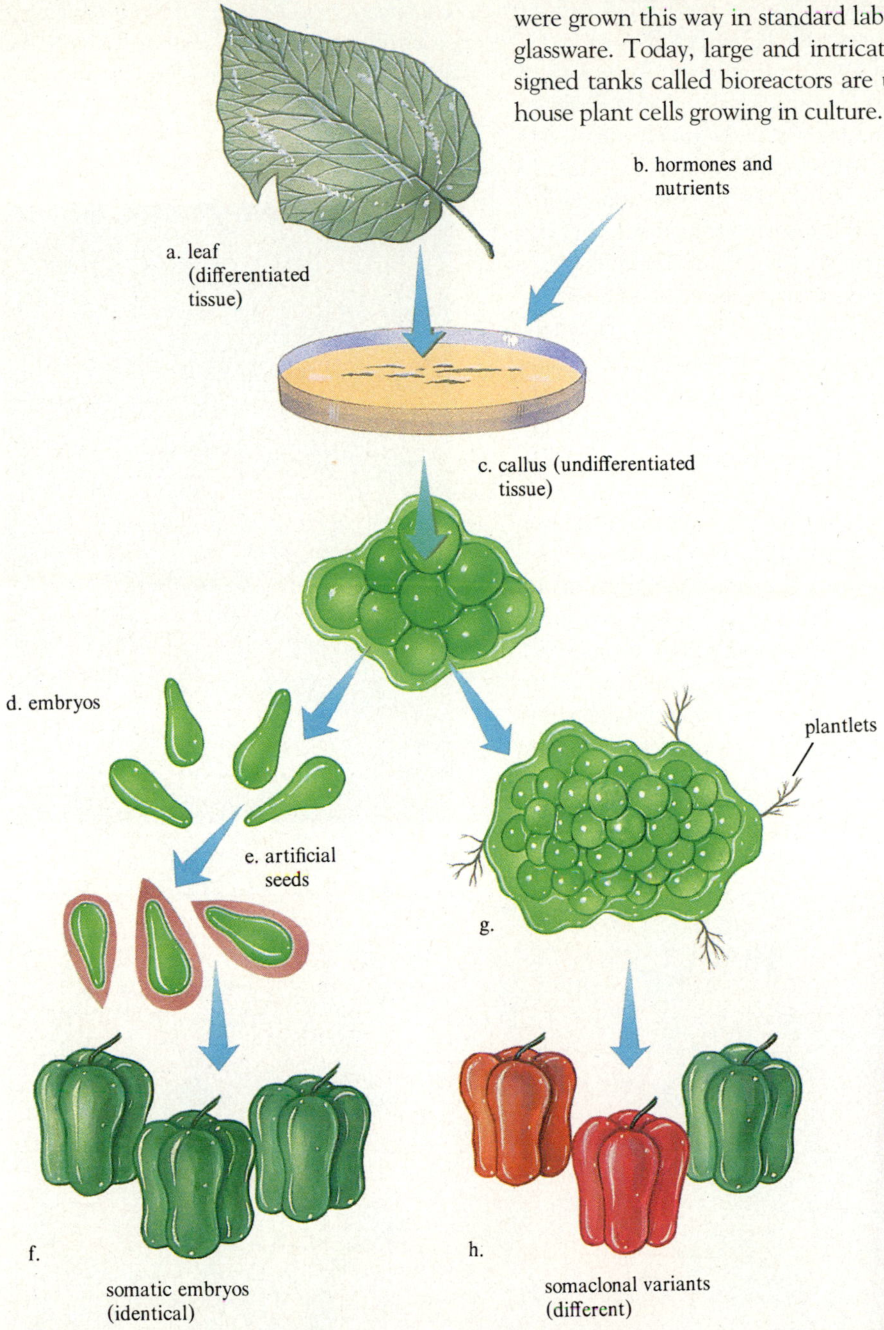

Clonal Propagation

Uniform plants are also produced by **clonal propagation,** in which cells or protoplasts are cultured in the laboratory and then grown into genetically identical plants (clones) (fig. 32.8). As long ago as the 1930s, some plants were grown this way in standard laboratory glassware. Today, large and intricately designed tanks called bioreactors are used to house plant cells growing in culture.

Clonal propagation offers several advantages. It can speed growth of plants that are difficult to grow vegetatively and of slow-growing valuable trees, such as oil palm, redwoods, and chestnuts. Plants that are clonally propagated are grown in disease-free conditions and can be grown year round. The ornamental flower industry clonally propagates orchids, for example, because the flowers are uniform in appearance. So far clonal propagation has been used mostly for tropical root and tuber plants, such as bananas, plantains, cassava, potato, sweet potato, and yam, but also for asparagus, carrot, potato, and strawberry. Clonally propagated oil palm, orchids, and potatoes are grown commercially. Like artificial seeds, clonally propagated plants are often too costly to be practical.

Cell Culture for Variety

Somaclonal Variation

Embryos and plantlets have been grown from callus since the 1950s. When researchers attempted to grow uniform embryos and plantlets, they were sometimes confounded by the appearance of new variants. A callus covered with tiny green tomato plantlets might sprout one that is darker or lighter than the others. This occasional variability,

a. leaf (differentiated tissue)

b. hormones and nutrients

c. callus (undifferentiated tissue)

d. embryos

plantlets

e. artificial seeds

g.

f. somatic embryos (identical)

h. somaclonal variants (different)

Figure 32.6

The fate of a callus—embryos or plantlets. New plants grown from cell culture are valuable either for their uniformity or their variation, depending upon the goal of the researcher. In somatic embryogenesis, plant cells are cultured into callus (*a-c*), which is then exposed to nutrients and hormones to give rise to genetically identical plant embryos (*d*). The embryos, when packaged in a protective shell to form artificial seeds (*e*), guarantee uniform, consistent crop (*f*). In somaclonal variation, the culture medium encourages variety. Plants are regenerated from the resulting callus (*g*), some of which display new traits (*h*).

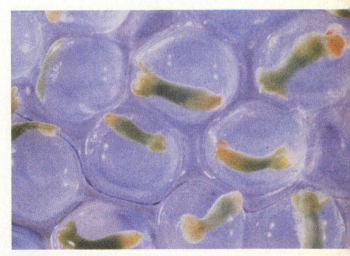

Figure 32.7

These artificial seeds consist of somatically derived alfalfa embryos encapsulated in a calcium alginate gel. As supplied to growers, the gel package would also include nutrients, hormones, pesticides, and other components needed for embryo-to-plant development. Artificial seeds, however, are more expensive than natural seeds.

a.

b.

c.

d.

Figure 32.8
Identical (cloned) carrots can be grown from callus. *a.* To clone carrots, sections of root are cored, and thin slices are placed in a culture dish containing nutrients and hormones to stimulate callus formation. *b.* After a few days, the carrot root cells lose their specific characteristics and form a callus (shown at 5 weeks). *c.* After about 3 months, the callus begins producing differentiated tissue, which is transferred to another medium to encourage growth of shoots and roots. *d.* Eventually, the new carrot plantlets are strong enough to be moved from their sterile medium into regular potted soil.

once regarded as a liability, has been turned into an entirely new technology in its own right, called **somaclonal variation.** Unusual plants arising from protoplast or cell culture are called somaclonal variants because they are derived from a single somatic cell (the one that gave rise to the callus) and are therefore clones of it and each other.

In 1981, researchers in Australia suggested that somaclonal variants could be agriculturally useful. Normally new plant varieties arise literally one in a million by spontaneous mutation, but somaclonal variants arise much more frequently. In 1983, researchers at DNA Plant Technologies, a New Jersey company, decided to intentionally look for variants from callus. They took a normal, medium-sized red tomato plant, chopped up bits of leaf tissue, grew the bits into callus, and regenerated 230 plantlets. After growth to maturity, 13 of the 230 plants were markedly different from the original tomato plant. One variant had tangerine-colored fruits; two others lacked a joint between the stem and the tomato, making harvesting easier; and two other variants had a high solids content (fig. 32.9).

One would have to look through millions of naturally grown tomato plants to find 13 genetic variants. How does the culture process uncover genetic variation? Possibly a genetic variant not noticeable if it exists only in one leaf cell among thousands becomes obvious when the cell that contains it gives rise to an entire new plant. (If this could happen in humans, imagine that a skin cell in a Caucasian underwent a mutation giving it a dark color. It would not be noticeable in the person, but if that mutated cell was used to regenerate a new person, he or she would

a.

b.

Figure 32.9
Somaclonal variation produces interesting new tomatoes. *a.* A high-solids tomato, the product of somaclonal variation, is of interest to the canned-food industry because less boiling is required to produce tomato paste, sauce, and soup. *b.* The same technique has also yielded larger than normal and differently pigmented varieties.

Figure 32.10
Rice plants are grown from cultured sex cells in gametoclonal variation. The inset shows various stages of the process—pollen-bearing anthers cut from rice plants are placed in culture, *left*, where the pollen grains form callus, *center*, and eventually produce plantlets, *right*. When they are strong enough, the plantlets are moved to pots and examined for beneficial variants.

have dark skin.) Alternatively, there is evidence that culturing alters the pattern of protective chemical groups on chromosomes, which may lead to cells with new traits.

Somaclonal variation technology makes it possible to alter or add traits one at a time to an existing genetic background. High-solids tomatoes derived from somaclonal variants go quicker from field to soup can, because less water needs to be boiled off. Crunchier carrots and stringless celery from somaclonal variants are sold at supermarkets and fast-food restaurants. Another healthful somaclonal variant is popcorn with built-in buttery taste.

Gametoclonal Variation

Whereas somaclonal variation uses somatic cells, sex cells can also be used to grow callus, from which plantlets can be coaxed to form. Genetically variant plantlets that grow from callus initiated by sex cells are said to arise from **gametoclonal variation** (fig. 32.10). Because such a callus consists of mass-produced sex cells, each cell has half the number of chromosomes found in somatic cells of that particular species. A plant regenerated from such a gamete-derived callus cannot itself form gametes, and so it cannot reproduce. To get around this drawback, gametoclonally derived plantlets are exposed to the drug colchicine, which duplicates the chromosomes, creating a polyploid. Obtaining such a homozygous plant by conventional breeding would take at least 5 or 6 years; using cell culture, it takes 1 or 2 years.

Mutant Selection

Researchers can choose specific characteristics of new plant variants arising in cell cultures by exposing cells or protoplasts to noxious substances and then selecting only those cells that survive. The surviving cells possess a gene (or genes) that enables them to manufacture a biochemical providing resistance to the substance. Looking for genetic variants that offer a desired characteristic is called **mutant selection.** If a plant can be regenerated from a cell that has been mutant selected, then that plant and its progeny may also be resistant.

A practical application of mutant selection is to tailor seeds to be resistant to particular herbicides, so that a seed company can sell an irresistible package—seed along with an herbicide that is biologically guaranteed not to harm it (fig. 32.11).

Altering Organelles

Combinations of nuclei, cytoplasms, and organelles not known in nature can be devised to yield interesting new variants. Chloroplasts and mitochondria are good candidates for such **organelle transfer** because they contain their own genes, some of which confer such traits as male sterility (important in setting up crosses), herbicide resistance, and increased efficiency in obtaining and using energy.

Cybridization is a technique that produces a plant cell having cytoplasm derived from two cells but containing a single nucleus. A cybrid is created by fusing two protoplasts, then destroying the nucleus of one with radiation. Researchers then select fused cells that contain one nucleus and the desired combination of organelles from the original cells. In another approach, individual chloroplasts or mitochondria are isolated and encapsulated in a fatty bubble called a liposome (see Reading 5.2). The liposome can transport its contents across the cell membrane into a selected cell. Introducing a chloroplast in this manner creates a cell called a **chlybrid**; sending in a mitochondrion produces a **mibrid** (figs. 32.12 and 32.13).

KEY CONCEPTS

Cultured protoplasts or explants can be cultured to give rise to calli, from which somatic embryos or plantlets may grow. Genetically identical somatic embryos can be encapsulated to form artificial seeds, and genetically identical plants are grown from calli by clonal propagation. Plantlets grown from calli can develop from somatically mutated cells, yielding somaclonal variants that may have interesting new qualities. Gametoclonal variation is seen in plantlets grown from calli initiated with sex cells. Use of colchicine in such plantlets produces homozygous polyploids. Mutant selection identifies cells and plants resistant to certain harmful substances. New varieties of plant cells can be generated by introducing new combinations of mitochondria and chloroplasts.

Within the Nucleus—Recombinant DNA Technology

In **recombinant DNA technology,** single genes are transferred from a cell of one type of organism to a cell of another. The first recombinant organisms were bacteria engineered to carry and express the genes of higher organisms, such as the bacterium *E. coli* altered to produce human insulin. Multicellular organisms that contain a "foreign" gene in each of their cells, resulting from foreign DNA introduced at the fertilized egg stage, are called **transgenic.** Figure 13.15 shows a transgenic tobacco plant, engineered to display a firefly's "glow." Recombinant DNA technology—on the simplest bacteria or in complex plants and animals—works because all species use the same genetic code. That is, all organisms use the same sequences of DNA to order the cell to manufacture the same amino acids. For example, a gene from a bean plant placed in

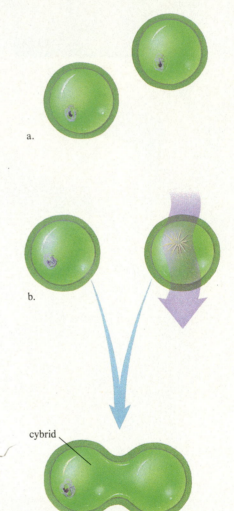

Figure 32.12
Cybridization, a technique similar to protoplast fusion, produces a plant cell having cytoplasm and organelles derived from two cells but containing only one nucleus. Just before two protoplasts are fused (*a*), the nucleus of one is destroyed by radiation (*b*). The fusion product (*c*) is called a cybrid.

Figure 32.11
Mutant selection yields herbicide-resistant corn. Corn developed by mutant selection to resist the herbicide imidazolinone, *left,* is compared with a nonresistant strain after treatment of the field with herbicide.

a sunflower cell instructs the cell to produce the highly nutritious bean proteins, in a sunflower, a feat that has improved the protein quality of sunflower seeds.

Recombinant DNA technology in plants begins by identifying and isolating an interesting gene. Bacteria are often the source of such genes, which can confer on plants built-in resistances to disease, insecticides, herbicides, and environmental extremes. The donor DNA as well as the "vector" DNA, which transports it into the plant cell, are then cut with the same restriction enzyme so that they can attach to each other at the ends to form a recombinant molecule. The vector and its cargo gene are then sent into the plant cell. Chapter 13 discusses the steps of recombinant DNA technology in greater detail.

In dicots, foreign genes are introduced in a **Ti plasmid** (which stands for "tumor inducing"), a ring of DNA found in the microorganism *Agrobacterium tumefaciens* (fig. 32.14). In its natural state the Ti plasmid invades plant cells and causes a cancerlike growth called crown gall disease (fig. 7.10). However, the tumor-causing genes of the plasmid can be chemically removed without impairing the plasmid's ability to enter a plant cell's nucleus. The "disabled" Ti plasmid brings into the plant cell whatever foreign genes are stitched into it.

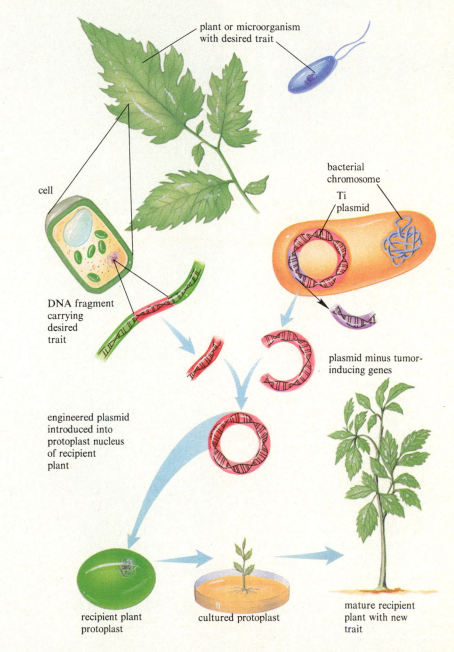

Figure 32.13
Chlybrids and mibrids. Chloroplasts can be isolated from cells of a parent plant (*a*) and encased in liposomes, which are microscopic spheres of lipid (*b*). When mixed with protoplasts of selected cells, the liposomes fuse with the cell membrane (*c*), delivering their contents to the cellular interior and creating "chlybrid" cells. Mitochondria introduced in this way produce "mibrid" cells.

Figure 32.14
Making a transgenic plant. A fragment of DNA carrying the desired gene—conferring resistance to an herbicide, for example—is isolated from its natural source and spliced into a Ti plasmid from which the tumor-inducing genes have been removed. The plasmid incorporating the foreign DNA is then allowed to invade a protoplast of the recipient plant, where it enters the nucleus and integrates into the plant's DNA. Finally, by means of cell culture, the protoplast is regenerated into a mature, transgenic plant that expresses the desired trait and passes it on to its progeny.

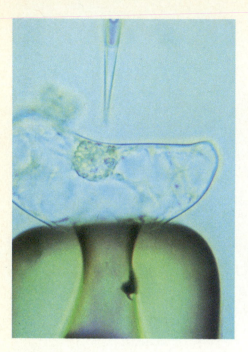

Figure 32.15
Injecting monocot cells with foreign DNA. One way to move foreign DNA into a plant cell nucleus is by direct injection with a microscopic glass needle.

Genetic engineering of the monocots requires more creative approaches than that of the dicots, because many naturally occurring plasmids do not enter monocot cells. One solution is to use monocot protoplasts, because removing the cell wall makes the cell membrane more likely to admit foreign DNA. In a technique called **electroporation**, a brief jolt of electricity opens up transient holes in the cell membrane of monocots that may permit entry of foreign DNA. Genetic material can also be injected into monocot cells using microscopic needles (fig. 32.15) or sent across the cell membrane within liposomes.

Another way to introduce DNA into a plant cell is with **electric discharge particle acceleration,** also known as a "gene gun." A gunlike device shoots tiny metal particles, usually gold, that have been coated with the foreign DNA. Some of the projectiles enter the target cells. This method has been used to "shoot" soybean seed meristem cells with a gene from *E. coli* that stains cells expressing it a vibrant blue, allowing the gene transfer to be detected (fig. 32.16).

Once foreign DNA is introduced into a target cell, it must enter the nucleus and then be replicated along with the cell's own

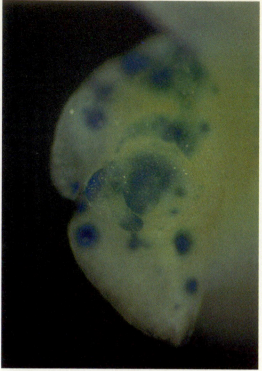

a.

b.

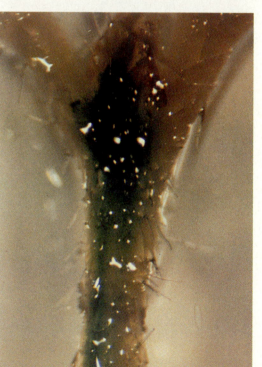

c.

d.

Figure 32.16
Transgenic soybeans created using a gene gun. A gene gun was used to send the *E. coli* gene for beta-glucuronidase into cells of soybean seed meristems. *a.* The blue spots on the meristem indicate cells that have taken up the foreign gene because this enzyme produces a blue color in the presence of its substrate. *b.* Nonengineered soybean meristem is shown for comparison. *c.* The plantlet has some engineered cells, and (*d*) this plantlet has taken up the bacterial gene in nearly all of its cells, as indicated by the dark blue stain.

a.   b.

Figure 32.17

Two routes to herbicide resistance. Petunias and tobacco were both genetically engineered to resist the herbicide glyphosate but in different ways. Glyphosate kills plants by suppressing the activity of an essential enzyme, EPSP synthase. *a.* The petunias in the back row were given a viral gene that allows them to overproduce the enzyme sufficiently to counteract the effect of a commercial glyphosate spray. In contrast, the unmodified petunias in the front row show no resistance to the spray. *b.* The glyphosate-sprayed tobacco plants in the center row carry a bacterial gene for a form of EPSP synthase that functions even in the presence of glyphosate. In the left row are engineered tobacco plants that were not sprayed; in the right row are unmodified tobacco plants that have succumbed to the glyphosate spray.

Table 32.1
Recombinant DNA Solutions to Agricultural Challenges

Challenge	Possible Solution
Crops damaged by frost	Spray crops with bacteria genetically engineered to lack surface proteins that promote ice crystallization. Bacteria can also be engineered to encourage ice crystallization; used to increase snow buildup in winter sports facilities.
Crops damaged by herbicides and pesticides	Isolate resistance genes from an organism that is not affected by the chemical and engineer the gene into crop plant.
Crops need costly nitrogen fertilizer because atmospheric nitrogen is not biologically usable	Short term: genetically engineer nitrogen-fixing *Rhizobia* bacteria to overproduce enzymes that convert atmospheric nitrogen to a biologically usable form in root nodules of legumes. Alter *Rhizobia* to colonize a wider variety of plants. Long term: transfer *Rhizobia* nitrogen-fixation genes into plant cells and regenerate transgenic plants.
A plant food is low in a particular amino acid	Transfer gene from another species that controls production of a protein rich in the amino acid normally lacking in the crop plant.
A crop plant is killed by a virus	Genetically engineer crop plant to manufacture a protein on its cell surface normally found on the virus's surface. Plant becomes "immune" to virus.
Public concern about the safety of synthetic pesticides	Engineer *Bacillus thuringiensis* to overproduce its natural pesticide, which destroys insects' stomach linings. Transfer *B. thuringiensis* bioinsecticide gene to crop plant.
Fruits and vegetables ripen quickly once picked	Suppress or slow production of ripening enzymes such as cellulase.

DNA and transmitted when the cell divides. Finally, a mature plant must be regenerated from the engineered cell and express the desired trait in the appropriate tissues and at the right time in development. Then the plant must pass the characteristic on to the next generation. That's a tall order! A quicker way to use genetic engineering to endow a plant with a new capability is to manipulate bacteria that normally live on a crop plant's roots (fig. 32.17). Table 32.1 lists some ways that recombinant DNA technology can be used to solve agricultural challenges.

KEY CONCEPTS

Transgenic plants are generated by introducing foreign DNA into a cell and regenerating a plant from that cell. The plant must express the foreign gene appropriately and transmit it to future generations. Methods of gene transfer include the Ti plasmid, electroporation, microinjection, liposomes, and gene guns.

Biotechnology Provides Different Routes to Solving a Problem

Different biotechnological approaches can address a single problem. For example, how might you devise a crop that cannot be damaged by the herbicide used to protect it from weeds? The traditional approach is to find a weed that is resistant to the herbicide and related to the crop plant. The hardy weed and its domesticated relative are then crossbred until a variant arises that retains the desired qualities of each parent plant—resistance to the herbicide, plus the characteristics that make the plant a valuable crop. In the past, if an herbicide-resistant crop could not be bred, then the herbicide was simply not used.

Today, instead of changing herbicides to fit crops (called the "spray and pray" approach), biotechnologists are altering crops to fit herbicides. In mutant selection, resistant cells cultured in the presence of the herbicide are isolated and used to regenerate resistant plants. A callus grown in the presence of the herbicide would yield embryos or plantlets that are resistant. The recombinant

Reading 32.1 *Plant Biotechnology Moves from the Laboratory to the Land*

IT IS A FRIGID EVENING IN JANUARY 1987, AND SEVERAL ANGRY RESIDENTS OF TULELAKE, CALIFORNIA, ARE MEETING IN A TOWN HALL TO DISCUSS WHAT TO THEM IS A FRIGHTENING PROSPECT. Researchers at the nearby University of California at Berkeley want to paint potato plants, on town land, with genetically altered bacteria to see whether the bacteria will render the potatoes frost resistant. The residents have been given a very complete, 500-page environmental impact statement by the researchers. While it looks like the proposed experiment is relatively safe and has been checked out in the laboratory and greenhouse extensively, the people are nonetheless disturbed. Words like "mutant" and "recombinant DNA" invoke fear; and many are worried by the uncertainty of the scientists' language and the fact that they cannot guarantee that the bacteria will not spread beyond the test plot, harm native plants, or cause disease in them or their animals.

The story of the "ice-minus" bacteria of Tulelake actually begins back in 1977, when a graduate student at the University of Wisconsin at Madison, Steven Lindow, found that ice forms on potato leaves by gathering around "ice-nucleating proteins." The proteins are part of the surface of the bacterium *Pseudomonas syringae*. What would happen to the potato plants, Lindow wondered, if the bacteria could not produce the ice-forming protein? He found a naturally occurring *P. syringae* mutant that made fewer than normal ice-nucleating proteins; he made the mutant more severe by deleting about a third of the responsible gene's base pairs. In greenhouse experiments, Lindow validated his hypothesis—potato leaves coated with unaltered, wild type *P. syringae* froze at 28°F (-2.2°C); leaves coated with the genetically engineered ice-minus bacteria did not freeze until the mercury dipped to 23°F (-5°C). By 1982, Lindow wanted to test his bacteria in the field, thinking ahead that frost-resistant bacteria could cut into the $1.5 billion in damage caused by frozen crops in the United States each year.

Lindow's plans for the logical next step—the field test—were sidelined for 4 years by a lawsuit brought by the Foundation on Economic Trends in Washington, D.C. Meanwhile, Lindow continued his work—he brought native Tulelake plants into the greenhouse, where he exposed them to ice-minus bacteria; he studied local wind patterns, consulted wildlife experts, and talked with Tulelake townspeople, who did not, at first, seem to object to what he planned to do. The Environmental Protection Agency and the National Institutes of Health applauded Lindow's efforts to ensure safety.

But in 1985, the young scientist hit another snag. A company called Advanced Genetic Sciences injected similarly altered bacteria, called Frostban, into trees on the roof of their Oakland facility—without approval of the EPA. The Frostban experiment hit the press, and a wave of apprehension spread northwards to Tulelake. The town meetings began.

Finally, in the spring of 1987, the first "deliberate release" of genetically engineered bacteria was allowed. A Sacramento County Superior Court Judge declared the Frostban bacteria safe on April 23, and the next day, 2,400 strawberry plants were sprayed with it in Brentwood. But vandals ripped out the plants overnight. On April 19, Steven Lindow planted in Tulelake 3,000 potato seedlings that had been coated as seeds with ice-minus bacteria. Again, vandals struck, removing half of the plants. Researchers replanted most of them the next day. Then, on May 28, Lindow sprayed ice-minus bacteria on the seedlings.

The ice-minus bacteria indeed protected the potato plants. Elaborate monitoring experiments showed that, even many months later, none of the 6 trillion released bacteria had wandered beyond the 30 meters of bare soil surrounding the test plot. And so began the era of deliberate release of organisms altered by humans.

Scientists are developing methods to counter some possible dangers of releasing genetically altered organisms to the environment. For example, bacteria that are manipulated to contain genes providing a valuable resistance factor to crop seeds can also be given a gene that makes them glow or change color in the presence of a particular substance. Recombinant *Pseudomonas fluorescens* bacteria coated onto winter wheat are altered to cause a color change on standard bacterial growth plates when exposed to the sugar lactose. Using this tracing system, the bacteria were shown to have traveled 7 inches (17.8 centimeters) horizontally and 12 inches (30.5 centimeters) vertically in 10 weeks along the roots of the wheat plants.

A way to control the spread of a genetically engineered organism is the "suicide plasmid," which causes altered bacteria coated on crop plants to self-destruct once they have completed their job. Recall that a plasmid is a small, circular piece of DNA found naturally in some bacterial cells (see fig. 13.25). A plasmid can be engineered to contain a gene that turns on production of a DNA-cutting enzyme when a particular biochemical is not present. Self-destruct plasmids are inserted into the engineered bacteria, which are coated onto seeds of crop plants. (For example, consider bacteria that produce an insecticide and are coated onto corn seeds.) A chemical that suppresses the DNA-cutting function of the plasmid is applied along with the bacteria. Once the chemical is degraded or washed away, the plasmid activates its DNA-cutting enzymes, and the bacteria are destroyed. The corn seeds have by this time germinated, insect free, and the bacteria can no longer pass on their engineered resistance to nearby weeds.

While geneticists alter crop plants one gene at a time and devise ways to introduce these plants into the environment as safely as possible, other biologists are concerned about the consequences of these efforts because they deviate from the sorts of genetic changes that occur naturally. For example, pests are known to evolve resistances to pesticides, usually in the form of resistance genes carried on plasmids. Such natural resistance usually proceeds in a gene-by-gene fashion over long periods of time—that is, a pest organism's resistance is a single gene change in response to the effect of the pesticide on the organism's physiology. How will organisms respond to crop plants that are engineered to produce several substances? How will they react to what appears to be a very sudden and drastic evolutionary change?

Some ecologists are looking at an even bigger picture. If organisms can be designed to grow in the presence of chemical pesticides, will we increase our use of such chemicals, possibly threatening other species not given protection? Similarly, if organisms can be biologically altered to withstand pollution, will efforts to clean up the environment be slowed or halted? Engineering more hardy species, some argue, is treating the symptoms of environmental problems rather than getting to the roots of the problems. These concerns perhaps summarize the potential impact of agricultural biotechnology on our society—in the long run it can provide valuable new variants; but in the short term, we must understand how altering these organisms will affect the living world.

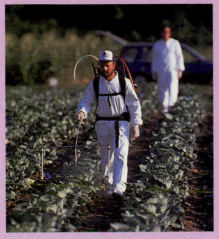

Figure 1
The very first field tests of genetically engineered microbes applied to plants were conducted by researchers clad in spacesuits and protective gear (*a*). *b*. Today, only a jumpsuit, gloves, goggles, and mask are required.

Table 1
Government Regulation of Transgenic Plants

Agency	Role
Department of Agriculture (USDA)	Approves field tests
Environmental Protection Agency (EPA)	Sets tolerable levels of pesticides in food crops
Food and Drug Administration (FDA)	Ask these questions: Is a genetically engineered food "generally recognized as safe?" and "Does the genetic engineering produce a food additive?"

DNA approach to herbicide resistance focuses on identifying the part of the crop plant's physiology that is damaged by the herbicide and then finding a gene (from any organism) that might enable the plant to prevent or undo whatever damage the herbicide does.

Beyond the Laboratory—Release of Altered Plants to the Environment

A genetically altered plant is more controllable on a laboratory shelf or in a greenhouse than when growing in a field, where it can interact with other species. However, field testing is an essential step in using the agricultural products of biotechnology.

The first "deliberately released" genetically engineered organisms were bacteria that prevent ice crystal formation on crop plants (Reading 32.1). Today, regulatory agencies approving field tests of genetically altered organisms are overrun with requests. The concerns of the agencies as well as the public are several. How long will the altered plant or bacterium survive? How quickly does it multiply? Has it been altered in a way not seen in nature? How far can the organism travel? Most important, what are the effects of the genetically engineered organism on the living and nonliving environment? Can the altered organism pass on its new characteristic—such as herbicide or disease resistance—to a weed?

KEY CONCEPTS

Sometimes an agricultural problem can be solved by several biotechnologies, including traditional breeding, creating a transgenic plant or a somatic hybrid, selecting a resistant mutant, or altering bacteria that live on a plant's roots. After an altered and fertile plant is grown to maturity, it must be field tested. Scientists must determine how a genetically engineered plant affects its environment.

SUMMARY

Plant biotechnology manipulates plants at the level of cells or DNA, producing either new variants or uniformity. Once an individual cell is altered or selected, it must be regenerated into a mature plant, that plant must express the sought-after trait and pass it on to the next generation, and the new variety must be able to withstand conditions in the greenhouse and in the field. Biotechnology differs from traditional plant breeding in that it is asexual, more precise, and faster.

In *protoplast fusion*, two cells are stripped of their cell walls and fused. If a plant can be regenerated from protoplast fusions of two species, an interesting hybrid may result. Culture of an explant produces a *callus*, an undifferentiated mass that can yield embryos or plantlets, which are genetically identical or occasionally variant, depending upon the particular mix of nutrients and plant hormones in which they are cultured. Identical embryos are used to fashion *artificial seeds*.

Identical plantlets offer uniform crops. Unusual plantlets, derived from *somaclonal* or *gametoclonal* variation, offer new plant types. Plant cells with novel combinations of cytoplasms, nuclei, and chloroplasts and mitochondria are derived by *cybridization*, in which protoplast fusion is followed by radiation treatment to inactivate one nucleus. Chloroplasts and mitochondria can also be introduced in *liposomes*.

In *recombinant DNA technology*, foreign genes are introduced into bacteria and these bacteria coated onto vulnerable plant parts; or *transgenic* plants are created by transferring foreign genes into fertilized ova and regenerating plants. Recombinant DNA technology in plants can offer resistances to temperature extremes, pests, and disease and alter nutritional qualities. Several environmental concerns are raised by introducing plant varieties derived from altering cells or DNA into the environment.

QUESTIONS

1. List the steps necessary for plants altered at the cell or DNA level to become useful agricultural varieties.

2. How are modern biotechnologies such as cell culture and recombinant DNA technology similar to and different from traditional plant breeding?

3. Name a plant biotechnology that is very precise and one that is very imprecise.

4. If you want to breed identical-looking flowers that are easy to pick, what biotechnology might you choose? Why?

5. List the steps involved in using somaclonal variation to develop an extra-sweet carrot plant.

6. What is an advantage and a drawback of gametoclonal variation?

7. How must dicots and monocots be handled differently in protoplast fusion? In recombinant DNA technology?

TO THINK ABOUT

1. What do you think is the major benefit of plant biotechnology? The major risk?

2. One explanation for the mechanism behind somaclonal variation is that the cell culturing process uncovers preexisting somatic mutations. What is an alternative explanation?

3. Suggest three biotechnology approaches to developing a potato plant that is resistant to the potato beetle, which eats its leaves.

4. On June 18, 1987, a plant pathologist at Montana State University, Gary Strobel, infected 14 elm trees, outdoors, with *Pseudomonas syringae* bacteria. In 1981 he had altered the bacteria to overproduce a protein that they normally manufacture and that kills the fungus that causes Dutch elm disease. As part of the experiment, Strobel injected the 14 trees as well as 14 unprotected control trees with the Dutch elm disease fungus. Strobel had already tried his bacteria on Dutch elm tree sap in the laboratory and greenhouse and found that they indeed killed the disease-causing fungus.

Because it was June, Strobel knew that he needed to conduct the field test immediately or wait another year. So he infected the trees, without clearance from university officials or the EPA. The officials as well as much of the scientific community were enraged by Strobel's disregard of regulations. Strobel, however, defended his view: "We can sit and talk about Dutch elm disease, or we can do something about it. I chose to do something about it."

a. What additional pieces of information do you need to fairly judge whether Gary Strobel was justified in carrying out his field test without standard approvals?

b. Do you think that Strobel acted wisely? Why or why not?

5. Considering what you now know about plant biotechnology, how would you feel about a crop plant that is genetically engineered to tolerate extreme heat being field tested next to your home? If you were the researcher, what measures would you take to ensure the safety of the experiment?

6. Studies have shown that fewer than 20% of Americans know what DNA is and what it does. Many genetic researchers are frustrated by people without knowledge of genetics attempting to regulate their experiments. What do you think can be done so that the public can become better informed about plant biotechnology—or about science in general?

SUGGESTED READINGS

Gould, Fred. January 1988. Evolutionary biology and genetically engineered crops. *BioScience*. Can we learn from evolution about how unaltered plants will respond to altered plants?

Hall, Stephen S. September 1987. One potato patch that is making genetic history. *Smithsonian*. The first release of a genetically altered bacterium onto plants was traumatic for residents of the town that housed the testing site. Today we take such tests for granted.

Hoffman, Carol A. June 1990. Ecological risks of genetic engineering of crop plants. *BioScience*. Genetic engineering of crop plants must proceed with caution because other species may be affected.

Lewis, Ricki. May 1986. Building a better tomato. *High Technology*. A survey of different biotechnological approaches to devising new plant varieties.

Miller, Henry I., and Stephen J. Ackerman. March 1990. Perspectives on food biotechnology. *FDA Consumer*. Biotechnology of plant foods is the latest approach to agriculture.

Potrykus, I. June 1990. Gene transfer to cereals: an assessment. *Biotechnology*. Altering cereals has been biotechnology's greatest challenge.

Ratner, Mark. May 1990. Identifying quantitative traits in plants. *Biotechnology*. How do plant biotechnologists know which combinations of traits are valuable.

Strobel, Gary. October 19, 1987. Strobel: "I have acted in good faith." *The Scientist*. Plant pathologist Gary Strobel released genetically modified bacteria that protect against Dutch elm disease—without appropriate regulatory approval. Was he justified in his action?

Appendix A
Microscopy

As the study of life has progressed steadily from observing organisms to probing the molecules of life, the technology to view living things has grown accordingly. Today's biologist has a range of microscope types to choose from, and the instrument used depends upon the nature of the biological material being observed (table 1). An *ultraviolet microscope* might be used to highlight stained chromosomes; a *polarizing microscope* to focus in on protein arrays of a cytoskeleton; a *phase contrast microscope* to view cells while they are still alive. A *scanning electron microscope* reveals the topography of cell and organelle surfaces. A *confocal microscope* presents startlingly clear peeks at biological structures in action, and a *scanning probe microscope* reveals surfaces of individual atoms.

All microscopes provide two types of power—*magnification* and *resolution* (also called resolving power). A microscope produces an enlarged, or magnified, image of an object. Magnification is defined as the ratio between the image size and the object size. Resolution refers to the smallest degree of separation at which two objects are viewed as distinct from one another, rather than as a blurry, single image. Resolution is important in distinguishing structures from one another. A *compound microscope* commonly used in college biology teaching laboratories can resolve objects that are 0.1 to 0.2 micrometers (4 to 8 millionths of an inch) apart. The resolving power of an electron microscope is 10,000 times greater than this.

Table 1
Compound Microscopes

Method	Basis	Advantages	Disadvantages
Phase contrast microscopy	Converts differences in the velocity of light through different parts of specimen into observable contrasts	Can be used on live cells	Not all subcellular structures are visible; halos seen around structures
Interference microscopy	Two beams of light hit specimen and join in image plane	No halos on structures; fine detail	Cumbersome to use; expensive
Differential-interference (Nomarski-optics) microscopy	Detects localized differences in velocities at which light passes through specimen	Fine transparent detail visible	
Polarizing microscopy	Ray of plane-polarized (i.e., unidirectional) light hits specimen, splits into two directions, at two different velocities, creating image of ordered molecular detail	Highlights detail at molecular level	Works best on highly oriented, crystalline or fibrous structures
Fluorescence microscopy	Light of one wavelength is selectively absorbed by certain molecules that reemit light of a longer wavelength		Only creates image of structures that absorb the wavelength of light used
Ultraviolet (uv) microscopy	Ultraviolet light used with lens made of quartz	High resolving power; excellent for viewing proteins and nucleic acids	

The Light Microscope

The compound light microscope focuses visible light through a specimen. Different regions of the object scatter the light differently, producing an image. In modern microscopes, three sets of lenses contribute to the generation of an image (fig. 1). The *condenser lens* focuses light through the specimen. The *objective lens* receives light that has passed through the specimen, generating an enlarged image. The *ocular lens,* or eyepiece, magnifies the image further. Total magnification is calculated by multiplying the magnification of the objective lens by that of the ocular lens. The coarse and fine adjustment knobs are manipulated to bring the magnified image into sharp focus. The mirror directs the light into the condenser lens, and the *diaphragm* controls the amount of light to which the specimen is exposed.

A limitation of a light microscope is that only one two-dimensional plane of the specimen can be observed at a time. Thus, when a light microscope is focused on the top of a specimen, different structures are visible than when it is focused at a deeper level. It can be difficult to envision the three-dimensional nature of the specimen from the two-dimensional views afforded by the light microscope. The problem is like focusing on particular parts of a scene with a camera. If the photographer focuses on his children in the foreground of a shot, he may miss entirely the antics of a cat and mouse that are several feet behind the children. Similarly, light microscope views at different depths within a cell can reveal different structures.

Electron Microscopes

Electron microscopes provide greater magnification, better resolution, and a better sense of depth than light microscopes. Instead of visible light, the *transmission electron microscope* (TEM) sends a beam of electrons through the specimen, using a magnetic field to focus the beam rather than a glass lens (fig. 2). Different parts of the specimen absorb different numbers of

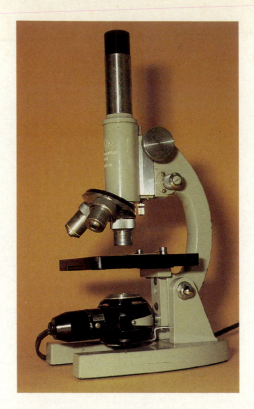

Figure 1
Light Microscope

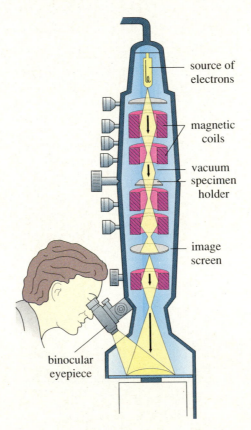

Figure 2
Electron Microscope

electrons. These contrasts are rendered visible to the human eye by a fluorescent screen coated with a chemical that gives off visible light rays when excited by electrons from the specimen.

Although the TEM has provided some spectacular glimpses into the microscopic structures of life, it does have limitations. For the TEM, the specimen must be killed, treated with chemicals, cut into very thin sections, and placed in a vacuum. This treatment can distort natural structures. A close cousin of the TEM eliminates these drawbacks. The *scanning electron microscope* (SEM) bounces electrons off of a three-dimensional specimen, generating a three-dimensional image on a device similar to a television screen. The resulting depth of field highlights crevices and textures. Although many SEM specimens are coated with a heavy metal to highlight their surfaces, some specimens (such as fruit flies) can be examined while alive, with no apparent harm.

A variation of the electron microscope is the *photoelectron microscope* (PEM), originally used to probe metal surfaces but now used to examine cells as well. The PEM bombards a specimen with ultraviolet light, ejecting the valence shell electrons of molecules on a cell or organelle surface. These electrons are accelerated and focused by an electron lens system. The excited electrons are quite sensitive to the surface detail of the specimen, and their deflection pattern provides a high-resolution view of minute surface details. The PEM is especially useful to zero in on specific molecules that have been labeled with fluorescent antibodies. PEM is an electron-based version of fluorescence microscopy.

While the SEM highlights large surface features, the PEM provides a closer look. It is like comparing a topographic map of a mountain (SEM) to a picture of a bump in the terrain of the mountain (PEM). A light microscope and all three electron microscopes can be used in conjunction to paint a detailed portrait of biological structures, which can clarify functions at the organelle or even the molecular level.

Labels on Figure 2:
source of electrons
magnetic coils
vacuum
specimen holder
image screen
binocular eyepiece

The Confocal Microscope

A limitation of light microscopy is that light reflected from regions of the sample near the object of interest interferes with the image, making it blurry or hazy. A *confocal microscope* avoids interference and enhances resolution by passing white or laser light through a pinhole and a lens to the object (fig. 3). The light is then reflected through a beam splitter and then through another pinhole, a detector, and finally a photomultiplier. The result is a scan of highly focused light on one tiny part of the specimen at a time, usually an area 0.25 μm in diameter and 0.5 μm deep. The microscope is called "confocal" because the objective and the condenser lenses are both focused on the same small area.

The idea of a confocal microscope was patented by Marvin Minsky in 1961, but it was not developed until the mid 1980s, when computers enabled many scans of different sites and at different depths to be integrated and translated into a dynamic image. By using fluorescent dyes that label specific cell parts and are activated by the incoming light, different structures can be distinguished. The first division of a fertilized sea urchin egg, for example, can be captured: the spindle fibers appear green, and the chromosomes being pulled in opposite directions are a vibrant blue. Confocal microscopy has also revealed changing concentrations of calcium ions in a neuron receiving a biochemical message; the cytoskeleton in action; platelets aggregating at the scene of an injury to form a clot; sperm fertilizing an ovum; and nerve cells infiltrating the developing brain of an embryo. When teamed with a tool borrowed from the physical sciences called Raman spectroscopy, confocal microscopy reveals details of chromosome structure, and can distinguish between the chemical bonds of a protein or nucleic acid.

Scanning Probe Microscopes

The world of microscopy was again revolutionized in 1981, with the invention of the *scanning tunneling microscope* (STM) by Gerd K. Binnig and Heinrich Rohrer. This device reveals detail at the atomic level. A very

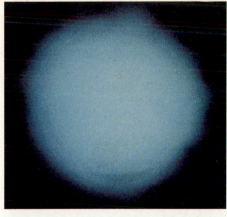

a.

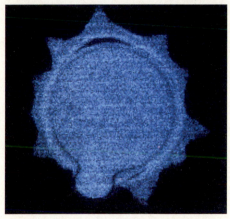

b.

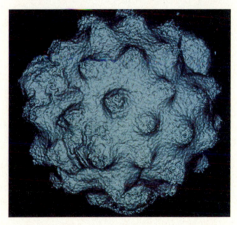

c.

Figure 3
a. Sea urchin embryo at first division stained with fluorescently labeled anti-tubulin antibody, taken with a conventional fluorescence microscope. *b.* Sea urchin embryo at first division stained with fluorescently labeled anti-tubulin antibody, taken with a confocal laser scanning microscope. *c.* Sea urchin embryo at first division, double stained to show tubulin in green and DNA in blue, taken with a tandem-scanning microscope.

sharp metal needle, its tip as small as an atom, is scanned over a molecule's surface. Electrons "tunnel" across the space between the sample and the needle, thereby creating an electrical current. The closer the needle, the greater the current. An image is generated as the scanner continually adjusts the space between needle and sample, keeping the current constant over the topography of the molecular surface. The needle's movements over the microscopic hills and valleys are expressed as contour lines, which in turn are converted and enhanced by computer into a colored image of the surface.

Electrons do not pass readily from many biological samples, limiting use of STM. However, the same principle of adjusting a probe over a changing surface is used in *scanning ion-conductance microscopy* (SICM), developed by Paul K. Hansma and Calvin Quate. It uses ions instead of electrons—useful in the many biological situations where ions travel between cells. The probe is made of hollow glass filled with a conductive salt solution, which is also applied to the sample. When voltage is passed through the sample and the probe, ions flow to the probe. The rate of ion flow is kept constant, and a portrait is painted by the compensatory movements of the probe. SICM is useful in studying cell membrane surfaces and muscle and nerve function.

Another type of scanning probe microscope, the *atomic force microscope* (AFM), was developed in 1986 by the inventors of the SICM. It uses a diamond-tipped probe that resembles the stylus on a phonograph but that presses a molecule's surface with a force millions of times gentler. As the force is kept constant, the probe moves, generating an image. AFM is especially useful for recording molecular movements, such as those involved in blood clotting and cell division.

New and improved microscopes do not always replace existing models but complement the information that they provide. Many researchers today create their own versions of microscopes to suit their particular experiments. All modern microscopes though, some of them quite technologically sophisticated, support the cell theory advanced by the early microscopists, who had only very crude light microscopes with which to work.

Appendix B
Units of Measurement
Metric/English Conversions

Length

1 meter = 39.4 inches = 3.28 feet
= 1.09 yard
1 foot = 0.305 meters = 12 inches
= 0.33 yard
1 inch = 2.54 centimeters
1 centimeter = 10 millimeter = 0.394 inch
1 millimeter = 0.001 meter = 0.01
centimeter = 0.039 inch
1 kilometer = 1,000 meters = 0.621 miles
= 0.54 nautical miles
1 mile = 5,280 feet = 1.61 kilometers
1 nautical mile = 1.15 mile

Area

1 square centimeter = 0.155 square inch
1 square foot = 144 square inches = 929
square centimeters
1 square yard = 9 square feet = 0.836
square meters
1 square meter = 10.76 square feet = 1.196
square yards = 1 million square
millimeters
1 hectare = 10,000 square meters = 0.01
square kilometers = 2.47 acres

1 acre = 43,560 square feet = 0.405
hectares
1 square kilometer = 100 hectares = 1
million square meters = 0.386 square
miles = 247 acres
1 square mile = 640 acres = 2.59 square
kilometers

Volume

1 cubic centimeter = 1 milliliter = 0.001
liter
1 cubic meter = 1 million cubic centimeters = 1,000 liters
1 cubic meter = 35.3 cubic feet = 1.307
cubic yards = 264 U.S. gallons
1 cubic yard = 27 cubic feet = 0.765 cubic
meters = 202 U.S. gallons
1 cubic kilometer = 1 million cubic meters
= 0.24 cubic mile = 264 billion gallons
1 cubic mile = 4.166 cubic kilometers
1 liter = 1,000 milliliters = 1.06 quarts =
0.265 U.S. gallons = 0.035 cubic feet
1 U.S. gallon = 4 quarts = 3.79 liters = 231
cubic inches
1 quart = 2 pints = 4 cups = 0.94 liters

Mass

1 microgram = 0.001 milligram = 0.000001
gram
1 gram = 1,000 milligrams = 0.035 ounce
1 kilogram = 1,000 grams = 2.205 pound
1 pound = 16 ounces = 454 grams
1 short ton = 2,000 pounds = 909 kilograms
1 metric ton = 1,000 kilograms = 2,200
pounds

Temperature

Celsius to Fahrenheit $°F = (°C \times 1.8) + 32$
Fahrenheit to Celsius $°C = (°F - 32) \div 1.8$

Energy and Power

1 kilocalorie = 1,000 calories

Appendix C
Metric Conversion

	Metric Quantities	Metric to English Conversion	English to Metric Conversion
Length	1 kilometer (km) = 1,000 (10^3) meters 1 meter (m) = 100 centimeters 1 centimeter (cm) = 0.01 (10^{-2}) meter 1 millimeter (mm) = 0.001 (10^{-3}) meter 1 micrometer* (μm) = 0.000001 (10^{-6}) meter 1 nanometer (nm) = 0.000000001 (10^{-9}) meter *formerly called micron	1 km = 0.62 mile 1 m = 1.09 yards = 39.37 inches 1 cm = 0.394 inch 1 mm = 0.039 inch	1 mile = 1.609 km 1 yard = 0.914 m 1 foot = 0.305 m = 30.5 cm 1 inch = 2.54 cm

Area	1 square kilometer (km^2) = 100 hectares
	1 hectare (ha) = 10,000 square meters
	1 square meter (m^2) = 10,000 square centimeters
	
	1 square centimeter (cm^2) = 100 square
	    millimeters
		1 km^2 = 0.3861 square mile
		1 ha = 2.471 acres
		1 m^2 = 1.1960 square yards
		      = 10.764 square feet
		1 cm^2 = 0.155 square inch
			1 square mile = 2.590 km^2
			1 acre = 0.4047 ha
			1 square yard = 0.8361 m^2
			1 square foot = 0.0929 m^2
			1 square inch = 6.4516 cm^2

Mass	1 metric ton (t) = 1,000 kilograms 1 metric ton (t) = 1,000,000 grams 1 kilogram (kg) = 1,000 grams 1 gram (g) = 1,000 milligrams 1 milligram (mg) = 0.001 gram 1 microgram (μg) = 0.000001 gram	1 t = 1.1025 ton (U.S.) 1 kg = 2.205 pounds 1 g = 0.0353 ounce	1 ton (U.S.) = 0.907 t 1 pound = 0.4536 kg 1 ounce = 28.35 g
Volume (solids)	1 cubic meter (m^3) = 1,000,000 cubic centimeters 1 cubic centimeter (cm^3) = 1,000 cubic millimeters	1 m^3 = 1.3080 cubic yards = 35.315 cubic feet 1 cm^3 = 0.0610 cubic inch	1 cubic yard = 0.7646 m^3 1 cubic foot = 0.0283 m^3 1 cubic inch = 16.387 cm^3
Volume (liquids)	1 liter (l) = 1,000 milliliters 1 milliliter (ml) = 0.001 liter 1 microliter (μl) = 0.000001 liter	1 l = 1.06 quarts (U.S.) 1 ml = 0.034 fluid ounce	1 quart (U.S.) = 0.94 l 1 pint (U.S.) = 0.47 l 1 fluid ounce = 29.57 ml
Time	1 second (sec) = 1,000 milliseconds 1 millisecond (msec) = 0.001 second 1 microsecond (μsec) = 0.000001 second		

Appendix D
Taxonomy

The millions of living and extinct species that have dwelled on earth can be grouped according to many schemes. Taxonomists group organisms to reflect both anatomical similarities and descent from a common ancestor. Two, three, four, five, and most recently, six kingdom classifications have been proposed. The five-kingdom scheme is outlined here with all phyla described briefly. Short statements explaining the rationale behind groupings of phyla are given wherever possible, and indented subheadings reflect these groupings. Scientific names are followed by more familiar names of organisms. Figures from the text accompany the listing to help you visualize and recall the wide diversity of life forms discussed in chapter 2.

Salmonella

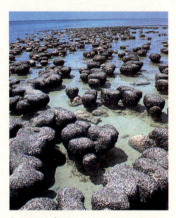

Stromatolites

Kingdom Monera The monerans are unicellular prokaryotes that obtain nutrients by direct absorption or by photosynthesis or chemosynthesis. Most monerans reproduce asexually, but some can exchange genetic material in a primitive form of sexual reproduction. (The six-kingdom classification system divides the monerans into two kingdoms, whose members are distinguished by genetic differences and by whether or not they produce methane as a metabolic by-product. The methane-producing bacteria are thought to be the most primitive organisms, having evolved before the atmosphere contained oxygen.)

Phylum Schizophyta The bacteria.
Phylum Cyanobacteria Photosynthetic bacteria, formerly called blue-green algae.

Kingdom Protista Protists are the structurally simplest eukaryotes, and they can be unicellular or multicellular. They can absorb or ingest nutrients or photosynthesize. Reproduction is asexual or sexual. Some forms move by ciliary or flagellar motion, and others are nonmotile. The protists' early development differs from that of the fungi, plants, and animals. The kingdom includes the protozoans, algae, and the water molds and slime molds.

Protozoans Unicellular, nonphotosynthetic, lack cell walls.
Phylum Sarcomastigophora Locomote by flagella and/or pseudopoda and includes the familiar *Amoeba proteus*.
Phylum Labyrinthomorpha Aquatic, live on algae.
Phylum Apicomplexa Parasitic, with characteristic twisted structure on anterior end at some point in life cycle.
Phylum Myxozoa Parasitic on fish and invertebrates.
Phylum Microspora Parasitic on invertebrates and primitive vertebrates.
Phylum Ciliophora Cilia present at some stage of the life cycle.

Algae Unicellular or multicellular, photosynthetic, some have cell walls. Distinguished by pigments.
Phylum Euglenophyta Unicellular and photosynthetic, with a single flagellum and contractile vacuole.
Phylum Chrysophyta Diatoms, golden-brown algae, and yellow-green algae. Unicellular and photosynthetic.
Phylum Pyrrophyta Dinoflagellates. Unicellular and photosynthetic.
Phylum Chlorophyta Green algae. Unicellular or multicellular, photosynthetic.
Phylum Phaeophyta Brown algae (kelps). Multicellular and photosynthetic.
Phylum Rhodophyta Red algae. Multicellular and photosynthetic.

Water and Slime Molds
Phylum Oomycota The water molds. Unicellular or multinucleate, with cellulose cell walls. Live in fresh water.
Phylum Chytridiomycota The chytrids. Multicellular, with chitinous cell walls. Aquatic.
Phylum Myxomycota Multinucleated, "acellular" slime molds.
Phylum Acrasiomycota Multicellular "cellular" slime molds.

Morel mushroom   Fossel ferns   Hydra

Kingdom Fungi With the exception of the yeasts, fungi are multicellular eukaryotes that decompose organisms to obtain nourishment. Chitinous cell walls. Phyla are distinguished by mode of reproduction.

    Phylum Zygomycota Reproduce with sexual resting spores.

    Phylum Ascomycota Yeasts, morels, truffles, molds, lichens. Reproduce with sexual spores carried in asci. Some ascomycetes cause food spoilage and some plant diseases; others are used in the production of certain foods, beverages, and antibiotic drugs.

    Phylum Basidiomycota Mushrooms, toadstools, puffballs, stinkhorns, shelf fungi, rusts, and smuts. Reproduce by spore-containing basidia.

Kingdom Plantae Plants are multicellular, land dwelling, photosynthetic, and reproduce both asexually and sexually in an alternation of generations. Cellulose cell walls. Plants have specialized tissues and organs but lack nervous and muscular systems.

    Nonvascular Plants (Bryophytes) Lack specialized conducting tissues and true roots, stems, and leaves. The gamete-producing reproductive phase predominates.

        Division Bryophyta Liverworts, hornworts, mosses.

    Vascular Plants (Tracheophytes) Xylem and phloem transport water and nutrients, respectively, throughout the plant body of roots, stems, and leaves. The spore-producing reproductive phase predominates.

        Primitive Plants Sperm cells travel in water to meet egg cells.

            Division Pterophyta Ferns.

            Division Psilophyta Whisk ferns.

            Division Lycophyta Club mosses and others.

            Division Spenophyta Horsetails.

        Seed Plants Sperm cells and egg cells enclosed in protective structures.

            Gymnosperms (naked seed plants) Male and female cones produce pollen grains and ovules.

                Division Coniferophyta Conifers.

                Division Cycadophyta Cycads.

                Division Ginkgophyta Ginkgos.

                Division Gnetophyta Gnetophytes.

            Angiosperms (seeds in a vessel) The flowering plants.

                Division Anthophyta Flowering plants.

Kingdom Animalia The animals are multicellular with specialized tissues and organs, including nervous and locomotive systems. No cell walls. Animals obtain nutrients from food. Phyla are distinguished largely on the basis of body form and symmetry, characteristics that are generally established in the early embryo.

    Mesozoa Simplest animals.

        Phylum Mesozoa Very simple, wormlike parasites of marine invertebrates. Consist of only 20 to 30 cells.

    Parazoa A separate branch from the evolution of protozoa to metazoa.

        Phylum Placozoa A single species, *Trichoplax adhaerens*, characterized by two cell layers with fluid in between them.

        Phylum Porifera The sponges. Specialized cell types organized into canal system to transport nutrients in and wastes out.

    Eumetazoa Animal phyla descended from protozoa.

        Radiata Radially symmetric body plan. Sedentary, saclike bodies with two or three cell layers and a diffuse nerve net.

            Phylum Cnidaria Hydroids, sea anemones, jellyfish, horny corals, hard corals.

            Phylum Ctenophora Sea walnuts, comb jellies.

        Bilateria Bilaterally symmetric body plan.

            Protostomia (first mouth) Embryonic characteristics:

                1. Mouth forms close to area of initial folding inward in very early embryo.

                2. Spiral cleavage: At third cell division, second group of four cells sits atop first group of four cells but rotated by 45°.

                3. Determinate cleavage: Cell fates determined very early in development. If a cell from a four-celled embryo is isolated, it will divide and differentiate to form only one-quarter of an embryo.

                4. The protostomes are further grouped by the way in which the body cavity (coelom) forms. A true coelom is a body cavity that develops within mesoderm, the middle layer of the embryo.

            Acoelomates No coelom.

                Phylum Platyhelminthes Flatworms.

                Phylum Nemertina Ribbonworms.

                Phylum Gnathostomulida Jawworms.

            Pseudocoelomates Body cavity derived from a space in the embryo between the mesoderm and endoderm. The body cavity is called "pseudo" because it does not form within mesoderm. In the adult, the pseudocoelom is a cavity but it is not lined with mesoderm-derived peritoneum (seen in more advanced forms).

                Phylum Rotifera The rotifers. Small (40µm–3mm), intricately shaped organisms that have a structure on their anterior ends that resembles rotating wheels. The rotifers occupy a variety of habitats.

Octopus

Sea urchin

Boobies and people

Phylum Gastrotricha Aquatic, microscopic, flattened organisms with a scaly outer covering.

Phylum Kinorhyncha Marine worms less than 1 mm long.

Phylum Nematoda Roundworms. Found everywhere, many parasitic.

Phylum Nematomorpha Horsehair worms. Juveniles are parasitic in arthropods; adults are free-living.

Phylum Acanthocephala Spiny-headed worms. Spiny projection from anterior end used to attach to intestine of host vertebrate. Range in size from 2 mm to more than a meter.

Phylum Entoprocta Nonmotile, sessile, mostly marine animals that look like stalks that are anchored to rocks, shells, algae, or vegetation on one end, with a tufted growth on the other.

Eucoelomates Coelom forms in a schizocoelous fashion, in which the body cavity forms when mesodermal cells invade the space between ectoderm and endoderm, and then proliferate so that a cavity forms within the mesoderm.

    Major Eucoelomate Protostomes Three phyla, with many species.

        Phylum Mollusca Snails, clams, oysters, squids, octopuses.

        Phylum Annelida Segmented worms.

        Phylum Arthropoda Spiders, scorpions, ticks, mites, crustaceans, millipedes, centipedes, insects.

    The Lesser Protostomes Seven phyla, including many extinct species. Little-understood offshoots of annelid-arthropod line.

        Phylum Pripulida Bottom-dwelling marine worms.

        Phylum Echiurida Marine worms.

        Phylum Sipunculida Bottom-dwelling marine worms.

        Phylum Tardigrada "Water bears." Less than 1 mm, live in water film on mosses and lichens.

        Phylum Pentastomida Tongue worms. Parasitic on respiratory system of vertebrates, mostly reptiles.

Phylum Onychophora Velvet worms. Live in tropical rain forest and resemble caterpillars, with 14 to 43 pairs of unjointed legs and a velvety skin.

Phylum Pogonophora Beard worms. Live in mud on ocean bottom.

Lophophorates Three phyla distinguished by a ciliary feeding structure called a lophophore.

    Phylum Phoronida Small, wormlike bottom-dwellers of shallow, coastal temperate seas. Live in a tube that they secrete.

    Phylum Ectoprocta Bryozoa, or "moss animals." Aquatic, less than 1/2 mm long, live in colonies but each individual lives within a chamber secreted by the epidermis. Bryozoa look like crust on rocks, shells, and seaweeds.

    Phylum Brachiopoda Lampshells. Attached, bottom-dwelling marine animals that have two shells and resemble mollusks, about 5 to 8 mm long.

Deuterostomia (second mouth) Embryonic characteristics:

1. Mouth forms far from area of initial folding inward in very early embryo.
2. Radial cleavage: At third cell division, second group of four cells sits directly atop first group.
3. Indeterminate cleavage: Cell fates of very early embryo not detmined. If a cell from a four-cell embryo is isolated, it will develop into a complete embryo.
4. Coelom formation is enterocoelous. Body cavity forms from outpouchings of endoderm that become lined with mesoderm.

Phylum Echinodermata Sea stars, brittle stars, sea urchins, sea cucumbers, sea lilies. Radial symmetry in adult but larvae are bilaterally symmetric. Complex organ systems, but no distinct head region.

Phylum Chaetognatha Arrow worms. Marine-dwelling with bristles surrounding mouth.

Phylum Hemichordata Acorn worms and others. Aquatic, bottom-dwelling, nonmotile, wormlike animals.

Phylum Chordata Tunicates, lancelets, hagfishes, lampreys, sharks, bony fishes, amphibians, reptiles, birds, mammals. Chordates have a notochord, dorsal nerve cord, gill slits, and a tail. Some of these characteristics may only be present in embryos.

Glossary

A

abscisic acid *ab-SIS-ik AS-id* A plant hormone that inhibits growth. 588

abscission zone *ab-SCISZ-on ZONE* A region at the base of the petiole from which leaves are shed. 562

abyssal zone *ah-BIS-el ZONE* The part of the bottom of the ocean where light does not reach. 737

acclimation *AK-klah-MA-shun* Changes in a plant in preparation for winter. 599

accommodation *ah-KOM-o-DAY-shun* Changes in the shape of the lens to suit the distance of the object being viewed. 356

acetyl CoA formation *AS-eh-til FOR-MAY-shun* The first step in aerobic respiration, occurring in the mitochondrion. Pyruvic acid loses a carbon dioxide and bonds to coenzyme A to form acetyl CoA. 122

acid *AS-id* A molecule that releases hydrogen ions into water. 46

acquired immune deficiency syndrome (AIDS) *ak-KWY-erd im-MUNE dah-FISH-en-see SIN-drome* Infection by the human immunodeficiency virus (HIV), which kills a certain class of helper T cells, causing profound immune suppression and resulting in opportunistic infections and cancer. 211

acromegaly *AK-ro-MEG-eh-lee* Abnormal thickening of bones in an adult due to excess growth hormone. 374

acrosome *AK-ro-som* A protrusion on the anterior end of a sperm cell containing digestive enzymes that enable the sperm to penetrate the protective layers around the oocyte. 163

actin *AK-tin* A type of protein in the thin myofilaments of skeletal muscle cells. 407

action potential *AK-shun po-TEN-shel* The measurement of an electrochemical change caused by ion movement across the cell membrane of a neuron. The message formed by this change is the nerve impulse. 317

active immunity *AK-tiv im-MUNE-eh-tee* Immunity generated by an organism's production of antibodies. 522

active site *AK-tiv SITE* The portion of an enzyme's conformation that directly participates in catalysis. 56

active transport *AK-tiv TRANZ-port* Movement of a molecule through a membrane against its concentration gradient, using a carrier protein and energy from ATP. 102

adaptation *AD-ap-TAY-shun* An inherited trait that enables an organism to survive a particular environmental challenge. 40

adaptive radiation *ah-DAP-tiv RAID-ee-AY-shun* The divergence of several new types of organisms from a single ancestral type. 626

adenine *AD-eh-neen* One of two purine nitrogenous bases in DNA and RNA. 57, 253

adenosine triphosphate *(ATP) ah-DEN-o-seen tri-FOS-fate* A molecule whose three high-energy phosphate bonds power many biological processes. 101, 109

adipose cell *ADD-eh-pos SEL* A cell filled almost entirely with lipid. 51

adrenal cortex *ad-REE-nal KOR-tex* The outer part of the adrenal glands. 377

adrenal glands *ad-REE-nal GLANZ* Paired, two-part glands that sit atop the kidneys and produce catecholamines, mineralocorticoids, glucocorticoids, and sex hormones. 377

adrenal medulla *ad-REE-nal mah-DUEL-ah* The inner part of the adrenal glands. 377

adrenocorticotropic hormone (ACTH) *ah-DREEN-o-KOR-tah-ko-TROP-ik HOR-moan* A hormone made in the anterior pituitary that stimulates secretion of hormones from the adrenal cortex. 375

adventitious roots *AD-ven-TISH-shus ROOTZ* Roots that form on stems or leaves, replacing the first root (the radicle). 563

aerial roots *AIR-ee-al ROOTZ* Adventitious roots that form and grow in the air. 564

afferent arterioles *AF-fer-ent are-TEAR-ee-olz* Branches of the renal artery approaching the proximal portion of a nephron. 506

agonist *AG-o-nist* A drug that activates a receptor, triggering an action potential, or helps a neurotransmitter to bind to the receptor. 325

agriculture *AG-rah-CUL-tur* The domestication of animals and the planting and cultivation of plants used as crops. 540

AIDS-related complex (ARC) *AIDS re-LAY-tid KOM-plex* The early stages of AIDS, characterized by weakness, swollen glands in the neck, and frequent fever. 523

alcoholic fermentation *AL-ko-HALL-ik FER-men-TAY-shun* An anaerobic step following glycolysis utilized by yeast. Pyruvic acid is converted to ethanol and carbon dioxide. 121

aldosterone *al-DOS-ter-own* The major mineralocorticoid hormone produced by the adrenal cortex. It maintains the level of Na+ in the blood by altering the amount reabsorbed in the kidneys. 378, 510

aleurone *AL-ah-roan* A protective layer of a seed. 541

algae *AL-gee* Photosynthetic eukaryotes, including the unicellular diatoms, euglenoids, and dinoflagellates and the multicellular red, brown, and green algae. 25

alkaloids *AL-kah-loids* Plant biochemicals that are used to treat cancer and to relieve pain. 547

allele *ah-LEEL* An alternate form of a gene. 159, 220

allergens *AL-er-gens* Substances that provoke an allergic response. 525

allergy *AL-er-gee* An inappropriate response of the immune system against a nonthreatening substance, caused by IgE antibodies binding to mast cells and releasing their allergy mediators. 525

allergy mediators *AL-er-gee MEED-ee-A-terz* Biochemicals, such as histamine and heparin, that are released from mast cells when an allergen is encountered and that cause the symptoms of an allergy. 525

allopatric *AL-o-PAT-rik* Two populations that are geographically isolated from one another. 638

allopatric speciation *AL-o-PAT-rik SPE-she-A-shun* The formation of new species initiated by geographic isolation. 638

allopolyploid *AL-lo-POL-ee-ploid* An organism with multiple chromosome sets resulting from fertilization of an individual of one species by an individual of a different species. 639

allosaurs *AL-lo-SORZ* Carnivorous dinosaurs that stood upright. 659

alternation of generations *ALL-ter-NAY-shun JEN-er-AY-shunz* The existence of a gamete-producing and a spore-producing phase in the life cycle of a plant. 28, 573

altruism *AL-tru-iz-um* A behavior that harms the individual performing it but helps another organism. 692

alveolar ducts *AL-vee-O-ler DUCTS* The narrowed ending of bronchioles, opening into clusters of alveoli. 451

alveoli *AL-vee-O-li* A microscopic air sac in the lung. 451

amaranth *AM-ah-RANTH* A tall plant that can supply many types of food. 547

amino acid *ah-MEEN-o AS-id* An organic molecule built of a central carbon atom bonded to a hydrogen atom, an amino group, a carboxylic acid, and an R group. A polymer of amino acids is a peptide. 19, 52

amino acid racemization *ah-MEEN-o AS-id RACE-eh-mah-ZA-shun* A technique that measures the rate at which amino acids in biological matter alter to isomeric forms. This measurement is used in absolute dating of fossils and remains up to 100,000 years old. 650

ammonia *ah-MOAN-ee-ah* The chemical compound NH₃, which is a nitrogenous waste generated by the deamination of protein. 502

amniocentesis *AM-nee-o-cen-TEE-sis* A prenatal diagnostic procedure, performed during the fourth month of pregnancy. Fetal cells and biochemicals are sampled and then examined to reveal certain abnormalities. 180, 300

amniote egg *AM-nee-oat EGG* An egg in which an embryo could develop completely, without the requirement of being laid in water. 659

ampullae *AM-pew-li* The enlarged bases of the semicircular canals in the inner ear, lined with hair cells that detect fluid movement and convert it into action potentials. 362

amygdala *ah-MIG-dah-lah* A part of the cerebrum involved in encoding factual memory. 341

anabolism *eh-NAB-o-liz-um* Synthetic metabolic reactions, using energy. 110

anal canal *AAN-al kah-NAL* The final section of the digestive tract. 477

analgesic *AN-al-JEE-sik* A pain-relieving treatment. 459

analogous *ah-NAL-eh-ges* Structures similar in function but not in structure that have evolved in unrelated organisms in response to a similar environmental challenge. 651

anaphase *AN-ah-faze* The stage of mitosis when centromeres split and the two sets of chromosomes move to opposite ends of the cell. In anaphase of meiosis I, homologs separate. 134

anaphylactic shock *AN-ah-fah-LAK-tik SHOCK* A potentially life-threatening allergic reaction in which mast cells release allergy mediators throughout the body, causing apprehension, rash, and a closing of the throat. 528

androecium *an-DREE-see-um* The innermost whorl of a flower's corolla, consisting of male reproductive structures. 574

aneuploid *AN-you-ploid* A cell with one or more extra or missing chromosomes. 280

angina pectoris *an-GINE-ah pek-TORE-is* A gripping, viselike pain in the chest. 436

angiosperms *AN-gee-o-spermz* The flowering plants. 29

Animalia *AN-ah-MAIL-ee-ah* Kingdom including eukaryotes that derive energy from food and have nervous systems. 22

anorexia nervosa *AN-eh-REX-ee-ah ner-VO-sah* An eating disorder characterized by self-imposed starvation due to a psychological problem involving self-image. 490

antagonist *an-TAG-o-nist* A drug that binds to a receptor, blocking the docking of a neurotransmitter. 325

antagonistic muscles *an-TAG-o-NIS-tik MUS-selz* The two muscles or muscle groups that flank a movable bone and move it in opposite directions. 414

anthers *an-THERZ* Oval bodies at the tips of stamens that produce pollen. 574

anthocyanins *AN-tho-CY-ah-ninz* Pigments produced in senescent plant cells. 599

antibodies *AN-tah-BOD-eez* Proteins secreted by B cells that recognize and bind to foreign antigens, disabling them or signaling other cells to do so. 518

anticodon *AN-ti-ko-don* A three-base sequence on one loop of a transfer RNA molecule that is complementary to an mRNA codon and therefore serves to bring together the appropriate amino acid and its mRNA instructions. 258

antidiuretic hormone (ADH) (vasopressin) *AN-ti-DI-yur-RET-ik HOR-moan* A hormone made in the hypothalamus and released from the posterior pituitary that acts on the kidneys and smooth muscle cells of blood vessels to maintain the composition of body fluids. 375, 510

antigen *AN-tah-gen* The specific parts of cells or chemicals that elicit an immune response. 517

antigen binding site *AN-tah-gen BIND-ing SITE* Specialized ends of antibodies that bind specific antigens. 519

antihistamines *AN-ti-HIS-tah-meens* Drugs that decrease mucus secretion and alleviate watery eyes and sneezing. 459

antisense strand *AN-ti-sense strand* The side of the DNA double helix for a particular gene that is not transcribed into mRNA. 257

anus *A-nus* The opening to the anal canal. 477

anvil *AN-vil* One of the bones in the middle ear. 359

aorta *a-OR-tah* The largest artery that leaves the heart. 432, 435

aortic semilunar valve *a-OR-tik SEM-i-LOON-er VALVE* The valve between the left ventricle and the aorta. 435

apatosaurs *ah-PAT-o-SORZ* Huge, land-dwelling, herbivorous dinosaurs, also called brontosaurs. 659

apical meristems *A-pik-el MER-eh-STEMZ* Unspecialized cells that divide; found in plants near the tips of roots and shoots. 552

apneustic center *ap-NUS-tik CEN-ter* The part of the brain controlling the ability to take a deep breath. 458

appendicular skeleton *AP-en-DIK-u-lar SKEL-eh-ten* In a vertebrate skeleton, the limb bones and the bones that support them. 397

appendix *ap-PEN-diks* A thin tube from the cecum. 475

aqueous humor *AWK-kwee-es U-mer* A nutritive, watery fluid between the cornea and the lens of the eye that focuses incoming light rays and maintains the shape of the eyeball. 356

archaeopteryx *AR-kee-OP-ter-iks* A type of dinosaur that could fly. 659

arteries *ARE-teh-reez* Large, elastic blood vessels that leave the heart and branch into arterioles. 428

arterioles *are-TER-ee-olz* Small, elastic blood vessels that arise from arteries and lead into capillaries. 428

arthritis *arth-RI-tis* Inflammation of the joints. 401

artificial insemination *AR-teh-FISH-el in-SEM-eh-NAY-shun* Placing donated sperm in a woman's reproductive tract to start a pregnancy. 205

artificial seed *ARE-tah-FISH-al SEED* A somatic embryo placed in a transparent polysaccharide gel containing nutrients and hormones, with an outer, biodegradable polymer coat. 606

artificial selection *AR-tah-FISH-al sah-LEK-shun* Influencing the genetic makeup of a population, as occurs in agriculture and selective breeding of domesticated animals. 540, 626

ascending limb *as-SEN-ding LIM* The distal portion of the loop of Henle, which ascends from the kidney's medulla. Cells here are impermeable to water, and they actively transport Na⁺ into the medullary space. 508

ascomycete *AS-ko-my-seat* A fungus with asci as sexual structures, such as the organism that causes athlete's foot. 27

asexual reproduction *A-sex-yu-al re-pro-DUK-shun* A cell's doubling its contents and then splitting in two to yield two identical cells. 42, 158

association areas *ah-SOC-ee-A-shun AIR-ee-ahs* Little-understood parts of the cerebral cortex that control learning and creativity. 337

asthma *AS-mah* Spasm of the bronchial muscles. 451

atherosclerosis *ATH-ee-ro-skle-RO-sis* The accumulation of fatty plaques inside coronary arteries. 436

atom *AT-um* A chemical unit, composed of protons, neutrons, and electrons, that cannot be further broken down by chemical means. 44

atria *A-tree-ah* The paired uppermost chambers of the heart, which receive blood returning to the heart and pump it to the ventricles below. 434

atrial natriuretic factor (ANF) *A-tree-al NAY-tre-yu-RET-ik FAK-ter* A hormone produced in the heart atria of mammals that regulates blood pressure and volume and the excretion of K⁺, Na⁺, and water. 383

atrioventricular node (AV node) *A-tre-o-ven-TRIK-yu-lar NOOD* Specialized muscle cells that branch into a network of Purkinje fibers, which conduct electrical stimulation six times faster than other parts of the heart. 438

atrioventricular valves *A-tree-o-ven-TRIK-ku-ler VALVZ* Flaps of tissue between each atrium and ventricle that move in response to the pressure changes accompanying the contraction of the ventricle. 434

atrophy *AH-tro-fee* Muscle degeneration resulting from lack of use or immobilization. 417

auditory nerve *AWD-eh-tore-ee NERV* Nerve fibers carrying action potentials from the cochlea in the inner ear to the cortex of the brain. 360

autoantibodies *AW-to-AN-tah-BOD-eez* Antibodies produced by an organism that attack tissue of the body, resulting in an autoimmune disease. 525

autonomic nervous system *AW-toe-NOM-ik NER-ves SIS-tum* Part of the motor pathways of the peripheral nervous system that leads to smooth muscle, cardiac muscle, and glands. 344, 439

autopolyploid *AW-toe-POL-ee-ploid* An organism with multiple chromosome sets derived from the same species. 639

autosome *AW-toe-soam* A non-sex chromosome. 225

autotroph(ic) *AW-toe-trof* An organism that manufactures nutrient molecules using energy harnessed from the environment. 22, 114

auxin *AWK-zin* A type of plant hormone that causes cell elongation in seedlings, shoot tips, embryos, and leaves. 580, 588

axial skeleton *AX-ee-al SKEL-eh-ten* In a vertebrate skeleton, the skull, vertebral column, ribs, and breastbone. 397

axil *AX-el* The regions between a leaf stalk and stem. 557

axon *AX-on* An extension from a neuron that conducts information away from the cell body toward a receiving cell. 315

B

B cells *B SELZ* A class of lymphocytes that produce antibodies. 518

bacteria *BACK-TEAR-ee-ah* Single-celled prokaryotic organisms. 22

balanced polymorphism *BAL-anced POL-ee-MORF-iz-um* A form of stabilizing selection that allows a genetic disease to remain in a population because heterozygotes enjoy a selective advantage. 637

bark *BARK* All of the tissues outside of the vascular cambium. 568

Barr body *bar BOD-ee* The dark-staining body seen in the nucleus of a cell from a female mammal, corresponding to the inactivated X chromosome. 239

basal ganglia *BASE-el GANG-lee-ah* Masses of nerve cell bodies in the cerebrum involved in forming memories required to perform certain skills. 341

basal metabolic rate *BA-sal MET-ah-BALL-ik RATE* The energy required by an organism to stay alive. 112

base *BASE* A molecule that releases hydroxide ions into water. 46

basidiomycete *bah-SID-ee-o-my-SEAT* A fungus with spore-containing basidia, including hallucinogenic mushrooms. 28

basilar membrane *BAY-seh-ler MEM-brane* The membrane beneath the hair cells in the cochlea of the inner ear that vibrates in response to sound. 360

behavioral isolation *be-HAAV-yu-ral l-so-LAY-shun* When members of two populations do not crossbreed because they perform different courtship rituals. 638

benthic zone *BEN-thik ZONE* The bottom of the ocean. 737

bicuspid valve *BI-kus-pid VALVE* The valve between the left atrium and the left ventricle. 435

bile *BILE* A substance produced by the liver and stored in the gallbladder that emulsifies fats. 472

binary fission *BI-nair-ee FISH-en* A type of asexual reproduction in which a cell divides into two identical cells. 22, 131

biofeedback *BI-o-FEED-bak* A technology giving people information on physiological processes they wish to control. 673

biogeochemical cycles *BI-o-GEE-o-KEM-ik-el SI-kelz* The pathways of chemicals between the atmosphere, the earth's crust, water, and organisms. 721

biogeography *BI-o-gee-OG-grah-fee* The physical distribution of organisms. 638

biological clock *BI-o-LOG-ik-kal CLOCK* An internal timing mechanism in an organism that controls its circadian rhythms. 600, 674

biomagnification *BI-o-MAG-nah-fah-KA-shun* The increasing concentration of a substance at higher trophic levels in a food chain. 721

biomass *BI-o-mass* The total dry weight of organisms in an area. 719

biome *BI-oam* A group of interacting terrestrial ecosystems characterized by a dominant collection of plant species, or a group of interacting aquatic ecosystems with similar salinities. 717

biosphere *BI-o-sfer* All of the parts of the earth that support life. 717

biotechnology *BI-o-tek-NAL-eh-gee* The alteration of cells or biological molecules with a specific application, including monoclonal antibody technology, genetic engineering, and cell culture. 268, 603

biotherapy *BI-o-THER-ah-pee* Use of body chemicals as pharmaceuticals. 534

biotic potential *bi-OT-ik po-TEN-shal* The maximum number of offspring an individual is physiologically capable of producing. 701

blade *BLADE* The flattened region of a leaf. 559

blastocyst *BLAS-toe-cyst* The preembryonic stage of human development when the organism is a hollow, fluid-filled ball of cells. 173

blastomere *BLAS-toe-mere* A cell in a preembryonic organism resulting from cleavage divisions. 172

blood *BLOOD* A complex fluid consisting of formed elements (blood cells and platelets) suspended in a watery plasma, in which are dissolved a variety of proteins and other biochemicals. 421

blood-brain barrier *BLOOD BRANE BARR-ee-er* Capillaries in the brain whose endothelial cells are so closely packed that many substances cannot cross from the blood to the brain tissue. 342

blood pressure *BLOOD PRESH-yur* The force exerted outward on blood vessel walls by the blood. 432

blood vessels *BLOOD VES-selz* Conduits that conduct blood throughout the body, including arteries, arterioles, capillaries, venules, and veins. 421

body *BOD-ee* The midsection of the stomach. 470

bolus *BO-lus* Food rolled into a lump by the tongue. 469

bomb calorimeter *BOMB KAL-or-IM-ah-ter* A chamber surrounded by water that is used to measure the caloric content of a food. 484

bone *BONE* A connective tissue consisting of bone-building osteoblasts, stationary osteocytes, and bone-destroying osteoclasts, embedded in a mineralized matrix infused with spaces and canals (lacunae, canaliculi, and Haversian canals). 86

Bowman's capsule *BOW-manz KAP-sul* The cup-shaped proximal end of the renal tubule which surrounds the glomerulus. 506

braced framework *BRACED FRAME-work* A skeleton built of solid structural components that are strong enough to resist pressure without collapsing. 390

brachiopods *BRAK-ee-o-PODZ* Clamlike organisms that appeared in the seas of the Cambrian period. 657

bracts *BRAKS* Floral leaves that protect developing flowers. 561

bronchi *BRON-ki* Two tubules that branch from the trachea as it reaches the lungs. 450

bronchioles *BRON-ki-olz* Microscopic branches of the bronchi within the lungs. 450

bronchitis *bron-KI-tis* Inflammation of the mucous membrane of the bronchi. 459

bryophytes *BRY-o-FIGHTS* Primitive plants that lack specialized tissues to conduct water and nutrients. 29, 571

bulimia *bu-LEEM-ee-ah* An eating disorder characterized by binging and purging. 492

bursae *BUR-si* Small packets within synovial joints that store synovial fluid, which helps to reduce friction between bones and nearby structures. 401

bursitis *bur-SI-tis* Inflammation of the bursae, possibly due to calcium deposits. 401

C

calcitonin *KAL-sah-TOE-nin* A thyroid hormone that decreases blood calcium levels. 375, 396

callus *KAL-lus* An undifferentiated white lump that grows from a cultured plant explant. 605

Calorie *CAL-o-ree* The amount of energy needed to raise the temperature of 1 kilogram of water by 1°C. 112

calyx *KA-liks* One of two outermost whorls of a flower, with no direct role in sexual reproduction. 574

Cambrian period *KAB-ree-an PER-ee-od* The time in earth history about 600 million years ago when many new types of organisms appeared. 656

canaliculi *kah-NAL-ku-LI* Narrow passageways in bone that connect spaces housing osteocytes. 393

cancer *CAN-sir* A group of disorders resulting from the loss of normal control over mitotic rate and number of divisions. 141

capacitation *cah-PASS-eh-TAY-shun* Activation of sperm cells in the human female reproductive tract. 171

capillaries *KAP-ah-lair-eez* The smallest blood vessels, with a lining one cell thick. 428

carbohydrases *KAR-bo-HI-dra-sez* Enzymes that chemically break down certain disaccharides into monosaccharides. 472

carbohydrate loading *KAR-bo-HI-drat LOAD-ing* A regimen of following a high-carbohydrate diet in the week before an endurance athletic event in an attempt to maximize muscle glycogen.

carbohydrates *CAR-bo-HIGH-drates* Compounds containing carbon, hydrogen, and oxygen, with twice as many hydrogens as oxygens. Carbohydrates include the sugars and starches. 49

carbonic anhydrase *kar-BON-ik an-HI-draze* An enzyme in red blood cells that catalyzes the conversion of carbon dioxide to carbonic acid. 457

Carboniferous period *KAR-bah-NIF-er-es PER-ee-od* The time from 345 to 275 million years ago, when the first amphibians and reptiles appeared on the land. 657

cardia *KAR-dee-ah* The neck of the stomach. 470

cardiac cycle *KAR-dee-ak SI-kel* The sequence of a contraction and relaxation that comprises the heartbeat. 438

cardiac muscle *CAR-dee-ak MUS-sel* Striated, involuntary, single-nucleated contractile cells found in the mammalian heart. 87, 405

cardioaccelerator area *KAR-dee-o-ak-SEL-er-ay-ter AIR-ee-ah* Part of the brain's vasomotor center that stimulates circulation by speeding the heart. 439

cardioinhibition area *KAR-de-o-IN-hah-BISH-un AIR-ee-ah* Part of the brain's vasomotor center that slows the heart. 439

carotenoid pigments *KAIR-et-teh-noid PIG-mentz* Yellow and orange plant pigments that become visible in autumn when chlorophyll production declines. 599

carpel *KAR-pel* Leaflike structures in a flower that enclose ovules. 574

carpels *KAR-pelz* The wrist bones. 400

carrying capacity *KARR-e-ing kah-PAS-eh-tee* The maximum number of individuals that can be supported by the environment for an indefinite time period. 705

cartilage *CAR-teh-lij* A supportive connective tissue consisting of chondrocytes embedded in collagen and proteoglycans. 84

Casparian strip *kas-PAHR-ee-an STRIP* The single layer of tightly packed cells comprising the endodermis of a plant. 564

catabolism *cah-TAB-o-liz-um* Metabolic reactions of degradation, releasing energy. 110

catecholamines *KAT-eh-KOL-ah-meenz* A class of hormones, including epinephrine and norepinephrine. 377

cecum *SEE-cum* A pouch at the entrance to the large intestine. 475

cell *SEL* The structural and functional unit of life. 40, 67

cell body *SEL BOD-ee* The central, rounded portion of a neuron from which an axon and dendrites extend. 315

cell cycle *SEL CY-kel* The life of a cell, in terms of whether it is dividing or in interphase. 131

cell membrane (plasmalemma) *SEL MEM-brane* An oily structure built of proteins embedded in a lipid bilayer, which forms the boundary of cells. 92

cell population *SEL POP-u-LAY-shun* A group of cells with characteristic proportions in particular stages of the cell cycle. 139

cell theory *SEL THER-ee* The ideas that all living matter is built of cells, cells are the structural and functional units of life, and all cells come from preexisting cells. 71

cellular respiration *SEL-u-ler RES-pir-AY-shun* Biochemical reactions involved in energy extraction in the mitochondrion. 119

cell wall *SEL WALL* A rigid boundary built of peptidoglycans in prokaryotic cells and cellulose in plant cells. 72

cementum *sah-MEN-tum* An outer layer of the tooth, anchoring it to the gum and jawbone. 469

Cenozoic era *CEN-o-ZO-ik ER-ah* The time from 65 million years ago, including the present. 661

central nervous system (CNS) *SEN-tral NER-vous SIS-tum* The brain and the spinal cord. 331

centrioles *CEN-tre-olz* Paired, oblong structures built of microtubules and found in animal cells, where they organize the mitotic spindle. 81

centromere *CEN-tro-mere* A characteristically located constriction in a chromosome. 133

cereals *SER-ee-alz* Members of the grass family Poaceae, which have seeds that can be stored for long periods of time. 541

cerebellum *SER-eh-BELL-um* A grooved area behind the brain stem and connected to the cerebrum above that receives impulses from the cerebral cortex and the peripheral nervous system and then unconsciously adjusts muscular responses so that they are smooth and coordinated. 335

cerebral cortex *sah-REE-bral KOR-tex* Gray matter comprising the outer layer of the cerebrum that integrates incoming information. 350, 458

cerebrospinal fluid *sah-REE-bro-SPI-nal FLU-id* Fluid similar to blood plasma that bathes and cushions the central nervous system. 342

cerebrum *seh-REE-brum* The higher region of the brain, controlling intelligence, learning, perception, and emotion. 337

cervical vertebrae *SER-vah-kel VER-tah-bray* Seven vertebrae in the neck. 398

cervix *SIR-viks* In the female human, the opening to the uterus. 157

chlorenchyma *klor-REN-kah-mah* Chloroplast-containing parenchyma cells. 553

chlorofluorocarbons (CFCs) *KLOR-o-FLOR-o-KAR-bunz* Compounds containing carbon, chlorine, and fluorine that destroy atmospheric ozone, which filters out ultraviolet radiation. 751

chlorophyll *KLOR-eh-fill* A green pigment used by plants to harness the energy in sunlight. 28, 81, 115

chloroplast *KLOR-o-plast* A plant cell organelle housing the reactions of photosynthesis. 81, 116

chlybrid *KLI-brid* A cell into which a chloroplast from another cell is introduced. 610

cholecystokinin (CCK) *KOL-e-sis-TOE-kah-nin* A hormone produced in the small intestine that signals the release of substances needed for fat digestion. 473

chorionic villi *KOR-ee-ON-ik VIL-i* Fingerlike projections extending from the chorion to the uterine lining. 179

choroid coat *KOR-oid KOAT* The middle layer of the human eyeball, containing many blood vessels. 354

chromatid *CRO-mah-tid* A continuous strand of DNA comprising an unreplicated chromosome or one-half of a replicated chromosome. 133

chromosome *KRO-mo-soam* A dark-staining, rod-shaped structure in the nucleus of a eukaryotic cell built of a continuous molecule of DNA, wrapped in protein. 76, 218

chyme *KIME* Semisolid food in the stomach. 470

chymotrypsin *KEE-mo-TRIP-sin* A pancreatic enzyme that participates in protein digestion in the small intestine. 472

cilia *SIL-ee-ah* Protein projections from cells. Cilia beat in unison, moving substances. 83, 104

ciliary body *SIL-ee-AIR-ee BOD-ee* A highly folded, specialized structure in the center of the choroid coat of the human eye that houses the ciliary muscle, which controls the shape of the lens. 354

ciliary muscle *SIL-e-AIR-ee MUS-sel* A muscle at the center of the choroid coat in the human eye that alters the shape of the lens. 354

circadian rhythms *sir-KA-dee-en RITH-umz* Regular, daily rhythms of particular biological functions. 677

circalunadian *SIR-kah-lu-NAY-di-an* A biological rhythm that repeats approximately every day. 677

circannual *SIR-kah-AN-u-al* A biological rhythm that repeats approximately every year. 677

classical conditioning *KLAS-ik-kal kon-DISH-on-ing* A form of learning in which an animal responds in a familiar way to a new stimulus. 673

cleavage *KLEV-ij* A period of rapid cell division following fertilization but before embryogenesis. 172

climax community *KLI-max kom-MUUN-eh-te* A community that remains fairly constant if the land and climate are undisturbed. 722

clonal propagation *KLO-nel PROP-ah-GAY-shun* Uniform plants grown from cells or protoplasts cultured in the laboratory. 607

clones *KLONZ* Genetically identical individuals. 584

closed behavior program *CLOZED bee-HAIV-yur PRO-gram* A behavior that is largely genetically determined and rigid and not easily influenced by the environment. 667

closed circulatory system *CLOZED SIR-ku-lah-TORE-ee SIS-tum* A circulatory system in which the blood is contained in blood vessels. 422

coagulation *ko-AG-u-LAY-shun* Clotting of blood. 427

coccyx *COK-six* The final four vertebrae, which are fused to form the tailbone. 399

cochlea *COKE-lee-ah* The spiral-shaped, hindmost portion of the inner ear, where vibrations are translated into nerve impulses. 359

cochlear implant *COKE-lee-ar IM-plant* A device that delivers an electronic stimulus directly to the auditory nerve, bypassing the function of hair cells to provide an awareness of sound. 361

codominant *KO-DOM-eh-nent* Alleles that are both expressed in the heterozygote. 225

codon *KO-don* A continuous triplet of mRNA that specifies a particular amino acid. 258

coelom *SEE-loam* A central body cavity in an animal. 31

coevolution *KO-ev-eh-LU-shun* The interdependence of two types of organisms for survival. 619

coleoptile *KOL-ee-OP-tile* A sheathlike structure covering the plumule in monocots. 578

collateral circulation *ko-LAT-er-al SIR-ku-LAY-shun* Rerouting of blood in the heart into different arteries following damage to the heart. 436

collecting duct *ko-LEK-ting DUCT* A structure in the kidney into which nephrons drain urine. 509

collenchyma *kol-LEN-kah-mah* Elongated, living cells that differentiate from parenchyma and support the growing regions of shoots. 553

colon *KOL-en* The large intestine. 475

color blind *KUL-er BLIND* A condition in which one or more types of cone cells in the retina are missing. The individual cannot distinguish among all colors. 358

colorectal cancer *KOL-ah-REK-tal KAN-cer* Cancer of the large intestine and rectum. 477

colostomy *ko-LOS-toe-mee* Surgery that attaches the large intestine to an opening leading to a bag worn outside the body, where fecal matter collects. 477

commensalism *kom-MEN-sah-liz-um* A symbiotic relationship where one partner benefits and the other is unaffected. 14

community *kom-MUN-nah-tee* All of the organisms in a given area. 713

compact bone *KOM-pact BONE* A layer of solid, hard bone covering spongy bone. 393

complement system *KOM-plah-ment SIS-tum* A group of proteins that assist other immune defenses. 515

complementary *kom-ple-MENT-ah-ree* The tendency of adenine to hydrogen bond to thymine and guanine to cytosine in the DNA double helix. 253

complex carbohydrates *KOM-plex kar-bo-HI-drates* The polysaccharides, which are chains of sugars. Polysaccharides include starch, glycogen, cellulose, and chitin. 50

compound *KOM-pound* A molecule consisting of different atoms. 45

compound microscope *KOM-pound MI-kro-scope* A microscope built of two lenses. 70

concentration gradient *KON-sen-TRA-shun GRAY-dee-ent* The phenomenon of ions passively diffusing from an area in which they are highly concentrated to an area where they are less concentrated. 318

concordance *KON-KOR-dance* A measure of the inherited component

of a trait, consisting of the number of pairs of either monozygotic or dizygotic twins in which both members express a trait, divided by the number of pairs in which at least one twin expresses the trait. 292

conditioned stimulus *kon-DISH-ond STIM-u-lus* A new stimulus that is coupled to a familiar, or unconditioned, stimulus, so that an animal can learn an association between the two. 673

conductive deafness *kon-DUK-tiv DEF-nes* Hearing loss resulting from blocked transmission of sound through the middle ear. 360

cones *KONZ* Specialized neurons found in the central portion of the retina that detect colors. 355

cones *KONZ* The reproductive structures of pines. 583

conformation *KON-for-MAY-shun* The three-dimensional shape of a protein. 53

confusion effect *kon-FUZ-yun E-fekt* The confusion faced by a predator in the presence of a school of fish. 687

congestive heart failure *kon-JES-tiv HART FAIL-yur* A weakening of the heart, impairing circulation. 436

connective tissue *kon-NECK-tiv TISH-u* Tissues consisting of cells embedded or suspended in a matrix, including loose and fibrous connective tissues, cartilage, bone, and blood. 81

constant regions *KON-stant REE-genz* The sequence of amino acids comprising the lower portions of heavy and light antibody chains, which is very similar in different antibody types. 518

constipation *KON-stah-PAY-shun* The infrequent passage of hard feces, caused by abnormally slow movement of fecal matter through the large intestine. 476

contact inhibition *KON-tact IN-heh-BISH-un* The tendency of a cell to cease dividing once it touches another cell. 138

contest competition *KON-test KOM-pah-TISH-un* Indirect competition of individuals in a population for a limited resource, such as acquiring a territory that provides access to resources. 705

contractile vacuole *KON-tract-till VAK-u-ol* An organelle in paramecium that pumps water out of the cell. 100

convergent evolution *KON-ver-gent EV-o-LU-shun* Organisms that have evolved similar adaptations to a similar environmental challenge but are not related by descent. 625

cork cambium *KORK KAM-bee-um* The lateral meristem that produces the periderm, the outer protective covering on mature stems and roots. 568

cork cells *KORK SELZ* Waxy, densely packed cells covering the surfaces of mature stems and roots. 568

cornea *KOR-nee-ah* A modified portion of the human eye's sclera that forms a transparent curved window admitting light. 353

corolla *kah-ROLE-ah* One of two outermost whorls of a flower, with no direct role in sexual reproduction. 574

corona radiata *kah-ROAN-ah RAID-ee-AH-tah* Cells surrounding the secondary oocyte and the zona pellucida. 171

coronary arteries *KOR-eh-nair-ee AR-ter-eez* Paired arteries that diverge from the aorta and surround and enter the heart. 439

coronary circulation *KOR-eh-nair-ee SIR-ku-LA-shun* The network of blood vessels that supplies blood to the heart. 439

coronary heart disease *KOR-eh-nair-ee HART DIS-eez* Disease of the coronary arteries. 436

corpus callosum *KOR-pes ka-LAWS-um* Tracts of myelinated nerve fibers that form a bridge between the cerebral hemispheres. 340

corpus luteum *KOR-pis LU-te-um* A gland formed from an ovarian follicle from which an oocyte has recently been ovulated that produces estrogen and progesterone. 381

cortex *KOR-teks* In plants, the ground tissue that fills the area between the epidermis and vascular tissue in stems. 558

cortex *KOR-teks* The outermost part of the kidney, consisting of glomeruli, Bowman's capsules, and proximal and distal convoluted tubules of nephrons. 505

cortisol *KOR-teh-sol* A major glucocorticoid hormone produced in the adrenal cortex that helps enable the body to cope with prolonged stress. 378

cotyledons *KOT-ah-LEE-donz* Embryonic leaves in flowering plants that store energy used for germination. 562, 578

cotylosaurs *KOT-el-o-SORZ* Animals living in the early Permian period that were ancestors of the dinosaurs and modern reptiles, birds, and mammals. 659

countercurrent flow *COUNT-er-CURR-ent FLO* A system in which fluid flows in a continuous tubule in opposite directions, which maximizes the amount of a particular substance that diffuses out of the tubule. 447

countercurrent multiplier system *KAUN-ter-CUR-ent MUL-tah-PLI er SIS-tum* The movement of Na⁺ and water between the limbs of the loop of Henle and the medullary space in the kidney. The concentration of Na⁺ in the medullary space forces water to leave the descending limb, and it then reenters the bloodstream. 509

courtship ritual *KOURT-ship RIT-u-al* A stereotyped, elaborate, and conspicuous behavior that overcomes aggressive tendencies long enough for mating to occur. 696

covalent bond *KO-va-lent bond* The sharing of electrons between atoms. 47

cranial nerves *CRANE-e-al NERVZ* Twelve pairs of somatic nerves that arise from the brain. 344

creatine phosphate *KRE-ah-tin FOS-fate* A molecule stored in muscle fibers that can donate its high-energy phosphate to ADP to regenerate ATP.

Cretaceous period *kra-TAY-shus PER-ee-od* The time from 135 to 65 million years ago when angiosperms were abundant and the number of dinosaur species declined. 659

cretinism *KRE-tin-iz-um* A child who is physically and mentally retarded due to a thyroid gland underactive since birth.

cristae *KRIS-ty* The folds of the inner membrane of a mitochondrion along which many of the reactions of cellular respiration occur. 79, 122

critical period *KRIT-eh-kel PER-ee-od* The time during prenatal development when a specific structure can be altered by a gene or an external influence. 202

critical period *KRIT-eh-kel PER-ee-od* The time in an animal's life when it performs a particular imprinting behavior. 673

Cro-Magnons *kro-MAG-nonz* Lightweight, fine-boned, less hairy members of *Homo sapiens* who lived about 40,000 years ago in Europe and Asia. 663

crossing over *KROS-ing O-ver* The exchange of genetic material between homologous chromosomes during prophase of meiosis I. 159, 237

crossopterygians *cros-SOP-ter-REEG-ee-anz* The lobe-finned fishes, which first appeared in the Devonian period and were probably ancestral to amphibians. 657

cuticle *KU-tah-kal* A covering tissue over all of a plant except the roots. 554

cutin *KU-tin* A fatty material produced by a plant's epidermal cells that forms the cuticle. 554

cyanobacteria *si-AN-o-bak-TEAR-ee-ah* Prokaryotic organisms that contain pigments and can photosynthesize: Also called blue-green algae. 22

cybridization *SI-brid-di-ZAY-shun* The production of a cell having cytoplasm derived from two cells but containing a single nucleus. 610

cyclic ovulator *SI-klik OV-u-LAY-ter* A female mammal that undergoes a monthly cycle of fertility. 382

cyclosporin *SI-klo-SPOR-in* A fungus-derived drug that suppresses immunity and is of great value in assisting transplant recipients in accepting a new organ. 529

cystic fibrosis *SIS-tik fi-BRO-sis* An inherited condition in which excess mucus plugs up the lungs and pancreas. 460

cytokinesis *SI-toe-kin-E-sis* Distribution of cytoplasm, organelles, and macromolecules into two daughter cells in cell division. 131

cytokinins *SI-toe-KI-ninz* A class of plant hormones that promote cytokinesis (division of a cell following division of the genetic material) in seeds, roots, young leaves, and fruits. 588

cytoplasm *SI-toe-PLAZ-um* The jellylike fluid in which organelles are suspended in eukaryotic cells. 75

cytosine *SI-toe-seen* One of the two pyrimidine nitrogenous bases in DNA and RNA. 57, 253

cytoskeleton *SI-toe-SKEL-eh-ten* A framework built of arrays of protein rods and tubules found in animal cells. 75, 92

D

dark reactions *DARK re-AK-shuns* Reactions of photosynthesis that do not require light and that use the products of the light reactions (NADPH and ATP) to synthesize organic molecules. 117

day-neutral plants *DAY NU-trel PLANTZ* Plants that do not rely on photoperiod to flower. 596

dead space *DEAD SPACE* The air in the pharynx, trachea, and the upper third of the lungs, which is not used in gas exchange. 455

deciduous trees *dah-SID-u-us TREEZ* Trees that shed their leaves at the end of a growing season. 562

decomposers *DEE-kom-POZ-erz* Organisms that consume dead organisms and feces. 718

decongestants *DE-kon-JES-tentz* Drugs that shrink nasal membranes, easing breathing. 459

defibrillator *de-FIB-rah-LAY-ter* A device that sends an electric shock to the heart to restore a normal heartbeat. 436

degenerate *de-JEN-er-at* Different codons specifying the same amino acid. 261

dehydration synthesis *DE-hi-DRA-shun SYN-theh-sis* Formation of a covalent bond between two molecules by the loss of water. 50

dendrites *DEN-dritz* Short, branched, numerous extensions from a neuron that usually receive information from other neurons and transmit it toward the neuron cell body. 315

denitrifying bacteria *DE-ni-trah-FI-ing bak-TER-ee-ah* Bacteria that convert ammonia, nitrite, and nitrate to nitrogen gas. 721

density dependent factors *DEN-seh-tee DE-pen-dent FAK-terz* Factors that kill a greater percentage of a population as population size increases. 705

density independent factors *DEN-seh-tee IN-deh-PEN-dent FAK-terz* Factors that kill a certain percentage of a population regardless of population size, such as natural disasters. 705

dentine *DEN-tin* The bonelike material beneath a tooth's enamel. 469

deoxyhemoglobin *DE-OX-ee-HEEM-o-GLO-bin* Hemoglobin that is deep red after releasing its oxygen to tissues. 426

deoxyribonucleic acid (DNA) *de-OX-ee-RI-bo-nu-KLAY-ic AS-id* A double-stranded nucleic acid built of nucleotides containing a phosphate group, a nitrogenous base (A, T, G, or C), and the sugar deoxyribose. 57, 217

depolarized *DE-pol-er-ized* When the charge of the interior of a neuron at rest becomes less negative by the influx of Na⁺. 319

dermal tissue *DER-mal TISH-u* Tissue covering a plant's body. 554

descending limb *de-SEN-ding LIM* The proximal portion of the loop of Henle, which descends into the kidney's medulla. Cells here are permeable to water, which passively diffuses into the kidney's medulla in response to the Na⁺ that collects there after leaving the ascending limb. 508

desensitization *de-SEN-sah-teh-ZA-shun* Periodic injection of allergens under the skin in an attempt to plug receptors on mast cells with IgG so that allergy mediators are not released upon encountering the allergen. 526

Devonian period *deh-VOAN-ee-an PER-ee-od* The time following the Silurian period, 395 to 345 million years ago, when fishes first became abundant. 657

diabetes insipidus *DI-ah-BEE-teez IN-sip-eh-dis* A disruption of the synthesis or release of antidiuretic hormone, producing intense thirst and copious, watery urine. 375

diabetes mellitus *DI-ah-BEAT-es MEL-eh-tis* A medical condition in which the body does not produce sufficient insulin or cannot react to the insulin present. 379

diaphragm *DI-ah-fram* A broad sheet of muscle separating the thoracic cavity from the abdominal cavity. 453

diarrhea *DI-ah-REE-ah* The frequent and too-rapid passage of loose feces, caused by abnormally fast movement of fecal matter through the large intestine. 476

diastole *di-AS-toll-ee* The heart's relaxation. 438

diastolic pressure *DI-ah-stol-ik PRESH-yur* The blood pressure at its lowest, when the ventricles relax. 432

dicots *DI-kotz* Flowering plants that have two seed leaves. 557, 578

dihybrid *DI-HI-brid* An individual heterozygous for two particular genes. 222

dilution effect *dah-LU-shun E-fekt* A behavior in which ostriches with mates sit on eggs of females lacking permanent mates, which decreases the chances of their own eggs being eaten. 687

diplodocus *DIP-lo-DOE-kus* Huge, land-dwelling, herbivorous dinosaurs. 659

diploid *DIP-loid* A cell with two copies of each chromosome. 157

directional selection *dah-REK-shun-al sah-LEK-shun* When a previously prevalent characteristic of the individuals of a population is altered in response to a changing environment as the number of better-adapted individuals increases. 637

disaccharide *DI-SAK-eh-ride* A sugar built of two bonded monosaccharides, including sucrose, maltose, and lactose. 50

disruptive selection *dis-RUP-tiv sah-LEK-shun* When either of two extreme expressions of a trait are the most fit. 637

distal convoluted tubule *DIS-tel KON-vo-LU-tid TU-bule* The region of the kidney distal to the loop of Henle and proximal to a collecting duct where Na⁺ is reabsorbed into the peritubular capillaries by active transport, blood pH is maintained, and wastes are secreted. 509

diverticulosis *DI-ver-TIK-ku-LO-sis* A weakening of parts of the large intestinal wall. 476

DNA hybridization *HI-brid-i-ZAY-shun* Determining the relatedness of two types of organisms by observing how rapidly separated strands of their DNA form hybrids. 654

DNA polymerase *po-LIM-er-ase* A type of enzyme that participates in DNA replication by inserting new bases and correcting mismatched base pairs. 257

DNA replication *REP-leh-KAY-shun* Construction of a new DNA double helix using the information in parental strands as a template. 253-54

dominance hierarchy *DOM-eh-nance HI-er-AR-kee* A social ranking of members of a group of the same sex, which distributes resources with a minimum of aggression. 695

dominant *DOM-eh-nent* An allele that masks the expression of another allele. 220

dormant *DOR-mant* A period of decreased metabolism that often enables an organism to survive harsh climatic conditions. 599

double-blind *DUB-el BLIND* An experimental protocol where neither the participants nor the researchers know which subjects have received a placebo and which have received the treatment being evaluated. 5

double fertilization *DUB-el FER-til-i-ZAY-shun* The fertilization of both the egg and the polar nuclei in a flowering plant. 578

duodenum *DO-o-DEE-num* The first section of the small intestine. 472

dystrophin *DIS-tro-fin* A protein comprising only 0.002% of the total protein in skeletal muscle but vital

for this tissue's function. Lack of dystrophin leads to muscular dystrophy. 412

E

ecological isolation *E-ko-LOG-eh-kel I-so-LAY-shun* When members of two populations do not crossbreed because they prefer to mate in different habitats. 638

ecological succession *E-ko-LODG-ik-el suk-SESH-un* The process of change in an ecological community. 722

ecology *e-KOL-o-gee* The study of the relationships between organisms and their environments. 713

ecosystem *E-ko-SIS-tum* A unit of interaction among organisms and between organisms and their physical environments, including all living things within a defined area. 713

ecotones *E-ko-tonz* Bridges between ecosystems, such as marshes and meadows. 753

ectoderm *EK-TOE-derm* The outermost embryonic germ layer, whose cells become part of the nervous system, sense organs, outer skin layer, and its specializations. 175

ectopic pregnancy *ek-TOP-ik PREG-nan-see* The implantation of a zygote in the wall of a fallopian tube rather than in the uterus. 201

ectotherms *EK-toe-THERMZ* Animals that lose or gain heat to their surroundings by moving into areas where the temperature is suitable. 499

edema *eh-DEEM-ah* Swelling of a body part due to fluid buildup. 441

effector *E-fek-ter* A muscle or gland that receives input from a neuron. 315

efferent arterioles *EF-fer-ent are-TEAR-ee-olz* Branches of the renal artery leaving the proximal portion of a nephron. 506

electrical gradient *e-LEK-trik-el GRAY-dee-ent* The phenomenon of like charges repelling one another and opposite charges attracting one another. 318

electric discharge particle acceleration *e e-LEK-trik DIS-charge PAR-te-kel ak-SEL-er-AY-shun* A gunlike device that shoots tiny metal particles coated with DNA into cells. 612

electron *e-LEK-tron* A subatomic particle carrying a negative electrical charge, and a negligible mass, that orbits the atomic nucleus. 44

electron-spin resonance *e-LEK-tron SPIN REZ-o-nence* A technique that measures the formation of tiny holes in crystals over time, caused by exposure to ionizing radiation. This measurement is used in absolute dating of fossils up to 1 million years old. 650

electron-transport chain *ee-LEK-tron TRANZ-port CHANE* Linked oxidation-reduction reactions. 116

electroporation *ee-LEK-tro-por-AY-shun* Applying a brief jolt of

electricity to open up transient holes in cell membranes, allowing foreign DNA to be introduced. 612

element *EL-eh-ment* A pure substance, consisting of atoms containing a characteristic number of protons. 44

embolus *EM-bo-lis* A blood clot that travels in the bloodstream to another location. 428

embryo *EM-bree-o* The stage of prenatal development when organs develop from a three-layered organization. 155

embryonic induction *EM-bree-ON-ik in-DUK-shun* The ability of a group of specialized cells to stimulate neighboring cells to specialize. 180

embryo sac *EM-bree-o SAK* A mature megagametophyte, containing an egg. 574

emphysema *EM-fah-ZEE-ma* Impaired breathing caused by an inherited enzyme deficiency or smoking. The lung's alveoli become overinflated and burst. 459

enamel *ee-NAM-el* The hard covering of a tooth.

endocrine glands *EN-do-crin GLANZ* Structures that secrete hormones directly into the circulatory system. 368

endocytosis *EN-doe-si-TOE-sis* The engulfing of an extracellular substance by the cell membrane. 81, 102

endoderm *EN-doe-derm* The innermost embryonic germ layer, whose cells become the organs and linings of the digestive, respiratory, and urinary systems. 175

endodermis *EN-do-DER-mis* The innermost region of a root's cortex. 564

endogenous pyrogen *en-DODGE-eh-nes PIR-o-gen* A protein secreted by some white blood cells that stimulates the hypothalamus to spike a fever. 516

endometrium *EN-doe-MEE-tree-um* The inner uterine lining. 173

endoplasmic reticulum *EN-doe-PLAZ-mik reh-TIK-u-lum* A maze of interconnected membranous tubules and sacs, winding from the nuclear envelope to the cell membrane, along which proteins are synthesized (in the rough ER) and lipids synthesized (in the smooth ER). 77

endorphins *en-DORF-inz* Peptides produced in the human body that influence mood and the perception of pain. 326

endoskeleton *EN-do-SKEL-eh-ten* An internal scaffolding type of skeleton in vertebrates. 390

endosperm *EN-do-sperm* A triploid tissue that provides nutrients to the embryo in a seed. 541, 578

endosymbiont theory *EN-doe-SYM-ee-ont THER-ee* The idea that eukaryotic cells evolved from large prokaryotic cells that engulfed once free-living bacteria. 87

endotherms *EN-doe-THERMZ* Animals that regulate their

temperatures by using metabolic heat. 499

energy nutrients *EN-er-gee NU-tre-entz* Dietary fats, carbohydrates, and proteins. 482

energy pyramid *EN-er-gee PIR-ah-mid* A depiction of trophic levels, with each level represented by a bar whose length is proportional to the number of kilocalories available from that food for growth and development. 719

energy RDA *EN-er-gee* The recommended dietary allowance for the energy nutrients, which are carbohydrates, proteins, and fats. 485

entrainment *en-TRANE-ment* The resynchronization of a biological clock by the environment. 600, 674

environmental resistance *en-VIR-on-MEN-tal ree-SIS-tance* All factors that reduce birth rate or increase death rate in a population. 704

enzyme *EN-zime* A protein that catalyzes a specific type of chemical reaction. 54

epicotyl *EP-eh-KOT-el* The stemlike region above the cotyledons. 578

epidemiology *EP-eh-dee-mee-OL-o-gee* The analysis of data derived from real-life, nonexperimental situations. 7

epidermis *EP-eh-DER-mis* The covering on the primary plant body. 554

epididymis *EP-eh-DID-eh-mis* In the human male, a tightly coiled tube leading from each testis, where sperm mature and are stored. 155

epiglottis *EP-eh-GLOT-is* A piece of cartilage that covers the glottis, routing food to the digestive tract and air to the respiratory tract. 449

epinephrine (adrenaline) *EP-eh-NEF-rin (ah-DREN-ah-lin)* A catecholamine hormone produced in the adrenal medulla and sent into the bloodstream, where it raises blood pressure, constricts blood vessels, and slows digestion, as part of the "fight or flight" response to a threat. 377

epiphyseal plates *EP-eh-FEEZ-ee-al PLATZ* In children, thin disks of cartilage at the ends of long bones from which new growth occurs. 395

epistasis *EP-eh-STAY-sis* A gene masking another gene's expression. 231

epithelial tissue *EP-eh-THEL-e-al TISH-u* Tissue built of cells that are packed close together to form linings and boundaries. 81

epithelium *EP-eh-THEL-e-um* Cells that form linings and coverings. 81

epochs *EP-okz* Time periods within periods, which are within eras. 654

equational division *ee-QUAY-shun-el deh-VISZ-un* The second meiotic division, when four haploid cells are generated from the two haploid cells that are the products of meiosis I by a mitosislike division. 157

eras *ER-ahs* Very long periods of time of biological or geological activity. 654

erythropoietin *eh-RITH-ro-PO-eh-tin* A hormone produced in the kidneys when the oxygen supply is insufficient that stimulates red blood cell production in the red bone marrow. 426

esophagus *ee-SOF-eh-gus* A muscular tube leading from the pharynx to the stomach. 469

essential nutrients *e-SEN-shal NU-tree-entz* Nutrients that must be obtained from the diet because the body cannot synthesize them. 484

estrogen *ES-tro-gen* A hormone made in the ovaries that increases the rate of mitosis in the uterine lining. 381

estuary *ES-tu-AIR-ee* The point where the fresh water of a river meets the salty water of an ocean. 735

ethology *ee-THOL-o-gee* The study of how natural selection shapes behavior to enable an animal to survive. 668

ethylene *ETH-eh-leen* A simple organic molecule that functions as a hormone in plants, produced in large amounts by a stigma when a pollen tube begins growing. It hastens fruit ripening. 579, 588

etiolated *E-ti-o-LAY-tid* Seedlings that have abnormally elongated stems, small roots, and leaves and a pale color, because they were grown in the dark. 598

eukaryotic cell *u-CARE-ee-OT-ik SEL* A complex cell containing organelles, which carry out a variety of specific functions. 17

eurypterids *yu-RIP-ter-idz* Scorpionlike organisms that appeared in the seas of the Cambrian period. 657

eusocial *YU-sosh-al* A population of animals that communicate with each other, cooperate in caring for young, has overlapping generations, and demonstrates division of labor. 684

eutrophic *yu-TRO-fik* An aging lake, containing many nutrients and decaying organisms, often tinted green with algae. 734

evolution *Ev-eh-LU-shun* The process by which the genetic composition of a population of organisms changes over time. 621

evolutionary tree diagrams *EV-o-LU-shun-air-ee TREE DI-ah-gramz* A depiction of DNA sequence differences indicating evolutionary relationships between different types of organisms. 654

exchange system *ex-CHANGE SIS-tum* A diet planning system based on classifying foods according to their percentages of carbohydrate, protein, and fat. 487

excitatory synapse *ex-SI-TAH-tore-ee SIN-apse* A synapse across which a particular neurotransmitter travels and depolarizes the postsynaptic membrane. 324

exocytosis *EX-o-si-TOE-sis* The fusing of secretion-containing organelles, which travel to the inside surface of the cell membrane, where they transport a substance out of the cell. 79, 102

exon *EX-on* The bases of a gene that code for amino acids. 265

exoskeleton *EX-o-SKEL-eh-ten* A braced framework skeleton on the outside of an organism. 390

experimental control *ex-PEAR-eh-MEN-tel KON-trol* An extra test that does not directly address the hypothesis but can rule out causes other than the one being investigated. 5

expiration *EX-spir-AY-shun* Exhalation. 455

explants *EX-plantz* Small pieces of plant tissue grown in a laboratory dish with nutrients and plant hormones. 605

expressivity *EX-pres-SIV-eh-tee* The degree of expression of a phenotype. 227

extinction *ex-TINK-shun* The disappearance of a type of organism. 621

extinction *ex-TINK-shun* The loss of a conditioned response. 673

extracellular digestion *EX-tra-SEL-yu-lar di-JEST-shun* Dismantling of food by hydrolytic enzymes in a cavity within an organism's body. 465

extraembryonic membranes *EX-tra-EM-bree-on-ik MEM-BRANZ* Structures that support and nourish the mammalian embryo and fetus, including the yolk sac, allantois, and amnion. 168

F

facilitated diffusion *fah-SIL-eh-tay-tid dif-FU-shun* Movement of a substance down its concentration gradient with the aid of a carrier protein. 101

facultative photoperiodism *FAK-kel-TAY-tiv FO-toe-PER-ee-o-DIZ-um* Plants for which an inductive photoperiod speeds flowering. 596

fallopian tubes *fah-LO-pee-an TUBES* In the human female, paired tubes leading from near the ovaries to the uterus, where oocytes can be fertilized. 157

fall turnover *FALL TURN-o-ver* The mixing of upper and lower layers in a lake by wind, which mixes nutrients and oxygen. 734

fast twitch-fatigable fibers *FAST TWITCH fah-TEEG-ab-bel FI-berz* Skeletal muscle fibers that contract rapidly but tire easily due to scarce oxygen. 414

fast twitch-fatigue resistant fibers *FAST TWITCH fah-TEEG re-ZIS-tent FI-berz* Skeletal muscle fibers that contract rapidly, do not tire easily, and have abundant oxygen. 413

fats *FATS* Organic compounds containing carbon, hydrogen, and oxygen but with less oxygen than carbohydrates. 51

feedback loop *FEED-bak LOOP* A complex interaction between the product of a biochemical reaction and the starting material. 370

femur *FE-mer* The thigh bone. 400

fibrillation *FIB-rah-LAY-shun* Wild twitching of the heart muscle. 436

fibroblast *FI-bro-blast* A cell of connective tissue that secretes the proteins collagen and elastin. 83

fibrous root system *FI-bres ROOT SIS-tum* A plant in which the first root (the radicle) is short-lived. 563

fibula *FIB-u-lah* The smaller of the two bones of the lower leg. 400

fixed action pattern (FAP) *FIXED AK-shun PAT-ern* An innate, stereotyped behavior. 668

flagella *fla-GEL-ah* Taillike appendages on prokaryotic cells. 72, 104

flavin *FLA-vin* A yellow pigment in plants that is probably the photoreceptor for phototropism. 592

flowers *FLAU-erz* The reproductive structures of angiosperms. 574

fluid mosaic *FLU-id mo-ZAY-ik* Description of a biological membrane, referring to the arrangement of proteins embedded in the oily lipid bilayer. 97

follicle cells *FOL-ik-kel SELZ* Nourishing cells surrounding oocytes. 155

follicle stimulating hormone (FSH) *FOL-eh-kul STIM-u-la-ting HOR-moan* A hormone made in the anterior pituitary that controls oocyte maturation, the development of ovarian follicles, and their release of estrogen. 374

food chain *FOOD CHANE* A series of organisms in which one eats another. 717

food group plan *FOOD GROUP PLAN* A diet plan based on classifying foods into four groups—meat and meat substitutes, milk and milk products, fruits and vegetables, and grains. 486

food webs *FOOD WEBZ* The interconnection of food chains to form webs. 718

formed elements *FORMED EL-eh-mentz* Blood cells and platelets.

fossils *FOS-silz* Evidence of past life. 622

founder effect *FAUN-der ah-FEKT* A type of genetic drift occurring when small groups of people leave their homes to found new settlements, taking with them a subset of the original population's genes. 633

fountain effect *FOUN-ten E-fekt* The splitting in two and regrouping of a school of fish, which confuses a predator. 687

fovea centralis *FO-ve-ah cen-TRAL-is* An indentation in the retina directly opposite the lens containing only cones and important to the acuity of an animal's sight. 355

free nerve ending *FREE NERV EN-ding* A type of receptor in the skin that responds to touch. 363

free radicals *FREE RAD-eh-kelz* Highly reactive by-products of metabolism that can damage tissue. 188

fruit *FROOT* A ripened plant ovary enclosing a seed. 580

fundamental niche *FUN-dah-MEN-tel NITCH* All the places and ways in which members of a species can live. 707

fundus *FUN-dus* The domelike top of the stomach. 470

Fungi *FUN-ji* The taxonomic kingdom of eukaryotes with chitin cell walls and no nervous systems and distinguished by their reproductive structures. 22, 26

G

G_1 phase *FAZE* The stage of interphase when proteins, lipids, and carbohydrates are synthesized. 133

G_2 phase *FAZE* The stage of interphase when membrane components are synthesized and stored. 133

gallbladder *GALL-blad-er* A structure leading from the liver and toward the small intestine that stores bile. 477

gamete *GAM-eet* A sex cell. The sperm and ovum. 28

gametoclonal variation *gah-ME-toe-KLON-al VAR-ee-AY-shun* Genetically variant plantlets grown from callus initiated by sex cells. 609

gametophyte *gah-MEE-toe-fight* The part of a plant's life cycle when sex cells are manufactured. 28, 573

ganglia *GANG-lee-ah* Cell bodies of neurons. 331

ganglion cells *GANG-lee-on SELZ* Cells comprising the third layer of the retina in the human eye. 356

gastric juice *GAS-trik JUICE* The fluid secreted by stomach cells; responsible for chemical digestion there. 470

gastric lipase *GAS-trik LI-pace* A stomach enzyme that chemically digests certain lipid molecules. 470

gastrin *GAS-trin* A hormone secreted by stomach cells that stimulates more gastric juice to be secreted. 470

gastrointestinal tract *GAS-tro-in-TES-ti-nal TRAKT* A continuous tube along which food is physically and chemically digested into its constituent nutrients. 467

gene *JEAN* A sequence of DNA that specifies the sequence of amino acids in a particular polypeptide. 217

gene library *JEAN LI-brair-ee* The genome of an organism, cut into pieces that are each cultured in recombinant bacteria. 274

gene pool *JEAN PUL* All the genes in a population. 631

generative nucleus *GEN-er-rah-tiv NU-klee-us* A haploid cell resulting from the mitotic division of a microspore, in male plant reproduction. 574

genetic code *jeh-NET-ik KODE* The correspondence between specific DNA base sequences and the amino acids that they specify. 259

genetic drift *jah-NET-ik DRIFT* Changes in gene frequencies caused by the separation of a small group from a larger population. 632

genetic heterogeneity *jeh-NET-ik HET-er-o-jeh-NE-eh-tee* Different genotypes that have identical phenotypes. 231

genetic load *jah-NET-ik LOAD* The collection of deleterious alleles in a population. 634

genetic marker *jeh-NET-ik MAR-ker* A detectable piece of DNA that is closely linked to a gene of interest, whose precise location is not known. 237, 303

genome *jeh-NOME* All of the DNA in a cell of an organism. 253

genotype *JEAN-o-type* The genetic constitution of an individual. 220

geological time scale *GE-o-LODG-ik-kel TIME SKAL* A division of time into major eras of biological and geological activity, then periods within eras, and finally epochs within some periods. 654

geotropism *GEE-o-TRO-piz-um* A plant's growth response toward gravity. 592

gerontology *JER-on-TOL-o-gee* Study of the biological changes of aging at the molecular, cellular, organismal, and population levels. 187

gibberellins *JIB-ah-REL-linz* A class of plant hormones that promote cell elongation and division in seeds, roots, shoots, and young leaves. 588

globin *GLO-bin* A polypeptide chain that binds iron and forms part of a molecule of hemoglobin. 426

glomerular filtrate *glo-MER-u-ler FIL-trate* In a nephron in the kidney, the material that diffuses from the glomerulus to the Bowman's capsule. 508

glomerulus *glo-MER-u-lus* A ball of capillaries lying between the afferent arterioles and efferent arterioles in the proximal region of a nephron. 506

glottis *GLOT-is* The opening from the pharynx to the larynx. 449

glucagon *GLU-ka-gon* A pancreatic hormone that breaks down glycogen into glucose, raising blood-sugar levels. 378

glucocorticoids *GLU-ko-KOR-tah-koidz* Hormones secreted by the adrenal cortex that enable the body to survive prolonged stress. 378

glycolysis *gli-KOL-eh-sis* A catabolic pathway occurring in the cytoplasm of all cells. One molecule of glucose is split and rearranged into two molecules of pyruvic acid. 119

glycoprotein *GLY-ko PRO-teen* A molecule built of a protein and a sugar. 97

goiter *GOI-ter* A lump in the neck caused by a thyroid gland that swells due to lack of iodine in the diet. 376

Golgi apparatus *GOL-gee AP-ah-rah-tis* A system of flat, stacked, membrane-bound sacs where sugars are polymerized to starches or bonded to proteins or lipids. 77

gonadotropic hormones *go-NAD-o-TRO-pik HOR-moan* Hormones made in the anterior pituitary that affect the ovaries or testes. 374

gout *GOUT* An inborn error of purine metabolism in which uric acid accumulates in the joints. 502

grana *GRAN-ah* Stacks of flattened thylakoid discs comprising the inner membrane of a chloroplast. 81, 116

graptolites *GRAP-toe-litz* Organisms that lived in the Ordovician period, whose fossilized remains resemble pencil markings. 657

gray matter *GRAY MAT-ter* Cell bodies and interneurons that are not myelinated and are often involved in integration. 321

greenhouse effect *GREEN-haus E-fekt* Elevation in surface temperature of the earth by accumulation of carbon dioxide, which allows solar radiation of short wavelengths in but does not release the longer wavelength, infrared heat that the energy is converted to. 749

gross primary production *GROSS PRI-mar-ee pro-DUK-shun* The total amount of energy converted to chemical energy by photosynthesis in a certain amount of time in a given area. 717

ground tissue *GROUND TISH-u* The tissue comprising most of the primary body of a plant, filling much of the interior of roots, stems, and leaves. 552

growth factor *GROWTH FAK-ter* Locally acting proteins that assist in would healing. 137

growth rings *GROWTH RINGZ* Demarcations seen in cross sections of wood, indicating yearly growth. 566

guanine *GWAN-een* One of the two purine nitrogenous bases in DNA and RNA. 57, 253

guard cells *GUARD SELZ* Cells that control the opening and closing of stomata in plants. 554

gymnosperms *JIM-no-spermz* Plants whose sex cells are on cones. 29

gynoecium *gin-NEE-see-um* The second innermost whorl of a flower, consisting of female reproductive structures. 574

H

habitat *HAB-eh-tat* The place where an organism lives. 706

habituation *ha-BIT-ju-AY-shun* The simplest form of learning, in which an animal learns not to respond to certain irrelevant stimuli. 672

hair cells *HAIR SELZ* Mechanoreceptors in the inner ear that lie between the basilar membrane and the tectorial membrane and trigger action potentials in fibers of the auditory nerve. 360

half-life *HAF-life* The time it takes for half of the isotopes in a sample of an element to decay into the second isotopic form. This measurement is used in absolute dating of fossils. 650

hammer *HAM-er* One of the bones in the middle ear. 359

haploid *HAP-loid* A cell with one copy of each chromosome. 157

hardwoods *HARD-woodz* Woods of dicots, such as oak, maple, and ash. 566

Hardy-Weinberg equilibrium *HAR-dee WINE-berg EE-kwah-LEE-BREE-um* Maintenance of the proportion of genotypes from one generation to the next, signifying that for a particular gene, evolution is not occurring. 632

Haversian canal *hah-VER-shun kah-NAL* In bone, a central portal housing blood vessels. 393

heart *HART* A muscular pump that forces blood through conduits throughout the body. 421

heart murmur *HART MUR-mer* A sound heard in the chest when heart valves do not function normally. 434

heartburn *HART-burn* A burning sensation in the upper chest caused by acidic chyme squeezing into the esophagus. 471

heartwood *HART-wood* Wood in the center of a tree, where wastes collect. 566

heavy chain *HEV-ee CHANE* The two larger polypeptide chains comprising a Y-shaped subunit of an antibody. 518

Heimlich maneuver *HEIM-lik mah-NU-ver* A motion of pushing up and in under a choking person's rib cage, which can dislodge the item caught in the throat. 450

helper T cells *HEL-per T SELZ* Lymphocytes that produce lymphokines and stimulate the activities of other T cells and other cell types. 521

heme *HEEM* An iron-containing complex that is the oxygen-binding part of the hemoglobin molecule. 426

hemizygous *HEM-ee-ZY-gus* A gene carried on the Y chromosome in humans. 238

hemoccult test *HEM-ok-kult TEST* An examination of fecal matter for blood, which can indicate a disorder. 477

hepatic portal system *heh-PAH-tik POR-tel SIS-tum* A special division of the circulatory system that enables the liver to harness the chemical energy in digested food rapidly. 432

hepatic portal vein *heh-PAH-tik POR-tel VANE* The vein that leads to the liver. 432

hepatitis *HEP-ah-TI-tis* Inflammation of the liver, usually caused by a viral infection. 478

heterogametic sex *HET-er-o-gah-MEE-tik SEX* The sex with two different sex chromosomes, such as the human male. 245

heterotroph(ic) *HET-er-o-TROF* An organism that obtains nourishment from another organism. 22, 114

heterozygous *HET-er-o-ZI-gus* Possessing two different alleles for a particular gene. 220

hippocampus *HI-po-KAM-pes* A part of the cerebral cortex thought to be involved in forming memories. 341

histamine *HIS-tah-meen* An allergy mediator that widens blood vessels and causes certain allergy symptoms. 515

homeostasis *HOME-ee-o-STA-sis* The ability of an organism to maintain constancy of body temperature, fluid balance, and chemistry. 498

hominid *HAWM-eh-nid* Animals ancestral to humans only. 662

hominoids *HAWM-eh-noidz* Animals ancestral to apes and humans that dwelled in Africa about 20 to 30 million years ago. 661

homogametic sex *HO-mo-gah-MEE-tik SEX* The sex with two identical sex chromosomes, such as the human female. 245

homologous *ho-MOL-eh-gus* Similarly built structures in different organisms that have the same general function, indicating that they are inherited from a common ancestor. 651

homologous pairs *ho-MOL-eh-gus PAIRZ* Chromosome pairs that have the same sequence of genes. 159

homozygous *HO-mo-ZI-gus* Possessing two identical alleles for a particular gene. 220

hormone *HOR-moan* A biochemical manufactured in a gland and transported in the blood to a target organ, where it exerts a characteristic effect. 137, 368

human chorionic gonadotropin *YU-man KOR-ee-on-ik go-NAD-o-TRO-pin* A hormone secreted by the preembryo and embryo that prevents menstruation. 173, 381

human lung surfactant *HU-man LUNG sir-FAK-TANT* A mixture of phospholipid molecules that inflates alveoli in the lungs. 453

humerus *YOOM-eh-ris* The upper arm bone. 400

humoral immune response *HUME-er-al IM-mune ree-SPONZ* The secretion of antibodies by B cells in response to detecting a foreign antigen. 518

hunter-gatherer *HUN-ter GATH-er-er* A person who collects and eats native vegetation. 539

hybridoma *HI-bra-DOE-mah* An artificial cell created by fusing a B cell with a cancer cell that secretes a particular antibody indefinitely. 531

hydrocarbon *HI-dro-kar-bon* A molecule containing carbon and hydrogen. 47

hydrochloric acid *HI-dro-KLOR-ik AS-id* A strong acid found in the stomach, where it provides the pH needed to activate pepsin, which chemically digests protein. 470

hydrogen bond *HI-dro-gen bond* A weak chemical bond between negatively charged portions of molecules and hydrogen ions. 48

hydrolysis *hi-DROL-eh-sis* Splitting of a molecule in two by adding water. 50

hydrophilic *HI-dro-FILL-ik* Attraction of part of a molecule to water. 95

hydrophobic *HI-dro-FOOB-ik* Repulsion of part of a molecule from water. 95

hydrostatic skeleton *HI-dro-STAT-ik SKEL-eh-ten* The simplest type of skeleton, built of a liquid surrounded by a layer of flexible tissue. 390

hyperpolarize *HI-per-POLE-er-ize* The action of an inhibitory neurotransmitter, which causes the postsynaptic neuron's interior to become more negative than the resting potential by admitting Cl⁻. 324

hypertension *HI-per-TEN-shun* Higher than normal blood pressure. 434

hyperthyroidism *HI-per-THY-roid-iz-um* A swelling in the neck (toxic goiter) caused by an overactive thyroid gland, which accelerates metabolism. 377

hypertrophy *hi-PER-tro-fee* An increase in muscle mass, possibly due to exercise. 417

hyperventilation *HI-per-VEN-tah-LAY-shun* An increased breathing rate, which decreases the level of carbon dioxide in the blood. 458

hyphae *HI-fee* Threadlike filaments that are part of the bodies of multicellular fungi. 27

hypocotyl *HI-po-KOT-el* The stemlike region below the cotyledons. 578

hypodermis *HI-po-DER-mis* The outermost, protective layer of the cortex of a plant. 564

hypoglycemia *HI-po-gly-SEEM-ee-ah* A low level of glucose in the blood, producing weakness, anxiety, and shakiness. 379

hypotension *HI-po-TEN-shun* Lower than normal blood pressure. 434

hypothalamus *HI-po-THAL-eh-mus* A small area beneath the thalamus that controls many aspects of homeostasis, including hunger, thirst, body temperature, heartbeat, water balance, blood pressure, sexual arousal, and feelings of pain, pleasure, anger, and fear. The hypothalamus links the nervous and endocrine systems. 335

hypothesis *hy-POTH-eh-sis* An educated guess, based on prior knowledge. 3

hypothyroidism *HI-po-THY-ro-diz-um* A slowing of metabolism and heartbeat and lowering of blood pressure and body temperature resulting from an underactive thyroid gland. 376

I

ichthyosaurs *IK-thee-o-SORZ* Dinosaurs that lived in the seas. 659

idiotype *ID-ee-o-TYPE* The particular parts of an antibody's antigen binding site that are complementary in conformation to the conformation of a particular antigen. 519

ileum *IL-ee-um* The last section of the small intestine. 472

imbibition *IM-bah-BISH-un* The absorption of water by a seed. 580

impact theory *IM-pakt THER-ee* The idea that a meteor or comet crashed to earth, throwing soot into the atmosphere, which blocked the sun and hampered photosynthesis, leading to the extinctions of many types of organisms. 640

imprinting *IM-print-ing* A type of learning that occurs for a limited time, usually early in an animal's life, and is performed usually without obvious reinforcement. Chicks following a parent illustrates imprinting. 673

inborn error of metabolism *IN-born ER-er Mah-TAB-o-liz-um* A disorder caused by a missing or inactive enzyme. 287

inclusive fitness *in-KLU-siv FIT-nes* A definition of fitness including personal reproductive success as well as that of relatives sharing an individual's genes. 692

incomplete dominance *IN-kim-plete DOM-eh-nance* A heterozygote whose phenotype is intermediate between the phenotypes of the two homozygotes. 225

independent assortment *IN-deh-PEN-dent ah-SORT-ment* The random arrangement of homologs during metaphase of meiosis I. 160, 223

indoleacetic acid (IAA) *IN-doe-ah-SEE-tik AS-id* The most active auxin, a type of plant hormone that stimulates growth. 589

induced ovulator *in-DEUCED OV-u-LAY-ter* Inducement of ovulation by the presence of a male. 382

industrial melanism *in-DUS-tree-al MEL-an-iz-um* An adaptive response of insects to pollution, in which coloration that is protective against a sooty background is selected. 635

inferior vena cava *in-FEAR-ee-er VE-nah kah-vah* The lower branch of the largest vein that leads to the heart. 432, 434

infertility *IN-fer-TIL-eh-tee* The inability to conceive a child after a year of trying. 196

inflammation *IN-fla-MA-shun* Increased blood flow and accumulation of fluid and phagocytes at the site of an injury, rendering the area inhospitable to bacteria. 515

inhibitory synapse *in-HIB-eh-tore-ee SIN-apse* A synapse across which a particular neurotransmitter has difficulty depolarizing the postsynaptic membrane. 324

innate *in-ATE* Instinctive. 667

inner cell mass *IN-er SEL MASS* The cells in the blastocyst that develop into the embryo. 173

inner ear *IN-ner EAR* A fluid-filled chamber that houses structures important in providing hearing and maintaining balance. 359

insect-trapping leaves *IN-sect TRAP-ing LEEVZ* Leaves of carnivorous plants that attract, capture, and digest prey. 562

insertion *in-SER-shun* The end of a muscle on a movable bone. 414

insight learning *IN-site LEARN-ing* The ability to apply prior learning to a new situation without observable trial-and-error activity. This is reasoning. 674

insomnia *in-SAWM-nee-ah* A sleep disorder in which a person has difficulty falling or remaining asleep. 676

inspiration *IN-spir-AY-shun* Inhalation. 453

insulin *IN-sel-in* A pancreatic hormone that lowers blood-sugar level by stimulating body cells to take up glucose from the blood and to metabolize or store it. 378

insulin-dependent diabetes *IN-sel-in de-PEN-dent DI-ah-BEAT-es* Diabetes mellitus resulting from insufficient insulin, usually beginning in childhood. Without injecting insulin, this condition causes extreme thirst, blurred vision, weakness, fatigue, nausea, and weight loss. 379

insulin-independent diabetes *IN-sel-in IN-de-PEN-dent DI-ah-BEAT-es* Diabetes mellitus resulting from the body's inability to utilize insulin. It usually begins in adulthood, produces fatigue, itchy skin, blurred vision, slow wound healing, and poor circulation and can often be controlled by diet, exercise, and drugs. 379

intercalary meristems *in-TER-kah-LER-ee MER-eh-stemz* Dividing tissues in grasses between mature regions of stem. 552

intercalated disks *in-TER-kah-LAY-tid DISKS* Tight foldings in cardiac muscle cell membranes that join adjacent cells. 405

interferon *IN-ter-FEAR-on* A polypeptide produced by a T cell infected with a virus that diffuses to surrounding cells and stimulates them to manufacture biochemicals that halt viral replication. 515

intermediate-day plants *IN-ter-MEED-ee-at DAY PLANTZ* Plants that flower only when exposed to days of intermediate length, growing vegetatively at other times. 596

interneuron *IN-ter-neur-on* A neuron that connects one neuron to another to integrate information from many sources and to coordinate responses. 315

internodes *IN-ter-noodz* Portions of stem between nodes. 557

interphase *IN-ter-FAZE* The period when the cell synthesizes proteins, lipids, carbohydrates, and nucleic acids. 131

interstitial cell stimulating hormone (ICSH) *IN-ter-STISH-el STIM-u-la-ting HOR-moan* A hormone made in the anterior pituitary that stimulates late development of sperm cells and the synthesis of testosterone. 375

intertidal zone *IN-ter-TI-dal ZONE* The region bordering an estuary where the tide recedes and returns. 735

intracellular digestion *IN-tra-SEL-yu-lar di-JEST-shun* Digestion within food vacuoles in cells. 465

intron *IN-tron* Bases of a gene that are transcribed but are excised from the mRNA before translation into protein. 265

inversion *in-VER-shun* A chromosome with part of its gene sequence inverted. 280

ion *I-on* An atom that has lost or gained electrons, giving it an electrical charge. 46

ionic bond *i-ON-ik bond* Attraction between oppositely charged ions. 46

iris *I-rus* The thin, opaque, colored region of the choroid coat in the human eye. 354

irritability *IR-eh-tah-BIL-eh-tee* An immediate response to a stimulus. 40

islets of Langerhans *I-lets LANG-er-hanz* Clusters of cells in the pancreas that secrete hormones controlling the body's utilization of nutrients. 378

isotope *I-so-tope* A differently weighted form of an element. 45

J

J-shaped curve *J SHAPED KURV* The mathematical curve resulting from plotting exponential population growth over time. 701

jaundice *JAWN-dis* An overproduction of the bile pigment bilirubin, which causes the skin to turn yellow. 478

jejunum *jah-JU-num* The middle section of the small intestine. 472

Jurassic period *jur-AS-ik PER-ee-od* The time from 185 to 135 million years ago, when dinosaurs were abundant. 659

K

karyokinesis *KAR-ee-o-kah-NEE-sus* Division of the genetic material. 131

karyotype *KAR-ee-o-type* A size-order chart of chromosomes. 298

keystone herbivore hypothesis *Ke-stone ER-bah-vor hi-POTH-eh-sis* The theory that the demise of large herbivores 11,000 years ago led to overgrowth of vegetation, which changed the environment sufficiently to kill many small herbivores. 643

kidney failure *KID-nee FAIL-yur* Damaged renal tubules, which eventually hamper the function of nephrons, resulting in the buildup of toxins in the blood. 511

kidney stones *KID-nee STONZ* Salts that precipitate out of newly formed urine and collect as solid masses in the kidney tubules or the renal pelvis. 511

kidneys *KID-neez* Paired organs built of millions of tubules responsible for excretion of nitrogenous waste and osmoregulation. 504

kilocalories *KIL-o-KAL-o-reez* The energy needed to raise one gram of water one degree Celsius. 484

kwashiorkor *KWASH-ee-OR-ker* Starvation resulting from a switch from breast milk to food deficient in nutrients. 490

L

lactic acid formation *LAK-tik AS-id for-MAY-shun* The conversion of pyruvic acid from glycolysis into lactic acid, occurring in some anaerobic bacteria and tired mammalian muscle cells. 121

lactose intolerance *LAK-tos in-TOLL-eh-rence* Digestive difficulties caused by a deficiency of the enzyme lactase. 472

larynx *LAR-inks* The "voice box" and a conduit for air. 449

latent learning *LA-tent LEARN-ing* Learning without any obvious reward or punishment; not apparent until sometime after the learning experience. 674

lateral meristems *LAT-er-al MER-eh-STEMZ* Actively dividing plant cells that grow outward, thickening the plant. 552

leaf abscission *LEAF ab-SCISZ-on* The shedding of a tree's leaves as a normal part of its life cycle. 562

lean tissue *LEEN-TISH-u* Body weight consisting of muscle, bone, connective tissue, and water. 493

learning *LEARN-ing* A change in behavior as a result of experience. 672

lens *LENZ* The structure in the eye through which light passes and is focused.

lentic system *LEN-tik SIS-tum* Fresh water biomes that have standing water, such as lakes and ponds. 733

lichen *LI-ken* An organism formed by the union of a fungus and a green alga. 16

ligaments *LIG-ah-mentz* Tough bands of fibrous connective tissue that form the joint capsule. 401

light chain *LITE CHANE* The two smaller polypeptide chains comprising a Y-shaped subunit of an antibody. 518

light reactions *LITE re-AK-shunz* The light-requiring reactions of photosynthesis that harness photon energy and use it to convert ADP to ATP. 117

limnetic zone *lim-NET-ik ZONE* The layer of open water in a lake or pond that is penetrated by light. 734

linkage *LINK-ege* The location of genes on the same chromosome. 237

lipases *LI-pay-ses* Enzymes that chemically digest fats. 472

lipid bilayer *LIP-id BI-lay-er* A two-layered structure formed by the alignment of phospholipids, reflecting their hydrophobic and hydrophilic tendencies. 95

lipids *LIP-idz* Organic molecules that are insoluble in water, including the fats. 51

littoral zone *LIT-or-al ZONE* The shallow region along the shore of a lake or pond where light can penetrate to the bottom with sufficient intensity to allow photosynthesis. 734

liver *LIV-er* The largest solid organ in the body, which detoxifies the blood, stores glycogen and fat-soluble vitamins, synthesizes blood proteins, and monitors blood-sugar level, plus other functions. 477

logistic growth curve *lo-JIS-tik GROWTH KURV* An S-shaped mathematical curve reflecting the slowing of population growth as the carrying capacity is reached, in response to environmental resistance. 705

long-day plants *LONG-day PLANTZ* Plants that require light periods longer than some critical length to flower. 596

long-term synaptic potentiation *LONG TERM sin-AP-tik PO-ten-she-A-shun* The hypothesis that long-term memory results from repeated and frequent stimulation of the same neurons, which strengthens their synaptic connections. 341

loop of Henle *LUP HEN-lee* A loop of a nephron, lying between the proximal and distal convoluted tubules, where water is conserved and the urine becomes concentrated by a countercurrent multiplier system that returns water to the blood. 508

lordosis *lor-DOE-sis* An abnormal forward curvature of the spine. 399

lotic system *LO-tik SIS-tum* Fresh water biomes with running water, such as rivers and streams. 733

lumbar vertebrae *LUM-bar VER-tah-bray* The five vertebrae in the small of the back.

lungs *LUNGZ* Paired structures that house the bronchial tree and the alveoli, the sites of gas exchange. 453

luteinizing hormone (LH) *LU-tah-ni-zing HOR-moan* A hormone made in the anterior pituitary that promotes ovulation. 375

luteinizing hormone releasing hormone (LHRH) *LU-ten-I-zing HOR-moan ree-LEAS-ing HOR-moan* A hormone sent from the hypothalamus to the anterior pituitary, where it stimulates release of follicle stimulating hormone and luteinizing hormone. 381

lymph *LIMF* Blood plasma minus some large proteins, which flows through lymph capillaries and lymph vessels. 441

lymphatic system *lim-FAH-tik SIS-tum* A circulatory system consisting of lymph capillaries and lymph vessels that transports lymph, which consists of blood plasma minus large proteins. 441

lymph capillaries *LIMF CAP-eh-LAIR-eez* Dead-ended, microscopic vessels that transport lymph. 441

lymph nodes *LIMF NOODZ* Structures in the lymphatic system that contain white blood cells and protect against infection. 441

lymphocytes *LIM-fo-SITZ* White blood cells that provide immune protection, including the B cells, which secrete antibodies, and the T cells, which secrete lymphokines and control the activities of each other and other cell types. 517

lymphokines *LIM-fo-KINES* Biochemicals secreted by lymphocytes that attack cancer cells or cells coated with viruses. 517

lymph vessels *LIMF VES-selz* Vessels that transport lymph and eventually empty into veins. 441

lysosome *LI-so-soam* A sac in a eukaryotic cell in which molecules and worn-out organelles are enzymatically dismantled. 80

M

macroevolution *MAK-ro-ev-eh-LU-shun* Large-scale evolutionary changes, such as speciation and extinction. 621

macronutrients *MAK-ro-NU-tri-entz* The carbohydrates, fats, and proteins that are obtained from food and required in large amounts. 482

macrophages *MAK-ro-FAH-ges* Very large, wandering phagocytic cells. 515

maiasaurs *MI-ah-SORZ* Duck-billed dinosaurs that lived in Montana about 80 million years ago. 659

major histocompatibility complex (MHC) *MA-jer HIS-toe-kum-PAT-ah-BIL-eh-tee KOM-plex* A family of genes in mammals that specifies cell surface proteins involved in cell-cell recognition. 518

map sense *MAP SENS* A sense that tells an organism its location relative to its home. 681

marasmus *mah-RAS-mus* Starvation due to profound nutrient deficiency. 490

marrow cavity *MAR-o KAV-eh-tee* A space in the shaft of a long bone housing fatty yellow marrow. 393

marsupials *mar-SU-pee-alz* Pouched mammals. 661

mast cells *MAST SELZ* Large cells that are burst by allergens binding to IgE on their surfaces, releasing allergy mediators that cause allergy symptoms. 515

maximum intrinsic rate of increase *MAX-ah-mum in-TRIN-sik RATE IN-krees* The rate of growth of a population when each member produces as many offspring as is possible and the environment does not restrict reproduction. 701

medulla *mah-DUEL-ah* The middle portion of the kidney, consisting of loops of Henle and collecting ducts of nephrons. 505

medulla *mah-DULE-ah* The part of the brain stem closest to the spinal cord; regulates such vital functions as breathing, heartbeat, blood pressure, and certain reflexes. 334

megagametophytes *MEG-ah-gah-MEE-toe-fightz* The large, female egg-producing gametophytes in a plant. 573

megakaryocyte *MEG-ah-KAR-ee-o-site* A huge bone marrow cell that breaks apart to yield platelets. 427

megasporangia *MEG-ah-spor-AN-gee-ah* Structures in which megaspores form. 573

megaspore mother cell *MEG-ah-spor MOTH-er SEL* A cell within an ovule that divides meiotically to produce four haploid cells, three of which degenerate. 574

megaspores *MEG-ah-sporz* Structures in plants that give rise to the female gametophytes. 573

meiosis *Mi-O-sis* Cell division resulting in a halving of the genetic material. 131

melanocyte stimulating hormone (MSH) *mah-LAN-o-site STIM-u-lat-ing HOR-moan* A hormone produced in between the anterior and posterior lobes of the pituitary in some vertebrate species that controls skin pigmentation. 375

melatonin *MEL-ah-TOE-nin* A hormone produced by the pineal gland that may control other hormones by a sensitivity to lightness and darkness. 382, 677

memory cells *MEM-or-ee SELZ* Mature B cells that are specific to an antigen already encountered and respond quickly by secreting antibodies when that antigen is encountered subsequently. 518

meninges *MEN-in-gees* A triple layer of membranes that covers and protects the central nervous system. 342

mesentery *MEZ-en-tear-ee* An epithelial sheet that supports digestive structures in the human.

mesoderm *MEZ-o-derm* The middle embryonic germ layer, whose cells become bone, muscle, blood, dermis, and reproductive organs. 175

messenger RNA (mRNA) *MESS-en-ger* A molecule of ribonucleic acid that is complementary in sequence to the sense strand of a gene. 76, 258

metabolism *meh-TAB-o-liz-um* The biochemical reactions that acquire and utilize energy. 109

metacarpals *MET-ah-KAR-pelz* Bones of the hand. 400

metaphase *MET-ah-faze* The second stage of cell division, when chromosomes align down the center of a cell. In mitosis the chromosomes form a single line. In meiosis I, the chromosomes line up in homologous pairs. 134

metastasis *meh-TAH-STAH-sis* The spreading of cancer from its site of origin to other parts of the body. 145

metazoan *MET-ah-ZO-en* An ancient, simple multicellular animal ancestral to modern animals. 31

mibrid *MI-brid* A cell into which a mitochondrion from another cell is introduced. 610

microevolution *MIKE-ro-ev-eh-LU-shun* The more subtle, incremental single-trait changes that underlie speciation. 621

microfilaments *MI-kro-FILL-ah-ment* Tiny rods built of actin found within cells, especially contractile cells. 104

microgametophytes *MIKE-ro-gah-MEE-toe-fightz* The small, male sperm-producing gametophytes in a plant. 573

micronutrients *MIKE-ro-NU-tree-entz* The vitamins and minerals that are obtained from food and required in small amounts. 482

microsporangia *MI-kro-spor-AN-gee-ah* Structures in which microspores form. 573

microspore mother cells *MI-kro-spor MOTH-er SELZ* Cells in pollen sacs that divide meiotically to produce four haploid microspores. 574

microspores *MI-kro-sporz* Structures in plants that give rise to the male gametophytes. 573

microtubules *MI-kro-TO-bules* Long, hollow tubules, built of the protein tubulin, that provide movement within cells. 81, 104

microvilli *MI-kro-VIL-i* Tiny projections on the surfaces of epithelial cells, which comprise intestinal villi. 473

midbrain *MID-brane* The part of the brain stem above the pons where white matter connects with higher brain structures and gray matter contributes to sight and hearing. 335

middle ear *MID-el EAR* The part of the ear consisting of three bones, the hammer, anvil, and stirrup, that transmit and amplify sound. 359

mineralocorticoids *MIN-er-rel-KOR-tah-KOIDZ* Hormones produced in the adrenal cortex that maintain blood volume and electrolyte balance by stimulating the kidneys to return Na^+ and water to the blood and to excrete K^+. 378

mitochondria *MI-toe-KON-dree-ah* Organelles within which the reactions of cellular metabolism occur. 79

mitosis *mi-TOE-sis* A form of cell division in which two genetically identical cells are generated from one. 131

molecular evolution *mo-LEK-yu-ler EV-o-LU-shun* The tracing of sequence differences in proteins and nucleic acids between living species to establish degrees of evolutionary relatedness. 652

molecule *MOLL-eh-kuel* A structure resulting from the combination of atoms. 45

Monera *mo-NER-ah* The taxonomic kingdom including the bacteria and the cyanobacteria. 22

monoclonal antibodies *MON-o-KLON-al AN-tah-BOD-eez* Antibodies descended from a single B cell and therefore are identical. B cells are fused with cancer cells to create hybridomas, which are artificial cells that secrete a particular antibody indefinitely. 531

monocots *MON-o-kotz* Flowering plants that have one seed leaf. 557, 578

monogamy *mah-NAUG-o-mee* The formation of a permanent male-female pair. 696

monohybrid *MON-o-HI-brid* An individual heterozygous for a particular gene. 221

monosaccharide *MON-o-SAK-eh-ride* A sugar built of one 5- or 6-carbon unit, including glucose, galactose, and fructose. 49

monosomy *MON-o-soam-ee* A cell missing one chromosome. 280

monotremes *MON-o-tremz* Egg-laying mammals. 661

morula *MORE-u-lah* The preembryonic stage of a solid ball of cells. 172

mosaic catastrophism *mo-ZAY-ik CAT-as-TROF-iz-um* A variation of Neptunism that holds that a series of great floods molded the earth's features and caused various extinctions and speciations. 621

motor areas *MO-ter AIR-ee-ahs* Parts of the cerebral cortex that send impulses to skeletal muscles. 337

motor (efferent) neuron *MO-ter (EF-fer-ent) NEUR-on* A neuron that transmits a message from the central nervous system toward a muscle or gland. It has a long axon and short dendrites. 315

motor pathways *MO-ter PATH-wayz* Nerve tracts in the peripheral nervous system that carry impulses from the central nervous system to muscles or glands. 342

motor unit *MOW-ter U-nit* A nerve cell and all of the muscle fibers it contacts. 411

mucigel *MUUS-eh-gel* A slimy, lubricating substance produced by cells of a root cap. 563

muscle fasciculi *MUS-sel fah-SIK-u-li* Bundles of muscle fibers. 406

muscle spindles *MUS-sel SPIN-delz* Receptors in skeletal muscle that monitor the degree of muscle tone or how many fibers are contracted at a given time. 416

muscle tone *MUS-sel TONE* The contraction of some fibers in skeletal muscle at any given time. 416

muscular tissue *MUS-ku-lar TISH-u* Tissue built of contractile cells, providing motion. 81

mutant *MU-tent* A phenotype or allele that is not the most common for a certain gene in a population. 220

mutant selection *MU-tant sah-LEK-shun* Searching for genetic variants that offer a desired characteristic. 609

mutation *mu-TAY-shun* A change in a gene or chromosome. 232, 261

mutualism *MU-tu-al-iz-um* A symbiotic relationship in which both partners benefit. 14

mycelium *MI-seal-ee-um* An assemblage of hyphae in a fungus. 27

mycorrhizae *MI-ko-RI-zee* A mutualistic association between a plant's roots and fungi that absorb nutrients from soil. 564

myelin sheath *MI-eh-lin SHEATH* A fatty material that insulates some nerve fibers in vertebrates, allowing rapid transmission of nerve impulses. 320

myofibrils *MI-o-FI-brilz* Cylindrical subunits of a muscle fiber. 407

myofilaments *MI-o-FILL-eh-mentz* Actin or myosin "strings" that comprise myofibrils. 407

myosin *MI-o-sin* A type of protein comprising the thick myofilaments of skeletal muscle cells. 407

myxedema *MIX-eh-DEEM-ah* Lethargy, dry sparse hair, and a puffy face, caused by an underactive thyroid beginning in adulthood. 376

N

naked-gene hypothesis *NA-kid JEAN hi-POTH-eh-sis* The theory that nucleic acids evolved before proteins. 62

narcolepsy *NAR-co-LEP-see* A sleep disorder in which a person suddenly falls asleep during the day. 676

nasal conchae *NAZ-al KON-chi* Three shelflike bones in each nasal cavity that partition it into channels. 448

nastic movements *NAS-tic MOVE-mentz* Nondirectional plant motions. 594

natural killer cells *NAT-chu-ral KILL-er SELZ* Lymphocytes that cause infected cells and possibly cancer cells to burst.

natural products chemists *NAT-u-ral PROD-uks KEM-ists* Chemists who examine biochemicals for substances with therapeutic or other value. 547

natural selection *NAT-rul sah-LEK-shun* The differential survival and reproduction of organisms whose genetic traits better adapt them to a particular environment. 626

nautiloids *NAWT-eh-loidz* Organisms that appeared in the seas of the Cambrian period. 657

Neanderthals *nee-AN-der-thalz* Members of *Homo sapiens* who lived about 75,000 years ago in Europe and Asia. 663

negative feedback *NEG-ah-tiv FEED-bak* The turning off of an enzyme's synthesis or activity caused by accumulation of the product of the reaction that the enzyme catalyzes. 111

negative feedback loop *NEG-ah-tiv FEED-bak LOOP* A biochemical pathway in which accumulation of a product inhibits earlier reactions. 370

negative reinforcement *NEG-eh-tiv REE-in-FORC-ment* A painful stimulus given to encourage an animal to avoid a particular behavior. 673

neonatology *NE-o-nah-TOL-eh-gee* The study of the newborn. 204

neoteny *ne-OT-eh-nee* Retaining juvenile features of an ancestral species. 669

nephron *NEF-ron* A microscopic, tubular subunit of a kidney, built of a renal tubule and peritubular capillaries. 505

Neptunism *NEP-tune-iz-um* The idea that a single great flood organized the features of the earth's surface present today. 621

neritic zone *NER-it-ik ZONE* The coastal region of an ocean. 737

nerve fiber *NERVE FI-ber* An axon. 315

nervous tissue *NER-vis TISH-u* A tissue whose cells (neutrons and neuroglia) form a communication network. 81

net primary production *NET PRI-mar-ee pro-DUK-shun* The energy left over for growth and reproduction after an animal has eaten. 717

neural (synaptic) integration *NEUR-el (sin-AP-tik) IN-tah-GRAY-shun* The summing of incoming inhibitory and excitatory messages by a neuron. This information determines whether or not an action potential will occur. 324

neural tube *NEUR-el TUUB* The embryonic precursor of the central nervous system. 181

neuron *NEUR-on* A nerve cell, consisting of a cell body, a long "sending" projection called an axon, and numerous "receiving" projections called dendrites. 86

neurosecretory cells *NUR-o-SEK-rah-tore-ee SELZ* Cells in the hypothalamus that function as neurons at one end but like endocrine cells at the other by receiving neural messages and secreting the hormones ADH and oxytocin. 372

neurotransmitter *NEUR-o-TRANZ-mit-er* A chemical passed from a nerve cell to another nerve cell or to a muscle or gland cell, relaying an electrochemical message. 86, 321

neutron *NEW-tron* A particle in an atom's nucleus that is electrically neutral and has one mass unit. 44

neutrophils *NU-tro-FILLZ* Short-lived phagocytic white blood cells that help combat the initial stages of infection. 515

niche *NITCH* The ways in which an organism interacts with the living and nonliving environment. 706

nitrifying bacteria *NI-trah-FI-ing bak-TER-ee-ah* Bacteria that convert ammonia from dead organisms to nitrite. 721

nitrite bacteria *NI-trit bak-TER-ee-ah* Bacteria that convert nitrite to nitrate.

node of Ranvier *NODE RON-vee-ay* A short region of exposed axon between adjacent Schwann cells on neurons of the peripheral nervous systems of vertebrates. 321

nodes *NOODZ* Areas of leaf attachment. 557

nondisjunction *NON-dis-JUNK-shun* The unequal partition of chromosomes into gametes during meiosis. 280

nonessential nutrients *NON-ee-SEN-shal NU-tree-entz* Nutrients found in food but that can also be synthesized in the body. 484

norepinephrine (noradrenaline) *NOR-EP-eh-NEF-rin (NOR-ah-DREN-ah-lin)* A catecholamine hormone produced in the adrenal medulla and sent into the bloodstream, where it raises blood pressure, constricts blood vessels, and slows digestion, as part of the "fight or flight" response to a threat. 377

notochord *NO-toe-kord* A semirigid rod running down the length of an animal's body. 33, 181

nucleoid *NEW-klee-oid* The part of a prokaryotic cell where the DNA is located. 72

nucleolus *new-KLEE-o-lis* A structure within the nucleus where RNA nucleotides are stored. 76, 134

nucleotide *NEW-klee-o-tide* The building block of a nucleic acid, consisting of a phosphate group, a nitrogenous base, and a five-carbon sugar. 57, 252

nucleus (atomic) *NEW-klee-is* The central region of an atom, consisting of protons and neutrons. 44

nucleus (cellular) *NEW-klee-is* A membrane-bound sac in a eukaryotic cell that contains the genetic material. 22

nutrient *NU-tri-ent* A substance that is obtained from food and used in an organism to promote growth, maintenance, and repair of tissues. 482

nutrient dense *NU-tri-ent DENSE* Foods that offer a maximum amount of nutrients with a minimum number of kilocalories. 487

nyctinasty *NIK-tah-NAS-tee* A nastic (nondirectional) movement caused by daily rhythms of light and dark. 595

O

obese *o-BESE* A person who is 20% above "ideal" weight based on population statistics considering age, sex, and build. 492

obligate photoperiodism *OB-lah-get FO-toe-PER-ee-o-DIZ-um* Plants that will not flower unless they are exposed to the correct photoperiod. 596

oceanic zone *O-she-AN-ik ZONE* The deep, open part of an ocean. 737

olfactory bulb *ol-FAK-tore-ee BULB* A part of the brain that relays a message from olfactory receptor cells. 350

olfactory receptor cells (epithelium) *ol-FAK-tore-ee re-CEP-ter SELZ* Neurons specialized to detect odors, found in a small patch of tissue high in the nostrils. 350

oligotrophic *OL-ah-go-TRO-fik* A lake with few nutrients, usually a sparkling blue. 734

ommatidia *O-mah-TID-ee-ah* The visual units comprising a compound eye. 352

oncogene *ON-ko-jean* A gene that normally controls cell division but when overexpressed leads to cancer. 145

oocyte *O-o-site* The female sex cell before it is fertilized. 155

oogenesis *O-o-GEN-eh-sis* The differentiation of an egg cell, from a diploid oogonium, to a primary oocyte, to two haploid secondary oocytes, to ootids, and finally, after fertilization, to a mature ovum. 165

open behavior program *O-pen bee-HAIV-yur PRO-gram* A behavior that is flexible and easily altered by learning. 667

open circulatory system *O-pen SIR-qu-lah-TORE-ee SIS-tum* A circulatory system in which blood is not always contained in blood vessels. 422

operant conditioning *OP-er-aunt kon-DISH-on-ing* Trial-and-error learning, in which an animal voluntarily repeats any behavior that brings success. 673

operculum *o-PER-ku-lum* A flap of tissue protecting gills. 447

optic nerve *OP-tik NERV* Nerve fibers leading from the retina to the visual cortex of the brain. 356

Ordovician period *OR-do-VEESH-ee-an PER-ee-od* The period following the Cambrian period, 500 to 435 million years ago. 657

organ *OR-gan* A structure built of two or more tissues that functions as an integrated unit. 40

organelles *OR-gan-nellz* Specialized structures in eukaryotic cells that carry out specific functions. 17, 22

organelle transfer *OR-gan-el TRANZ-fer* Engineering combinations of nuclei and organelles in plant cells not seen in nature. 610

origin *ARE-eh-jen* The end of a muscle on an immobile bone. 414

osmoreceptors *OZ-mo-ree-CEP-terz* Specialized cells in the hypothalamus that sense the concentration of water in the blood. 375

osmosis *oz-MO-sis* Passive diffusion of water. 100

ossification *OS-eh-feh-KAY-shun* The process by which cartilage in embryonic bones is replaced with bone tissue. 394

osteocytes *OS-tee-o-sitz* Mature bone cells. 393

osteoporosis *OS-tee-o-por-O-sis* Bones that break easily because calcium is removed from them faster than it is replaced, possibly caused by hyperthyroidism. 377

otolith *O-toe-lith* Calcium carbonate granules in the vestibule of the inner ear whose movements provide information on changes in velocity. 363

outcrossing *OUT-cross-ing* The transfer of pollen grains from one flower to the stigma of another flower. 574

oval window *O-vel WIN-dow* A membrane between the middle ear and inner ear. 359

ovaries *O-var-ees* The paired, female gonads, which house developing oocytes. 155, 374

ovary *O-var-ree* In a flowering plant, the carpels and the ovules they enclose. 574

over dominant *O-ver DOM-en-nant* A heterozygote that is more vigorous that either homozygote. 226

ovulation *OV-u-LAY-shun* The release of an oocyte from the largest ovarian follicle just after the peak of luteinizing hormone in the blood in the middle of a woman's menstrual cycle. 381

ovules *OV-yulz* In flowering plants, a megasporangium containing a megaspore mother cell, which undergoes meiosis to produce four cells, three of which degenerate. 574

oxidation *OX-en-DAY-shun* A chemical reaction in which electrons are lost. 48

oxygen debt *OX-eh-gen DET* The body's need for oxygen to complete the metabolism of lactic acid following heavy exercise that has temporarily shifted metabolism to the anaerobic pathway. 410

oxyhemoglobin *OX-ee-HEEM-o-GLO-bin* Hemoglobin that is bright red because it has just picked up oxygen in the lungs. 426

oxytocin *OX-eh-TOE-sin* A hormone made in the hypothalamus and released from the posterior pituitary that stimulates muscle contraction in the mammary glands and the uterus. 375

P

pacemaker *PACE-may-ker* Specialized cells in the wall of the right atrium that set the pace of the heartbeat. Also called the sinoatrial node. 438

Pacinian and Meissner's corpuscles *pah-SIN-ee-en MICE-nerz KOR-pus-elz* Receptors in the skin that provide information on touch. 363

paleontologist *PAY-lee-on-TOL-ah gist* A scientist who studies evidence of past life. 640, 648

palisade mesophyll *PAL-eh-sade MEZ-o-fil* Long, columnar cells along the upper side of a leaf specialized for light absorption. 561

pancreas *PAN-kre-as* A structure that has an endocrine component, which produces somatostatin, insulin, and glucagon, and a digestive component, which produces a pancreatic juice containing trypsin, chymotrypsin, pancreatic amylase, pancreatic lipase, and nucleases. 477

parasitism *PAR-eh-sah-TIZ-um* A symbiotic relationship where one partner benefits from the other, while harming it. 15

parasympathetic nervous system *PAR-ah-SIM-pah-THE-tik NER-ves SIS-tum* Part of the autonomic nervous system that controls vital functions such as respiration and heart rate when at rest. 344, 439

parathyroid glands *PAR-ah-THY-roid GLANZ* Four small groups of cells embedded in the thyroid gland that secrete a hormone that releases calcium from bones and enhances calcium absorption through the digestive tract and kidneys, actions that regulate calcium level in blood and tissue fluid. 377, 396

parathyroid hormone *PAR-ah-THY-roid HOR-moan* The hormone produced by the parathyroid glands; regulates calcium level in the blood and tissue fluid by releasing calcium from bones and enhancing calcium absorption through the digestive tract and kidneys. 377

parenchyma *pah-REN-kah-mah* Abundant, unspecialized plant cells that can divide. 553

passive immunity *PAS-siv im-MUNE-eh-tee* Immunity generated by an organism's receiving antibodies manufactured by another organism. 522

patella *pah-TEL-lah* The bony part of the kneecap. 400

pectoral girdle *PEC-tor-al GIR-del* The two clavicles and two scapulae bones that form the shoulders. 400

pedigree *PED-eh-gree* A chart showing the relationships of relatives and which ones have a particular trait. 297

pelagic zone *pah-LA-gik ZONE* The water above the ocean floor. 737

pelvic girdle *PEL-vik GIR-del* The two hipbones. 400

pelvis *PEL-vis* The innermost portion of the kidney, which stores urine. 505

pelycosaurs *PEL-eh-ko-SORZ* The sailed lizards, which were distant ancestors of mammals. 659

penetrance *PEN-eh-trance* The percentage of individuals inheriting a genotype who express the corresponding phenotype. 227

pepsin *PEP-sin* A stomach enzyme that chemically digests protein. 470

pepsinogen *pep-SIN-o-jen* A precursor molecule that is split to yield pepsin, a stomach enzyme that chemically digests protein. 470

peptidase *PEP-tah-daze* A type of intestinal enzyme that completes protein digestion. 472

peptide bond *PEP-tide BOND* A chemical bond between two amino acids resulting from dehydration synthesis. 53, 262

peptide hormone *PEP-tide HOR-moan* A hormone composed of amino acids. It is water soluble but fat insoluble so cannot traverse a cell's membrane. Instead, it binds to a cell surface receptor and triggers a second messenger. 369

pericardium *PEAR-eh-KAR-dee-um* The tough, connective tissue sac enclosing the heart. 434

pericarp *PEAR-ah-karp* A protective layer of a seed. 541

perichondrium *PEAR-eh-KON-dree-um* A layer of connective tissue surrounding embryonic, cartilaginous bones. 394

pericycle *PEAR-ah-SI-kel* A ring of parenchyma cells in a root's cortex that produces branch roots that burst through the cortex and epidermis and into the soil. 564

periderm *PEAR-ah-derm* The outer protective covering on mature stems and roots. 568

periodontal membrane *PEAR-ah-DON-tal MEM-brane* An outer layer of the tooth, anchoring it to the gum and jawbone. 469

periods *PER-ee-odz* Time periods within eras. 654

peripheral nervous system (PNS) *per-RIF-er-al NER-vous SIS-tum* Nerves and cell bodies (ganglia) that transmit information to and from the central nervous system. 331

peristalsis *pear-eh-STAL-sis* Waves of muscle contraction along the digestive tract that propel food. 468

peritubular capillaries *pear-eh-TUUB-yu-lar CAP-eh-LAIR-eez* The capillaries that surround the renal tubule of the nephron, in the kidney. 505

permafrost *PER-mah-frost* The permanently frozen part of the ground in the tundra. 733

Permian period *PER-mee-an PER-ee-od* The time from 275 to 225 million years ago, when many species became extinct. Amphibians and reptiles were still abundant. 658

peroxisome *PER-ox-eh-soam* A membrane-bound sac budded off of the smooth ER housing enzymes important in oxygen utilization. 81

petals *PET-alz* Large and often colorful parts of flowers that sometimes help to attract pollinators. 574

petiole *PET-ee-ol* The stalklike portion of a leaf. 559

phagocytes *FAG-o-sitez* Scavenger cells that engulf and digest foreign cells. 515

phalanges *fah-LAN-gees* The finger bones. 400

pharynx *FAHR-inks* The throat. 449, 469

phelloderm *FEL-ah-derm* Living parenchyma cells in secondary growth. 568

phenocopy *FEEN-o-KOP-ee* An environmentally caused trait that resembles an inherited trait. 232

phenotype *FEEN-o-type* The observable expression of a genotype in a specific environment. 220

pheromones *FER-eh-moanz* Biochemicals secreted by an organism that stimulate a physiological or behavioral response in another individual of the same species. 385

phlebitis *flah-BI-tis* Inflammation of a vein wall. 438

phloem *FLO-um* Plant tissue that transports water and food materials. 29, 555

phospholipid *FOS-fo-LIP-id* A molecule built of a lipid and a phosphate that is hydrophobic at one end and hydrophilic at the other end. 94

photolysis *fo-TOL-eh-sis* A photosynthetic reaction in which electrons from water replace electrons lost by chlorophyll a. 116

photoperiodism *FO-toe-PER-ee-o-DIZ-um* A plant's ability to measure seasonal changes by the length of day and night. 596

photophosphorylation *FO-toe-FOS-for-eh-LAY-shun* A photosynthetic reaction in which energy released by the electron transport chain linking the two photosystems is stored in the high-energy phosphate bonds of ATP. 116

photoreceptors *FO-toe-ree-CEP-terz* Neurons that detect light by means of pigment molecules in contact with sensitive membranes. 351

photosynthesis *FO-toe-SIN-the-sis* The series of biochemical reactions that enable plants to harness the energy in sunlight to manufacture nutrient molecules. 24, 81, 113

photosystem *FO-toe-SIS-tum* A cluster of pigment molecules that enable green plants to absorb, transport, and harness solar energy. 116

phototropism *FO-to-TRO-piz-um* A plant's growth towards unidirectional light. 592

pH scale *SKALE* A measurement of how acidic or basic a solution is. 47

phylogenies *fi-LAWG-ah-nees* The evolutionary relationships between organisms. 648

phytochrome *FI-toe-krom* A pale blue plant pigment that exists in two interconvertible forms. The active form promotes flowering of long-day plants and inhibits flowering of short-day plants. 597

pica *PI-kah* A compulsive disorder in which people consume huge amounts of nonnutritive substances. 488

piloerection *PIL-o-ee-REK-shun* The raising of fur or feathers, which traps a layer of air near the body surface, serving as insulation. 500

pilus *PILL-us* A projection from a bacterial cell that transfers genetic information. 24

pineal gland *pin-EEL GLAND* A small oval structure in the brain, near the hypothalamus, that produces melatonin, a hormone that regulates the activities of other hormones, possibly by a sensitivity to patterns of lightness and darkness. 382, 677

pioneer species *PI-o-neer SPE-shez* The first species to colonize an area, such as lichens and mosses that begin soil formation. 722

pistil *PIS-til* The female reproductive structures and their covering in a flower. 574

pith *PITH* Ground storage tissue in the center of the stem in plants having concentric cylinders of xylem and phloem. 558

pituitary *pah-TU-eh-TEAR-ee* A pea-sized gland in the head. The anterior lobe releases growth hormone, thyroid stimulating hormone, adrenocorticotropic hormone, prolactin, and the gonadotropic hormones. The hypothalamus sends antidiuretic hormone and oxytocin to the posterior pituitary, from where they are released. Melanocyte stimulating hormone is secreted from the region of the pituitary between the lobes in some vertebrates. 371

pituitary dwarfism *pah-TU-eh-TEAR-ee DWARF-is-um* Short stature caused by a deficiency of growth hormone in childhood. 373

pituitary giant *pah-TU-eh-TEAR-ee GI-ant* A very tall child whose height results from a tumor that produces excess growth hormone. 374

placebo *pla-SEE-bo* A substance similar in taste and appearance to a substance under investigation, whose effects are known. 4

placenta *pla-CEN-tah* A specialized organ that develops in certain mammals, connecting mother to unborn offspring. 33, 168

placental mammals *plah-CEN-tel MAM-malz* Mammals that nurture the young in the female's body for a relatively long time, where they are nurtured by an organ called a placenta. 661

Plantae *PLAN-tye* Kingdom including land-dwelling multicellular organisms that extract energy from sunlight and have cell walls built of cellulose. 22

plant embryo *PLANT EM-bree-o* A plant after only a few cell divisions, forming part of a seed. 578

plasma *PLAZ-ma* A watery, protein-rich fluid that is the matrix of blood. 83, 424

plasma cells *PLAZ-mah SELZ* Mature B cells that secrete vast quantities of a single antibody type. 518

plasmid *PLAZ-mid* A small circle of double-stranded DNA found in some bacteria in addition to their DNA, commonly used as a vector for recombinant DNA. 270

platelet *PLATE-let* A cell fragment that is part of the blood and orchestrates clotting. 83, 424

plate tectonics *PLATE tek-TAWN-iks* A geological theory that views the earth's surface as several rigid plates that can move. 641

pleiotropic *PLY-o-TRO-pik* A genotype with multiple expressions. 231

Pleistocene overkill hypothesis *PLEIS-toe-seen O-ver-kill hi-POTH-eh-sis* The theory that the disappearance of many species of herbivores in North America 11,000 years ago was caused by humans hunting them. 642

plumule *PLU-mule* The epicotyl plus the first leaves of a young plantlet. 578

polar body *POLE-er BOD-ee* A small cell generated during female meiosis, enabling much cytoplasm to be partitioned into just one of the four meiotic products, the ovum. 165

polarized *PO-ler-ized* The state of a biological membrane when the electric charge inside differs from the electric charge outside. 317

polar nuclei *PO-lar NU-klee-i* The two nuclei in a cell of a plant's megagametophyte. 574

pollen grains *POL-en GRAANZ* Male microgametophytes. 574

pollen sacs *POL-en SAKS* The four microsporangia in an anther, the male part of a flower. 574

pollination *POL-eh-NA-shun* The transfer of pollen from an anther to a receptive stigma. 574

polygamy *pol-IG-ah-mee* A mating system in which a member of one sex associates with several members of the opposite sex. 696

polygyny *pol-IJ-ah-nee* A mating system in which one male mates with several females. 696

polymer *POL-eh-mer* A long molecule built of similar subunits. 50

polyploidy *POL-ee-PLOID-ee* A condition in which a cell has one or more extra sets of chromosomes. 278, 639

pons *PONZ* An oval mass in the brain stem where white matter connects the medulla to higher brain structures and gray matter helps control respiration. 335

population *POP-u-LAY-shun* Any group of interbreeding organisms. 631

population bottleneck *POP-u-LAY-shun BOT-el-nek* A type of genetic drift resulting from an event that kills many members of a population, and the numbers are restored by mating among a small number of individuals, restricting the gene pool compared to the original population. 633

population growth curve *POP-u-LAY-shun GROWTH CURVE* Description of the growth of a group of cells, influenced by nutrient and space availability and waste removal. Includes lag, log, stationary, and decline phases. 139

positive feedback loop *PAHZ-eh-tiv FEED-bak LOOP* A biochemical pathway in which accumulation of a product stimulates its production. 370

positive reinforcement *POS-eh-tiv REE-in-FORC-ment* A reward given for performing a particular behavior. 673

positron emission tomography (PET) *POS-eh-tron ee-MISH-on tah-MOG-rah-fee* A scanning technology that reveals biochemical activity in a living organism. 340

postsynaptic cell *POST-sin-AP-tik SEL* One of two adjacent neurons that are receiving a message. 321

Precambrian era *pre-KAB-ee-an ER-ah* The earliest part of earth history, from which few fossils are known. 654

presynaptic cell *PRE-sin-AP-tik SEL* One of two adjacent neurons that are transmitting a message. 321

primary body *PRI-mer-ee BOD-ee* A plant's axis, consisting of a root and a shoot. 552

primary consumers *PRI-mar-ee kon-SU-merz* Herbivores, which consume primary producers. 718

primary growth *PRI-mer-ee GROWTH* Lengthening of a plant due to cell division in the apical meristems. 552

primary immune response *PRI-mar-ee IM-mune ree-SPONZ* The immune system's response to its first encounter with a foreign antigen. 518

primary motor cortex *PRI-mare-ee MO-ter KOR-tex* A band of cerebral cortex extending from ear to ear across the top of the head that controls voluntary muscles. 337

primary nutrient deficiencies *PRI-mar-ee NU-tri-ent dee-FISH-en-seez* Too little of a particular nutrient due to an inadequate diet. 487

primary producers *PRI-mar-ee pro-DUCE-erz* Organisms that can use inorganic materials and energy to produce the organic material they require. These organisms form the first trophic level of food chains. 717

primary sensory cortex *PRI-mare-ee SEN-sore-ee KOR-tex* A band of cerebral cortex extending from ear to ear across the top of the head that receives sensory input from the skin. 337

primary structure *PRI-mer-ee STRUK-sure* The amino acid sequence of a protein. 53

primary succession *PRI-mar-ee suk-SESH-un* The arrival of life in an area where no community previously existed. 722

primary tissues *PRI-mer-ee TISH-yuz* Groups of cells with a common function. 552

primitive streak *PRIM-eh-tiv STREEK* The pigmented band along the back of a 3-week embryo that develops into the notochord. 181

principle of competitive exclusion *PRIN-sah-pul of kom-PET-ah-tiv ex-KLU-shun* The observation that two competing species will not continue to coexist indefinitely. 706

principle of superposition *PRIN-sah-pul SU-per-po-ZISH-un* The fact that lower rock layers are older than those above them. 621

prions *PRI-onz* Infectious protein particles. 43

profundal zone *pro-FUN-dal ZONE* The deep region of a lake or pond where light does not penetrate. 734

progeria *pro-JER-ee-ah* An inherited, accelerated aging disease. 188

progesterone *pro-JES-ter-own* A hormone produced by the ovaries that controls secretion patterns of other hormones involved in reproduction. 381

prokaryotic cell *pro-CARE-ee-OT-ik SEL* A structurally simple cell, lacking organelles. 22

prolactin *pro-LAK-tin* A hormone made in the anterior pituitary that stimulates milk production. 374

pronuclei *pro-NU-kle-eye* The genetic packages of gametes. 172

prophase *PRO-faze* The first stage of cell division, when chromosomes condense and become visible. During prophase of meiosis I, synapsis and crossing over occur. 134

prostaglandins *PROS-tah-GLAN-dinz* Lipid molecules that are released locally and transiently at the site of a cellular disturbance. They control a variety of body functions and are not well understood. 384

prostate *Pros-STATE* A male gland that produces a milky, alkaline fluid that activates sperm. 164

protein *PRO-teen* A long molecule built of amino acids bonded to each other. 19, 52

proteinoid theory *PRO-teh-noid THER-ee* The idea that proteins evolved before nucleic acids. 60

Protista *pro-TEES-tah* The taxonomic kingdom including the simplest eukaryotes—the protozoans, algae, water molds, and slime molds. 22

proton *PRO-ton* A particle in an atom's nucleus carrying a positive charge and having one mass unit. 44

protoplast fusion *PRO-toe-plast FU-zhun* The creation of new types of plants by combining their cells, from which the cell walls have been removed, and then regenerating a mature plant hybrid from the fused cell. 604

protozoans *PRO-toe-ZO-anz* Single-celled eukaryotes, often classified by their mode of movement, including the familiar amoeba, euglena, and paramecium. 25

proximal convoluted tubule *PROX-eh-mel KON-vo-LU-tid TU-bule* The region of the nephron proximal to Bowman's capsule where selective reabsorption of useful components of the glomerular filtrate occurs. 508

psilophytes *SIL-o-FIGHTS* Plants that first ventured onto the land, during the Silurian period 435 to 395 million years ago. 657

pulmonary artery *PULL-mo-NAIR-ee AR-ter-ee* The artery leading from the right ventricle to the lungs. 435

pulmonary semilunar valve *PULL-mo-NAIR-ee SEM-i-LOON-er VALVE* The valve leading from the right ventricle to the pulmonary artery. 435

pulmonary veins *PULL-mo-NAIR-ee VANEZ* Four veins leading from the lungs to the left atrium of the heart. 435

pulp *PULP* The soft inner portion of a tooth, consisting of connective tissue, blood vessels, and nerves. 469

punctuated equilibrium *PUNK-tu-A-tid EE-kwah-LEE-BREE-um* The view that evolution is characterized by long periods of relatively little change interrupted by bursts of rapid evolutionary change. 273

pupil *PU-pull* The opening in the iris that admits light into the human eye. 354

purine *PURE-een* A type of organic molecule with a double ring structure, including the nitrogenous bases adenine and guanine. 253

Purkinje fibers *per-KIN-gee FI-berz* Muscle fibers that branch from the atrioventricular node and transmit electrical stimulation rapidly. 438

Purkinje system *per-KIN-gee SIS-tum* The sinoatrial node, atrioventricular node, and Purkinje fibers, constituting a network of muscle fibers that triggers contraction of the ventricles. 439

pyloric stenosis *pi-LOR-ik stah-NO-sis* A birth defect in which the pyloric sphincter, which lies between the stomach and the small intestine, fails to open. 471

pylorus *pi-LOR-is* The bottom of the stomach. 470

pyramid of biomass *PIR-ah-mid BI-o-mass* A depiction of trophic levels indicating weight of organisms. 719

pyramid of numbers *PIR-ah-mid NUM-berz* A depiction of the number of organisms at each trophic level in a food chain. 719

pyrimidine *pie-RIM-eh-deen* A type of organic molecule with a single ring structure, including the nitrogenous bases cytosine, thymine, and uracil. 253

Q

quaternary structure *QUAR-teh-nair-ee STRUK-sure* The number and arrangement of polypeptide chains of a protein. 53

quiescent center *kwi-ES-cent CEN-ter* A reservoir of cells behind the root cap that can replace damaged cells in the adjacent meristem. 563

R

radicle *RAD-eh-sil* The first root to emerge from a seed. 563, 578

radiometric dating *RAD-ee-o MET-rik DA-ting* Using the measurement of natural radioactivity as a clock to date fossils. 650

radius *RAY-dee-is* One of the two lower arm bones. 400

realized niche *RE-ah-lized NITCH* The environment in which a species actually lives, which is restricted from its fundamental niche by competition with other species. 707

receptor *re-CEP-ter* A protein protruding from a cell membrane that forms a dock for other molecules. 321

receptor potential *re-CEP-ter po-TEN-shel* A change in membrane

potential in a neuron specialized as a sensory receptor, caused by the redistribution of ions, whose magnitude varies with the strength of the stimulus. 349

recessive *re-CESS-ive* An allele whose expression is masked by the activity of another allele. 220

recombinant DNA technology *re-KOM-bah-nent DNA tek-NAL-eh-gee* Transferring a gene from a cell of a member of one species to the cell of a member of a different species. 270, 610

Recommended Dietary Allowances (RDAs) *REK-o-MEN-ded DI-ah-TEAR-ee ah-LAOW-ance* Guidelines on healthy foods to eat issued by the Unites States government every 5 years. 485

rectum *REC-tum* A storage region leading from the large intestine. 477

red blood cell (erythrocyte) *RED BLOOD SEL* A disc-shaped cell, lacking a nucleus, that is packed with the oxygen-carrying molecule hemoglobin. 83, 424

red marrow *RED MAR-o* Immature blood cells and platelets that reside in cavities in spongy bone. 393

reduction *re-DUK-shun* A chemical reaction in which electrons are gained. 48

reduction division *re-DUK-shun dah-VISH-un* Meiosis I, when the diploid chromosome number is halved. 157

reflex *RE-flex* A rapid, involuntary response to a stimulus from within the body or from the outside environment. 331

reflex arc *RE-flex ARK* A neural pathway linking a sensory receptor and an effector, such as a muscle. 333

relative date *REL-ah-tiv DATE* An estimate of the time at which an organism lived based upon the location of its fossils in sedimentary rock. 650

releaser *rah-LEAS-er* The specific factor that triggers a fixed action pattern, also called a sign stimulus. 669

releasing hormone *re-LEES-ing HOR-moan* A hormone produced by the hypothalamus that influences the secretion of a hormone by another gland. 371

renal tubule *REE-nel TU-bule* The tubule portion of a nephron, along which toxins are added and nutrients recycled to the blood, forming urine. 505

renin *REN-in* A hormone that elevates the level of aldosterone, an adrenal hormone that enhances reabsorption of Na^+ in the kidney, salivary glands, sweat glands, and large intestine. 510

residual air *reh-ZID-u-el AIR* The air in the bottom third of the lungs, which is not exchanged with each breath. 455

respiratory chain *RES-pir-ah-TOR-ee CHANE* A series of electron-accepting enzymes embedded in the inner mitochondrial membrane. 123

resting potential *REST-ing po-TEN-shel* The electrical potential (-65 millivolts) on the inside of a neuron not conducting a nerve impulse. 317

restriction enzyme *re-STRIK-shun EN-zime* A bacterial enzyme that cuts DNA at a specific sequence. 270

restriction fragment length polymorphism *re-STRIK-shun FRAG-ment LENGTH POL-e-MORF-iz-um* Differences in restriction enzyme cutting sites between individuals. 303

reticular activating system (RAS) *rah-TIK-u-lar AK-tah-vay-ting SIS-tem* A diffuse network of cell bodies and nerve tracts extending through the brain stem and into the thalamus; screens sensory input approaching the cerebrum. 335

retina *RET-nah* A sheet of photoreceptors at the back of the human eye. 353, 355

retinal *RET-in-al* The pigment portion of rhodopsin, a molecule involved in black-and-white vision. 357

rhinoviruses *RI-no-vi-rus-ez* Viruses that cause the common cold. 459

rhodopsin *ro-DOP-sin* A pigment molecule stored in the rod cells of the retina in the eye. Light splits rhodopsin, which depolarizes the rod cell, provoking a nerve impulse. 357

rib cage *RIB KAGE* The part of the axial skeleton that protects the heart and lungs, consisting in the human of 10 pairs of ribs attached to the sternum, plus two floating ribs. 399

ribonucleic acid (RNA) *RI-bo-nu-KLAY-ik AS-id* A single-stranded nucleic acid built of nucleotides containing a phosphate, ribose, and nitrogenous bases adenine, guanine, cytosine, and uracil. 253

ribosomal RNA (rRNA) *RI-bo-SOAM-el* RNA that, along with proteins, comprises the ribosome. 258

ribosome *RI-bo-soam* A structure built of RNA and protein upon which a gene's message (mRNA) anchors during protein synthesis. 72, 258

rods *RODZ* Specialized neurons clustered around the edges of the retina that provide black-and-white vision and night vision. 355

root apical meristem *ROOT AP-eh-kel MER-eh-stem* Dividing tissue at root tips in a plantlet. 578

root cap *ROOT KAP* A thimble-shaped protective structure covering the tip of a root. 563

root hairs *ROOT HAIRZ* Trichomes that appear near root tips and absorb water and minerals from soil. 554

rosettes *ro-ZETTZ* Nonelongated stems, such as in banana. 557

round dance *ROUND DANC* A dance in which bees communicate to members of the colony that food is nearby and is of a certain sweetness. 692

rugae *RU-guy* Folds in the mucosa of the stomach. 470

S

S phase *FAZE* The synthesis phase of interphase, when DNA is replicated and microtubules are produced from tubulin. 133

saccule *SAK-yul* A pouch in the vestibule of the inner ear filled with a jellylike fluid and lined with hair cells, containing calcium carbonate otolith granules that move in response to changes in velocity, firing action potentials. 363

sacrum *SAY-krum* The five fused pelvic vertebrae. 398

saliva *sah-LI-va* A secretion in the mouth that is produced when food is smelled or tasted. 468

salivary amylase *SAL-eh-var-ee AM-eh-lase* An enzyme produced in the mouth that begins the chemical digestion of starch into sugar. 468

salivary glands *SAL-eh-vare-ee GLANDZ* Three pairs of glands near the mouth that secrete saliva, a fluid containing water, mucus, and salivary amylase. 468

saltatory conduction *SAL-teh-tore-ee kon-DUK-shun* The jumping of an action potential between nodes of Ranvier in myelinated nerve axons. 321

sapwood *SAP-wood* Wood located nearest the vascular cambium, which transports water and dissolved nutrients within a plant. 568

sarcolemma *SAR-ko-LEM-ah* The cell membrane of a skeletal muscle cell. 407

sarcoplasmic reticulum *SAR-ko-PLASZ-mik rah-TIK-u-lum* The endoplasmic reticulum of a skeletal muscle cell. 407

saturated (fat) *SAT-yur-ray-tid* A triglyceride with single bonds between the carbons of its fatty acid tails. 52

savanna *s ah-VAN-ah* A grassland. 729

scales *SKALZ* A subunit of a pinecone bearing two ovules. 583

scavengers *SKAHV-en-gerz* Animals that eat the leftovers of another animal's meal. 718

school *SKUL* A formation of fishes swimming at particular distances and angles from each other. 687

Schwann cells *SCHWAN SELZ* Fatty cells that wrap around neurons in the peripheral nervous system, forming myelin sheaths. 320

scientific method *SI-en-TIF-ik METH-id* A systematic approach to interpreting observations, involving reasoning, predicting, testing, and drawing conclusions, which are put into perspective with existing knowledge. 3

sclera *SKLER-ah* The outermost, white layer of the human eye. 353

sclereids *SKLER-ridz* Plant cells with a gritty texture found in pears and in the hulls of peanuts. 553

sclerenchyma *sklah-REN-kah-mah* Elongated supportive plant cells with thick, nonstretchable secondary cell walls. 553

scoliosis *SKOL-ee-O-sis* An abnormal spinal curvature in which the vertebrae shift sideways. 399

scotopsin *sco-TOP-sin* The protein portion of rhodopsin, a pigment molecule important in black-and-white vision. 357

scramble competition *SKRAM-bel KOM-pah-TISH-un* Direct competition of individuals in a population for a limited resource. 705

seasonal affective disorder (SAD) *SEE-son-al AF-fek-tiv DIS-or-der* A form of depression that occurs mostly in the winter and seems to respond to therapy of exposure to light. 677

seasonal ovulator *SEE-son-al OV-u-LAY-ter* A female mammal that has a period of sexual receptivity and fertility. 382

secondary consumers *SEK-on-DAIR-ee kon-SU-merz* Animals that eat herbivores, forming a third trophic level in a food chain. 718

secondary growth *SEK-on-DER-ee GROWTH* Thickening of a plant due to cell division in lateral meristems. 552

secondary immune response *SEK-on-DAIR-ee IM-mune ree-SPONZ* The immune system's response to subsequent encounters with a foreign antigen. 518

secondary nutrient deficiencies *SEK-on-dare-ee NU-tri-ent dah-FISH-en-seez* Too little of a particular nutrient due to an inborn metabolic condition. 488

secondary production *SEK-on-DAIR-ee pro-DUK-shun* The energy stored in the tissues of herbivores and carnivores. 718

secondary structure *SEK-en-DAIR-ee STRUCK-sure* The shape assumed by a protein caused by chemical attractions between amino acids that are close together in the primary structure. 53

secondary succession *SEK-on-DAIR-ee suk-SESH-un* The arrival of new species in an area that already has life. 723

second messengers *SEK-ond MESS-en-gerz* Biochemicals that modulate neurotransmitter action. 325

secretin *sah-KREE-tin* A hormone produced in the small intestine that triggers the release of bicarbonate from the pancreas, which neutralizes stomach acid. 473

seed *SEED* A temporarily dormant sporophyte individual surrounded by a tough protective coat. 578

seed coat *SEED COAT* A tough outer layer protecting a dormant plant embryo and its food supply in a seed. 579

segmentation *SEG-men-TA-shun* Localized muscle contractions in the small intestine that provide mechanical digestion. 472

segregation *SEG-rah-GAY-shun* The distribution of alleles of a gene into separate gametes during meiosis. 219

seismonasty *SIZ-mo-NAS-tee* A nastic (nondirectional) movement resulting from contact or mechanical disturbance. 594

selectively permeable *sah-LEK-tiv-lee PERM-ee-ah-bul* A biological membrane that admits only some substances. 317

semicircular canals *SEM-ee-SIR-ku-ler kah-NALZ* Fluid-filled structures in the inner ear that provide information on the position of the head. 362

semidwarf rices *SEM-i DWARF RI-ses* Highly productive varieties of rice. 545

semilunar valves *SEM-i-LOON-er VALVZ* A ring of tissue flaps in the arteries just outside each ventricle that maintains unidirectional blood flow. 434

seminal vesicles *SEM-en-el VES-eh-kels* In the human male, the paired structures that add fructose and prostaglandins to the sperm. 155

sense strand *SENSE STRAND* The side of the DNA double helix for a particular gene that is transcribed. 257

sensory adaptation *SEN-sore-ee ah-DAP-TAY-shun* The phenomenon of a sensation becoming less noticeable once it has been recognized. 349

sensory (afferent) neuron *SEN-sore-ee (AF-fer-ent) NEUR-on* A neuron that brings information toward the central nervous system, with long dendrites that transmit the message from the stimulated body part to the cell body near the spinal cord, and a short axon. 315

sensory areas *SEN-sore-ee AIR-ee-ahs* Parts of the cerebral cortex that receive and interpret messages from sense organs concerning temperature, body movement, pain, touch, taste, smell, sight, and sound. 337

sensory (neural) deafness *SEN-sore-ee (NEUR-al) DEF-nes* Hearing loss resulting from an inability of the cochlea to generate action potentials in response to detecting sound. 360

sensory pathways *SEN-sore-ee PATH-wayz* Nerve tracts in the peripheral nervous system that transmit impulses from a stimulus to the central nervous system. 342

sensory receptor *SEN-sore-ee re-CEP-ter* A specialized dendrite of a neuron that is specific to detecting a particular sensation and firing an action potential in response, which is transmitted to the spinal cord. 333

sepals *SEE-pelz* Leaflike structures that enclose and protect inner floral parts. 574

severe combined immune deficiency *sah-VEER kom-BIND im-MUNE dah-FISH-en-see* An inborn deficiency of T and B cells. 525

sex chromosome *SEX KRO-mo-soam* A chromosome that determines sex. 225

sex hormones *SEX HOR-moanz* Hormones that provide secondary sexual characteristics and prepare an animal for sexual reproduction, such as estrogen, progesterone, and testosterone. 378

sex-influenced inheritance *SEX IN-flu-enced in-HAIR-eh-tence* An allele that is dominant in one sex but recessive in the other. 225

sex-limited trait *SEX LIM-eh-tid TRAIT* A trait affecting a structure or function of the body that is present in only one sex. 225

sex-linked *SEX LINKED* A gene located on the X chromosome or a trait that results from the activity of such a gene. 238

sex ratio *SEX RAY-she-o* The ratio of males to females at conception (primary), birth (secondary), and 10-year intervals thereafter (tertiary). 246

sexual dimorphism *SEX-u-al di-MOR-fiz-um* The difference in appearance between males and females of the same species. 696

sexual reproduction *SEX-u-el RE-pro-DUK-shun* The combination of genetic material from two individuals to create a third individual. 42, 158

sexual selection *SEX-u-el sah-LEK-shun* Natural selection of traits that increase an individual's reproductive success. 627

shoot apical meristem *SHOOT AP-eh-kel MER-eh-stem* Dividing tissue at the tip of a shoot in a seedling. 578

short-day plants *SHORT-day PLANTZ* Plants that require light periods shorter than some critical length to flower. 596

sieve cells *SIV SELZ* Less specialized conducting cells in phloem. 555

sieve plate *SIV PLATE* End walls of aligned sieve tubes in a plant's phloem. 555

sieve pores *SIV PORZ* Perforations in phloem, through which solutes move from cell to cell. 555

sieve tube members *SIV TUUB MEM-berz* More complex and specialized conducting cells in phloem that form long sieve tubes. 555

Silurian period *sah-LUR-ee-an PER-ee-od* The period following the Ordovician period, 435 to 395 million years ago, when organisms first ventured onto the land. 657

simple carbohydrates *SIM-pel KAR-bo-HIGH-drates* Monosaccharides and disaccharides. 50

sinoatrial node (SA node) *SI-no-A-tree-al NOOD* Specialized cells in the wall of the right atrium that set the pace of the heartbeat. Also called the pacemaker. 438

skeletal muscle *SKEL-eh-tel MUS-sel* Voluntary, striated muscle consisting of single, multinucleated cells that are contractile due to sliding filaments of actin and myosin. 87, 405

skull *SKULL* A hard, bony structure protecting the brain. 397

sleep apnea *SLEEP AP-nee-ah* A sleep disorder in which breathing stops several hundred times a night, for 20 to 60 seconds each time.

sliding filament model *SLY-ding FILL-eh-ment MOD-el* The movement of protein myofilaments past each other to shorten skeletal muscle cells, leading to muscle contraction. 409

slow twitch-fatigue resistant fibers *SLO TWITCH fah-TEEG re-ZIS-tent FI-berz* Skeletal muscle fibers that contract slowly but are resistant to fatigue because of a plentiful supply of oxygen. 413

smooth muscle *SMOOTH MUS-sel* Involuntary, nonstriated contractile tissue found lining the digestive tract and other organs. 87, 405

sodium-potassium pump *SO-dee-um po-TAS-ee-um PUMP* A mechanism that uses energy released from splitting ATP to transport Na^+ out of cells and K^+ into cells. 317

softwoods *SOFT-woodz* Woods of gymnosperms, such as pine, spruce, and fir. 566

solution *so-LU-shun* A homogenous mixture of a substance (the solute) dissolved in water (the solvent). 98

somaclonal variation *SOAM-ah-KLON-al VAR-ee-AY-shun* Genetically variant embryos or plantlets grown from callus initiated by somatic cells. 608

somatic cell *so-MAT-ik SEL* A body cell; a cell other than the sperm or ovum. 131, 157

somatic embryo *so-MAT-ik EM-bree-o* A plant embryo grown from callus. 605

somatic hybrid *so-MAT-ik HI-brid* A plant regenerated from a protoplast fusion of cells from two types of plants. 605

somatic nervous system *so-MAT-ik NER-ves SIS-tum* Part of the motor pathways of the peripheral nervous system that leads to skeletal muscles. 342

somatostatin *so-MAH-toe-STAH-tin* A pancreatic hormone that controls the rate of nutrient absorption into the bloodstream. 378

Southern blotting *SOU-thern BLOT-ting* Use of DNA probes to identify specific fragments of DNA. 302

speciation *SPE-she-AY-shun* The appearance of a new type of organism. 621

species *SPE-shez* A group of similar individuals that interbreed in nature and are reproductively isolated from all other such groups. 19, 621

sperm *SPERM* The male sex cell. 155

spermatogenesis *sper-MAT-o-JEN-eh-sis* The differentiation of a sperm cell, from a diploid spermatogonium, to primary spermatocyte, to two haploid secondary spermatocytes, to spermatids, and finally to mature spermatozoa. 163

sphincters *SFINK-terz* Muscular rings that control the passage of a substance from one area to another. 470

sphygmomanometer *SFIG-mo-mah-NOM-eh-ter* A gauge that measures blood pressure by the displacement of a column of mercury. 432

spinal cord *SPI-nal KORD* A tube of neural tissue extending from the base of the brain to just below the lowest rib that carries impulses to and from the brain. 331

spinal nerves *SPI-nal NERVZ* Thirty-one pairs of somatic nerves that exit the spinal cord and emerge from between the vertebrae. 344

spinal reflex *SPI-nel RE-flex* A neural connection made entirely within the spinal cord. 333

spindle apparatus *SPIN-del AP-ah-RAH-tis* A structure built of microtubules that aligns and separates chromosomes in cell division. 133

spines *SPINZ* Leaves modified to protect plants from predators and excessive sunlight. 561

spleen *SPLEEN* An organ located in the abdomen that produces and stores lymphocytes and contains reserve supplies of red blood cells. 442

spongy bone *SPON-gee BONE* Flat bones and tips of long bones that have many large spaces between a web of bony struts. 393

spongy mesophyll *SPON-gee MEZ-o-fil* Irregularly shaped chlorenchyma cells separated by large spaces that are found below the palisade layer in leaves. 561

spontaneous generation *spon-TAY-nee-us JEN-er-RAY-shun* The idea, proven untrue, that living things can arise from nonliving matter. 59

sporophyte *SPOR-o-fight* The part of a plant's life cycle when spores are produced. 28, 573

spring turnover *SPRING TURN-o-ver* The rising of nutrient-rich lower layers of a lake and sinking of oxygen-rich layers from the top, often causing algal blooms. 734

stabilizing selection *STA-bil-I-zing sah-LEK-shun* When extreme phenotypes are less adaptive than an intermediate phenotype. 637

stable isotope tracing *STA-bel I-so-toap TRAC-ing* A technique that analyzes the proportions of certain isotopes in tissue samples, providing clues to which types of organisms consume others. 719

stamens *STA-menz* Male reproductive structures in flowers built of stalklike filaments bearing pollen-producing anthers at their tips. 574

stegosaurs *STEG-ah-SORZ* Herbivorous dinosaurs with panels down their backs. 659

stem cell *STEM SEL* A cell that divides often. 139

steroid hormone *STAIR-oid HOR-moan* A hormone composed of lipid that can pass through the target cell's membrane and enter the cell's nucleus. 369

stigma *STIG-mah* A pollen receptacle at the tip of a style in a flower. 574

stirrup *STIR-up* One of the bones in the middle ear. 359

stolons *STOL-onz* Stems that grow along the soil surface; also called runners. 558

stomata *sto-MAH-tah* Pores in a plant's cuticle through which water and gases are exchanged between the plant and the atmosphere. 559

storage leaves *STOR-age LEEVZ* Fleshy leaves that store nutrients. 562

stress test *STRESS TEST* An electrocardiogram taken while the subject is exercising. 440

stroma *STRO-ma* The nonmembranous inner region of the chloroplast. 116

stroma lamellae *STRO-ma la-MEL-i* Loosely packed inner membranes of the chloroplast, containing pigment molecules. 116

style *STILE* A stalk forming from an ovary in a flower. 574

subapical region *sub-APE-eh-kel REE-jen* The region behind the root cap, which is divided into zones of cellular division, cellular elongation, and cellular maturation. 563

subclinical *sub-KLIN-eh-kel* The stage of a nutrient deficiency when abnormalities can be detected with biochemical tests, but symptoms are not yet experienced. 488

suberin *SU-ber-in* A waxy, waterproof biochemical in the interior of a root's cortex. 564

succulent *SUK-ku-lent* Fleshy plant tissue that can store large amounts of water. 558

summation *sum-A-shun* An increase in the strength of contraction of a muscle that is stimulated a second time very soon after an initial stimulation. 413

superior vena cava *su-PER-ee-er VEE-nah KAH-vah* The upper branch of the largest vein that leads to the heart. 434

supernormal releaser *su-per-NOR-mal ree-LEAS-er* In animal behavior, a model that exaggerates a releaser and elicits a stronger response than the natural object. 670

suppressor T cells *su-PRES-ser T SELZ* T cells that inhibit the response of all lymphocytes to foreign antigens, shutting off the immune response when an infection is under control. 521

suprachiasmatic nuclei (SCN) *SU-pra-KI-as-MAT-ik NU-klee-i* Two clusters of 10,000 neurons each in the hypothalamus that control certain biological clocks in some species. 677

survival of the fittest *ser-VI-val of the FIT-tist* The idea that those individuals best able to reproduce healthy offspring contribute the most genes to the next generation. 627

symbiosis *SYM-bee-o-sis* An intimate relationship between two types of organisms. 14

sympathetic nervous system *SIM-pah-THE-tik NER-ves SIS-tum* Part of the autonomic nervous system that mobilizes the body to respond to environmental stimuli. 344, 439

sympatric species *SIM-pat-rik SPE-shez* Two closely related groups of organisms that occupy the same geographic region but cannot reproduce successfully with each other. 638

synapse *SIN-apse* A space between two adjacent neurons. 321

synapsis *SIN-ap-sis* The gene-by-gene alignment of homologous chromosomes during prophase of meiosis I. 159

synaptic knobs *sin-AP-tik NOBZ* The enlarged tips of branches at the ends of axons. 321

synaptic vesicles *sin-AP-tik VES-eh-kelz* Small sacs within synaptic knobs at the ends of axons that contain neurotransmitters. 321

synovial joint *sin-OV-ee-el JOINT* A capsule of fluid-filled fibrous connective tissue between freely movable bones. 401

synovial membrane *sin-OV-ee-el MEM-brane* The lining of the interior of a joint capsule, which secretes lubricating synovial fluid. 401

systole *SIS-toll-ee* The heart's contraction. 438

systolic pressure *SIS-tol-ik PRESH-yur* The blood pressure at its peak, when the ventricles contract. 432

T

taiga *TI-gah* The northern coniferous forest, north of the temperate zone. 729

taproot system *TAP-root SIS-tum* A plant in which the first root (the radicle) enlarges to form a major root that persists through the life of the plant. 563

target cell *TAR-get SEL* A cell that is affected directly by a particular hormone. 368

tarsals *TAR-salz* The ankle bones. 400

taste receptors *TASTE ree-CEP-terz* Specialized neurons that detect taste. 351

taxonomy *tax-ON-o-mee* The branch of biology concerned with classifying organisms on the basis of evolutionary relationships. Taxonomic levels include, in order, kingdom, phylum (or division), class, order, family, genus, and species. 19

tectorial membrane *TEK-TORE-ee-al MEM-brane* The membrane above the hair cells in the cochlea of the inner ear that is pressed by the hair cells responding to the basilar membrane's vibration in the presence of sound waves. 360

telophase *TELL-o-faze* The final stage of cell division, when two cells form from one and the spindle is disassembled. 135

temporal isolation *TEM-por-al I-so-LAY-shun* When members of two populations do not crossbreed because they have different mating seasons. 368

tendon *TEN-din* A heavy band of fibrous connective tissue that attaches a muscle to a bone. 406

tendrils *TEN-drilz* Shoots or modified leaves that support plants by coiling around objects. 558, 561

teosinte *TE-o-SIN-tee* A grass that may have been ancestral to corn. 544

teratogen *teh-RAT-eh-jen* A chemical or other environmental agent that causes a birth defect. 202

territory *TEAR-eh-TOR-ee* A portion of land defended by an individual. 694

tertiary consumers *TER-she-AIR-ee kon-SU-merz* Carnivores that eat other carnivores, forming a fourth trophic level. 718

tertiary structure *TER-she-air-ee STRUK-sure* The shape assumed by a protein caused by chemical attractions between amino acids that are far apart in the primary structure. 53

test cross *TEST CROSS.* Crossing an individual of unknown genotype to a homozygous recessive individual. 221

testes *TES-teez* The paired, male gonads, containing the seminiferous tubules, in which sperm are manufactured. 155, 374

tetanus *TET-nes* A smooth and continuous muscle contraction resulting from repeated strong stimulations that occur before the muscle has time to relax. Also, an infectious disease called "lockjaw."

tetraploid *TET-rah-ploid* An individual with four sets of chromosomes, usually resulting from self-fertilization in a diploid plant. 639

thalamus *THAL-eh-mus* A gray, tight package of nerve cell bodies and glia beneath the cerebrum that relays sensory input to the appropriate part of the cerebrum. 335

thecodonts *THEK-o-dontz* Descendants of the Permian cotylosaurs that were ancestors of the great dinosaurs. 659

therapsids *ther-AP-sidz* Reptiles living in the Mesozoic era, which had some characteristics of mammals. 659

thermal stratification *THER-mal STRAH-tah-fah-KAY-shun* Layers within lakes that have different temperatures. 734

thermocline *THER-mo-kline* A middle layer of a lake where water temperature changes rapidly and drastically. 734

thermoluminescence *THER-mo-LU-mah-NES-ence* A technique that measures the formation of tiny holes in crystals over time, caused by exposure to ionizing radiation. This measurement is used in absolute dating of fossils up to 1 million years old. 650

thigmomorphogenesis *THIG-mo-MOR-pho-GEN-ah-sis* A plant's responses to mechanical disturbances, including inhibition of cellular elongation and production of thick-walled supportive tissue. 596

thigmotropism *THIG-mo-TRO-piz-um* A plant's response toward touch. 592

thoracic vertebrae *thor-AS-ik VER-tah-bray* The 12 vertebrae in the upper back. 398

thorns *THORNZ* Stems modified for protection. 558

threat posture *THRET POS-tur* A visual display marking a territory. 694

thrombophlebitis *THROM-bo-flah-BI-tis* Inflammation of a vein wall complicated by the formation of blood clots. 438

thromboplastin *THROM-bo-plas-tin* A protein released from blood vessel walls following injury that, in the presence of calcium, converts the blood protein prothrombin into thrombin. 428

thrombus *THROM-bus* A blood clot that blocks a blood vessel or the heart. 428

thylakoids *THI-lah-koidz* Membranous discs comprising the inner membrane of a chloroplast. 81, 116

thymine *THI-meen* One of the two pyrimidine bases in DNA. 57, 253

thymus *THY-mis* A lymphatic organ in the upper chest where lymphocytes called T cells learn to distinguish foreign from self antigens. 442

thyroid gland *THI-roid Gland* A gland in the neck that manufactures thyroxine, a hormone that increases energy expenditure. 112

thyroid stimulating hormone (TSH) *THY-roid STIM-u-lat-ing HOR-moan* A hormone made in the anterior pituitary that stimulates the thyroid gland to release its two hormones. 375

thyroxine *thy-ROX-in* A thyroid hormone that increases the rate of cellular metabolism. 375

tibia *TIB-ee-ah* The larger of the two bones of the lower leg. 400

tidal volume *TI-del VOL-yum* The amount of air inhaled or exhaled during a normal breath. 455

tinnitus *tin-I-tus* A condition in which a persistent ringing sound is heard. 361

Ti plasmid *TI PLAZ-mid* A ring of DNA in the microorganism *Agrobacterium tumefaciens* that is used to introduce foreign plant genes in recombinant DNA technology. 611

tissue *TISH-u* In multicellular organisms, groups of cells with related functions. 40

tonsils *TAWN-silz* Collections of lymphatic tissue in the throat. 442

trachae *TRAY-ki* A branching system of tubules that brings the outside environment in close contact with an organism's cells so that gas exchange can occur. 446

trachea *TRAY-kee-ah* The respiratory tube just beneath the larynx, held open by rings of cartilage. Also called the windpipe. 449

tracheids *TRA-kee-idz* Less specialized conducting cells in plants that are elongate, are dead at maturity, and have thick walls. 555

tracheophytes *TRAY-key-o-fights* Plants that have specialized tubes to conduct water and nutrients. 29, 571

transcription *tranz-SKRIP-shun* Manufacturing RNA from DNA. 257

transfer RNA (tRNA) *TRANZ-fer* A small RNA molecule that binds an amino acid at one site and an mRNA codon at another site. 258

transgenic organism *TRANZ-jen-ik OR-gan-niz-um* Genetic engineering of a gamete or fertilized ovum, leading to development of an individual with the alteration in every cell. 146, 610

translation *tranz-LAY-shun* Assembly of an amino acid chain according to the sequence of base triplets in a molecule of mRNA. 257

translocation *TRANZ-lo-KAY-shun* Exchange of genetic material between nonhomologous chromosomes. 280

transverse (T) tubules *TRANZ-verse TU-bules* Portions of the sarcolemma that jut into the sarcoplasmic reticulum of a skeletal muscle cell. 407

Triassic period *tri-AS-ik PER-ee-od* The period from 225 to 185 million years ago, when small ancestors of the great dinosaurs flourished. 659

trichomes *TRI-koamz* Outgrowths of a plant's epidermis that provide protection. 554

triiodothyronine *TRI-i-ode-o-THY-ro-neen* A thyroid hormone that increases the rate of cellular metabolism. 375

trilobites *TRI-lo-bitz* Insectlike organisms that appeared in the seas of the Cambrian period. 657

trisomy *TRI-som-mee* A cell with one extra chromosome. 280

trophic level *TRO-fik LEV-el* A feeding level in a food chain or web. 717

trophoblast *TRO-fo-blast* A layer of cells in the preembryo that develops into the chorion and then the placenta. 173

tropical rain forest *TROP-e-kel RAIN FOR-est* A warm, moist terrestrial region where rainfall is 79 to 157 inches (200 to 400 centimeters) per year; life is diverse and plentiful, and nutrient cycling is rapid. 728

tropic hormone *TRO-pik HOR-moan* A hormone produced by one gland that influences the secretion of a hormone by another gland. 371

tropism *TRO-piz-um* Plant growth toward or away from an environmental stimulus. 591

tropomyosin *TRO-po-MI-o-sin* A type of protein in the thin myofilaments of skeletal muscle cells. 407

troponin *tro-PO-nin* A type of protein in the thin myofilaments of skeletal muscle cells. 407

trypsin *TRIP-sin* A pancreatic enzyme that participates in protein digestion in the small intestine. 472

tube nucleus *TUUB NU-klee-us* A haploid cell resulting from the mitotic division of a microspore, in male plant reproduction. 574

tubercle *to-BER-kel* A section of lung walled off by a fibrous connective tissue capsule as a result of tuberculosis. 461

tuberculosis *to-BER-ku-LO-sis* A bacterial infection of the lungs. 460

tubers *TU-berz* Swollen regions of stems that store nutrients. 558

tundra *TUN-drah* A band of land running across the northern parts of Asia, Europe, and North America, where the climate is harsh and few organisms live. 729, 733

turgor pressure *TER-ger PRESH-yur* Rigidity of a plant cell caused by water pressing against the cell wall. 100

twitch *TWITCH* A rapid contraction and relaxation of a muscle cell following a single stimulation. 413

twitch types *TWITCH TYPEZ* Varieties of skeletal muscle fibers distinguished by how quickly they contract and tire. 413

tympanal organ *TIM-PAN-al OR-gan* A thin part of an insect's cuticle that detects vibrations and therefore sound. 359

tympanic membrane *TIM-PAN-ik MEM-brane* The eardrum, a structure upon which sound waves impinge. 359

U

ulcer *UL-sir* A raw, craterlike sore. 470

ulcerative colitis *UL-sir-AH-tiv koal-I-tis* Inflammation of the inner lining of the colon and rectum, producing pain, bloody diarrhea, and weight loss. 477

ulna *UL-nah* One of the two lower arm bones. 400

umbilical cord *um-BIL-ik-kel KORD* A ropelike structure containing one artery and two veins that connects mother to unborn child. 168

unconditioned stimulus *un-kon-DISH-ond STIM-u-lus* A stimulus that normally triggers a particular response. 673

uniformitarianism *U-nah-FOR-mah-TER-ee-ah-niz-um* The view that the earth's surface is continually remolded. 621

unsaturated (fat) *un-SAT-yur-RAY tid* A triglyceride with double bonds between some of its carbons. 52

upwelling *up-WELL-ing* The movement upward of cooler, nutrient-rich bottom layers of the ocean, causing nutrients to bloom. 737

uracil *YUR-eh-sil* One of the two pyrimidine bases in RNA. 257

urea *u-REE-ah* A nitrogenous waste derived from ammonia. 502

ureter *u-REE-ter* A muscular tube that transports urine from the kidney to the bladder. 504

urethra *u-RETH-rah* The tube leading from the bladder through which urine exits the body. 505

uric acid *YUR-ik AS-id* A nitrogenous waste derived from ammonia. 502

urinary bladder *YUR-eh-NAIR-ee BLAD-er* A muscular sac in which urine collects. 505

urinary tract infection *YUR-eh-NAIR-ee TRACT in-FEK-shun* A bacterial infection of the urethra, with symptoms of frequent, painful urination and sometimes fever and lower abdominal pain. 511

uterus *U-ter-us* The muscular, saclike organ in the human female in which the embryo and fetus develop. 157

utricle *U-trah-kel* A pouch in the vestibule of the inner ear filled with a jellylike fluid and lined with hair cells, containing calcium carbonate otolith granules that move in response to changes in velocity, firing action potentials. 362

V

vaccine *VAK-seen* A killed or weakened form of, or part of, an infectious agent that initiates an immune response so that when the real agent is encountered, antibodies are already available to deactivate it. 529

vagus nerve *VA-ges NERVE* The one cranial nerve that innervates internal organs, rather than the head or neck. 344

variable regions *VAIR-ee-ah-bul REE-genz* The sequence of amino acids comprising the upper portions of heavy and light antibody chains, which varies greatly in different antibody types. 518

varicose veins *VAR-eh-kos VANEZ* Distension of the superficial veins in the legs. 438

vascular bundles *VAS-ku-ler BUN-delz* Organized groups of vascular tissues in stems. 557

vascular cambium *VAS-ku-ler KAM-bee-um* A thin cylinder of meristematic tissue found in roots and stems that produces most of the secondary plant body. 566

vas deferens *VAS DEF-er-enz* In the human male, a tube from the epididymis that continues to become the vas deferens, which joins the urethra in the penis. 155

vasoconstriction *VAZ-o-kon-strik-shun* The narrowing of blood vessels, which raises blood pressure. 433

vasoconstriction area *VAZ-o-kon-STRIK-shun AIR-ee-ah* Part of the brain's vasomotor center that stimulates circulation by constricting blood flow. 439

vasodilation *VAZ-o-di-LAY-shun* The widening of blood vessels, which lowers blood pressure. 433

vasodilation area *VAZ-o-di-LAY-shun AIR-ee-ah* Part of the brain's vasomotor center that dilates blood vessels. 439

vasomotor center *va-ZOM-eh-ter CEN-ter* A part of the brain that controls blood flow to the heart and heart rate by sending nerve impulses through the spinal cord to the sympathetic nervous system. 439

veins *VANEZ* Large blood vessels arising from venules that return blood to the heart. 428

veins *VANEZ* Strands of vascular tissue in leaves. 561

venous valves *VEEN-is VALVES* Flaplike structures in veins that keep blood flow in one direction. 432

ventricles *VEN-tree-kelz* Spaces in the brain into which cerebrospinal fluid is secreted. Also, the two muscular chambers of the heart located beneath the atria. 342

venules *VANE-yules* Vessels that arise from capillaries and drain into veins. 428

vertebral column *VER-teh-bral KOL-um* Bones along the back and neck that protect the spinal cord.

vertical stratification *VER-tah-kel STRAH-tah-fah-KAY-shun* The formation of layers of different types of organisms beneath the canopy of a tropical rain forest, caused by competition of organisms for sunlight. 728

vessel elements *VES-el EL-eh-mentz* More specialized conducting cells in plants that are elongate, are dead at maturity, and have thick walls. 555

vestibule *VES-teh-bule* A structure in the inner ear that provides information on the position of the head with respect to gravity and changes in velocity. 362

vestigial *ves-TEEG-el* A structure that seems not to have a function in an organism but resembles a functional organ in another type of organism. 651

villi *VIL-i* Tiny projections on the inner lining of the small intestine, which greatly increase surface area. 473

viroid *VEAR-oid* Infectious genetic material. 43

virus *VI-rus* An infectious particle consisting of a nucleic acid (DNA or RNA) wrapped in protein. 42

vital capacity *VI-tel kah-PASS-eh-tee* The maximal amount of air that can be moved in and out of the lungs during forceful breathing. 455

vitamin *VI-tah-min* An organic molecule essential in small amounts for the normal growth and function of an organism. 58

vitreous humor *VIT-ree-es U-mer* A jellylike substance behind the lens, comprising most of the volume of the eye. 356

vocal cords *VO-kel KORDZ* Two elastic bands of tissue stretched over the glottis, which vibrate as air passes, producing sounds. 449

W

waggle dance *WAG-gel DANC* A bee's dance signifying that food is farther from the hive than a round dance would indicate. The speed of the dance, the number of waggles during the straight part, and the duration of buzzing signal the distance to the food source. 692

white blood cell (leukocyte) *WHITE BLOOD SEL* A cell that helps fight infection. 83, 424

white matter *WHITE MAT-ter* Myelinated nerve fibers, found in pathways that transmit impulses over long distances. 321

wild type *WILD TYPE* A phenotype or allele that is the most common for a certain gene in a population. 220

X

X inactivation *X IN-ak-tah-VA-shun* The turning off of one X chromosome in each cell of a female mammal at a certain point in prenatal development. 239

xylem *ZI-lum* Tubules in a plant that transport water and minerals from the roots to the leaves. 29, 555

Z

zona pellucida *ZO-nah pel-LU-seh-dah* A thin, clear layer of proteins and sugars surrounding a secondary oocyte. 171

zone of cellular division *ZONE of SEL-yu-ler dah-VISH-on* The meristematic part of the subapical region in a plant's root. 563

zone of cellular elongation *ZONE of SEL-yu-ler e-long-GAY-shun* The middle part of the subapical region of a plant's root, where rapid cellular elongation lengthens the root. 563

zone of cellular maturation *ZONE of SEL-yu-ler MAT-ur-AY-shun* The hindmost region of the subapical region of a plant's root, where tiny root hairs protrude from epidermal cells. 563

zygomycete *ZI-go-my-SEAT* A fungus with sexual spores, such as bread mold. 27

zygote *ZI-goat* In prenatal humans, the organism during the first 2 weeks of development. Also called a preembryo. 172, 573, 578

Credits

Photographs

Title page © Dr. Lloyd M. Beidler/Science Photo Library/Photo Researchers, Inc.; **page vi:** © Jeff Henry/Peter Arnold, Inc.; **page viii:** © Science Photo Library/Science Source/Photo Researchers, Inc.

Table of Contents:
Page ix (all): © Dr. Lloyd M. Beidler/Science Photo Library/Photo Researchers, Inc.; **page x:** © William De Grado/Dupont; **page xii:** © Bruce Iverson; **page xiv:** © Petit Format/Nestle/Photo Researchers, Inc.; **page xv:** © Erika Stone/Peter Arnold, Inc.

Unit Openers
Unit 1: © Biophoto Associates/Science Source/Photo Researchers, Inc.; **Unit 2:** © Bruce Iverson; **Unit 3:** © Petit Format/Nestle/Photo Researchers, Inc.; **Unit 4:** © Erika Stone/Peter Arnold, Inc.; **Unit 5:** © Steven C. Kaufman/Peter Arnold, Inc.; **Unit 6:** © Andrew J. Martinez/Photo Researchers, Inc.; **Unit 7:** © W.H. Moller/Peter Arnold, Inc.; **Unit 8:** © A.P. Barnes/Planet Earth Pictures.

Chapter 1
1.1b: © Jeff Henry/Peter Arnold, Inc.; **1.4:** © Stranton K. Short/The Jackson Laboratory; **1.5:** Courtesy Biology Digest; **1.6:** © Thomas Novitsky/Cape Cod Associates; **1.7:** National Library of Medicine; **1.8:** © William E. Ferguson

Chapter 2
2.1: © M. I. Walker/Science Source/Photo Researchers, Inc.; **2.2:** J. Tucker/NASA, GFSC; **2.3:** Courtesy Dr. Allen R. J. Eaglesham; **page 16 (top):** © S. J. Krasemann/Peter Arnold, Inc.; **(bottom):** © Bruce Iverson; **2.6 (both):** © Barbara Mensch; **2.8:** © USDA/Science Source/Photo Researchers, Inc.; **2.9a:** © CNRI/Science Photo Library/Photo Researchers, Inc.; **2.9b:** © Dr. Tony Brain/Science Photo Library/Photo Researchers, Inc.; **2.9c (insert):** Carolina Biological Supply Company; **2.9c:** © Stanley F. Hayes, National Institutes of Health/Science Photo Library/Photo Researchers, Inc.; **2.11b:** © William E. Ferguson; **2.11c:** © Biophoto Associates/Science Source/Photo Researchers, Inc.; **2.14:** © Michel

Viard/Peter Arnold, Inc.; **2.15 (all):** © Bruce Iverson; **2.16:** © Jeff Rotman/Peter Arnold, Inc.; **page 32:** © Peter Arnold/Peter Arnold, Inc.; **2.17a:** © Fred Bavendam/Peter Arnold, Inc.; **2.17b:** © Tom Branch/Photo Researchers, Inc.; **2.17c:** © Ken Lucas/Biological Photo Service; **2.17d:** © Norm Thomas/Photo Researchers, Inc.; **2.17e:** © Fred Bavendam/Peter Arnold, Inc.; **2.17f:** © Andrew Martinez/Photo Researchers, Inc.; **2.17j:** © S. Nagendra/Photo Researchers, Inc.

Chapter 3
3.1: © Carl Purcell/Photo Researchers, Inc.; **3.3a:** © Bruce Iverson; **3.3b:** © Raymond A. Mendez; **3.4a:** © William E. Ferguson; **3.4b:** © Don Riepe/Peter Arnold, Inc.; **3.4c:** © B. I. Ullmann/Taurus Photos; **3.5 (both):** Theodore Diener/USDA Plant Virology Laboratory; **3.9:** From Ruth Kavenoff, Lynn C. Klotz, and Bruno H. Zimm, Symposia on Quantitative Biology (Cold Spring Harbor) 38 (1973): 4; **3.15b:** © Hans Pfletschinger/Peter Arnold, Inc.; **3.21:** © William De Grado/Dupont; **3.22:** © Leonard Lessin/Peter Arnold, Inc.

Chapter 4
4.1a,b: © Manfred Kage/Peter Arnold, Inc.; **4.1c:** © Edwin A. Reschke/Peter Arnold, Inc.; **4.3a:** © William E. Ferguson; **4.3b:** © Mark Cochran; **4.4 (all):** © Dr. Tony Brain/David Parker/Science Photo Library/Photo Researchers, Inc.; **4.7b:** © Dr. S. Kim/Peter Arnold, Inc.; **4.9b:** © Barry King, University of California, Davis/Biological Photo Service; **page 84 (top):** © J. & R. Weber/Peter Arnold, Inc.; **(second to the bottom):** © Edwin A. Reschke/Peter Arnold, Inc.; **4.15a:** © OMIKRON/Science Source/Photo Researchers, Inc.; **4.15b:** Carolina Biological Supply Company; **4.15c:** © Chuck Brown/Photo Researchers, Inc.; **4.15d:** © J. & R. Weber/Peter Arnold, Inc.

Chapter 5
5.1: © Dr. Arnold Brody/Science Photo Library/Photo Researchers, Inc.; **5.2:** © Dr. A. Liepins/Science Photo Library/Photo Researchers, Inc.; **5.3 (both):**

© Edwin A. Reschke/Peter Arnold, Inc.; **5.5:** © D. W. Fawcett/Photo Researchers, Inc.; **page 97:** Lysosome Company; **5.9 (all):** © S. J. Singer; **5.16a:** Reproduced with the permission of the American Lung Association; **5.17:** © C. Edelmann/La Villette/Photo Researchers, Inc.

Chapter 6
6.5: © Pat and Tom Leeson/Photo Researchers, Inc.; **page 119:** © William Ruf Photography; **6.11:** © Biophoto Associates/Science Source/Photo Researchers, Inc.; **6.14:** Bettmann Newsphotos

Chapter 7
7.1b: © David M. Phillips/Taurus Photos; **7.1c:** © Junebug Clark/Photo Researchers, Inc.; **7.1d:** © Lee D. Simon/Photo Researchers, Inc.; **7.4 (all):** © Edwin A. Reschke; **7.5 (all):** © Bruce Iverson; **7.6:** Dr. Martin Carter/Rockefeller University; **7.10:** Courtesy of Dr. Robert Turgeon and Dr. B. Gillian Turgeon, Cornell University; **page 142 (left):** GE Corporate Research and Development; **(right):** Becton Dickinson Labware; **7.11:** Courtesy Dr. Garth L. Nicolson; **7.13:** © Cecil H. Fox/Science Source/Photo Researchers, Inc.

Chapter 8
Page 158 (left) a–f: Carolina Biological Supply Company; **(right):** © David Scharf/Peter Arnold, Inc.; **page 159:** E. L. Wollman, F. Jacob, and W. Hayes, Symposia on Quantitative Biology (Cold Spring Harbor), vol. 21, p. 153, 1956; **8.10:** © David M. Phillips/The Population Council/Taurus Photos

Chapter 9
9.1: Carolina Biological Supply Company; **9.2:** © David Scharf/Peter Arnold, Inc.; **9.5 (all):** © R. G. Edwards; **page 177 (top):** Furnished courtesy of C. L. Markert; **(bottom):** © A. Villeneuve and B. Meyer; **9.13e:** © Petit Format/Nestle/Science Source/Photo Researchers, Inc.; **9.17:** © Mike Greeler/The Image Works; **9.19a-e, g, h:** UPI/Bettmann Newsphotos; **9.19f, 9.20:** AP/Wide World Photos; **9.21:** © Dr. Dennis Dickson, Albert Einstein School of Medicine/Peter Arnold, Inc.

Chapter 10
10.1a: AP/Wide World Photos; **10.1b:** Courtesy Cornell University; **page 195:** Courtesy University of California, Davis; **10.2:** © Dr. Tony Brain/Science Photo Library/Photo Researchers, Inc.; **10.4a:** © Jim Sulley/The Image Works; **10.4b:** © Alan Carey/The Image Works; **10.6:** © Topham/The Image Works; **10.7b-d:** Dr. Ann Pytkowicz Streissguth, University of Washington: Science 209 (18 July 1980) 353–61 © 1980 by the AAAS

Chapter 11
11.1a: W. Dorsey Stuart, University of Hawaii; **11.1b:** Hans Stubbe, Akademie der Wessenchagten der DDR; **11.6:** Courtesy Dr. Myron Neuffer, University of Missouri; **11.7a:** Field Museum of Natural History, Negative number 118; **11.7b:** R. L. Brinster, Cover of Cell, vol. 27, Nov. 1981. Reprinted with permission of Cell Press; **11.11:** Carolina Biological Supply Company; **11.12 (all):** The Bettmann Archive; **11.14:** © Lester V. Bergman and Associates, Inc.; **page 228:** American Institute of Applied Science, Syracuse, New York; **page 228c (both):** © Bob Coyle; **page 228d (both):** © Tom Ballard/EKM-Nepenthe; **11.15a:** © Jim Goodwin/Photo Researchers, Inc.; **11.15b-d:** © Phil Randazzo and Rudi Turner; **11.17:** © David Scharf/Peter Arnold, Inc.; **11.18b:** Courtesy Nobel Foundation/1977 Science/97/943. Unconventional Virurses: The Orgins and Dosaperanes of Kurin by D. Carlton Gajdusck. © 1977 of the AAAS

Chapter 12
12.3b: Historical Pictures Service, Chicago; **12.4 (all):** S. D. Sigamony; **12.5a,b:** Wilson and Foster, Williams Textbook of Endocrinology, 7th ed. © W.B. Saunders 1985; **12.5c,d:** National Jewish Hospital and Research Center; **12.6a:** © Horst Schaefer/Peter Arnold, Inc.; **12.6b:** © William E. Ferguson; **page 244 (top):** © Lee D. Simon/Photo Researchers, Inc.; **(bottom):** © Eric V. Grave/Photo Researchers, Inc.; **page 245 (top left):** © James Richardson/Visuals Unlimited; **top right (both):** Gerald M. Rubin, Cover of Cell, vol. 40, April 1985.

Reprinted with permission of Cell Press; (bottom): Courtesy Dr. Ricki Lewis; 12.8a: © James H. Karales/Peter Arnold, Inc.; 12.8b: © Bob Daemmrich/The Image Works; 12.8c: © Patsy Davidson/ The Image Works

Chapter 13

13.1a: © Lee D. Simon/Science Source/ Photo Researchers, Inc.; 13.1b: © John Carld' Annibale; 13.1c: © Stuart Lindsay, Ph.D; page 255: The Bettmann Archive; 13.8a: John Cairns, Symposia on Quantitative Biology (Cold Spring Harbor), vol. 28, p. 44, 1963; 13.8b: David Hogness/Stanford University; 13.15: D. W. Ow, Keith V. Wood, Marlene De Luca, Jeffrey R. Dewet, Donald R. Helsinki, Stephen H. Howell, "Transient and Stable Expression of the Firefly Luciferase Gene in Plant Cells and Trasgenic Plants." Science 234 (Nov. 14, 1986): 856–859, fig. 1. Copyright © 1986 by the AAAS; 13.17a, 13.18: Dr. O. L. Miller; 13.22: © Dr. Paul Englund; 13.23: From Federoff, N. 1984. Transposable Genetic Elements in Maize, Scientific American, June 84/98. Photos by Fritz W. Goro; 13.25: © Science Photo Library/Science Source/Photo Researchers, Inc.

Chapter 14

14.1: © Laura Dwight/Peter Arnold, Inc; 14.2a,b,d: Courtesy Dr. Fred Elder, Department of Pediatrics, University of Texas; 14.2c: Courtesy Ann Cork and Dr. J. M. Trujillo, Cytogenetics Laboratory, M. D. Anderson Cancer Center; 14.6a (both), b: From the British Medical Journal, vol. 12, Dec. 1886, p. 1189; 14.7: © Dr. McKusick/John Hopkins Hospital; page 286: March of Dimes Birth Defects Foundation; page 287 (both): Woody Guthrie Publications, Inc.; 14.11 (both): © Bill Longcore/Photo Researchers, Inc.; 14.13a: Library of Congress

Chapter 15

15.3: Photograph by permission of Linda Larsen from Human Chromosome Analysis: Methodology and Applications. American Journal of Medical Technology, 10:687 (1983); 15.5: © Michael Bender; 15.6 (both): Courtesy of Jason C. Birnholz, M.D., Rush-Presbyterian St. Lukes Medical Center, Chicago; 15.12: © Dr. Nancy Wexler; page 306 (left): March of Dimes Birth Defects Foundation; (right): © Leonard Lessin/Peter Arnold, Inc.; 15.14a: © Dr. R. L. Brinster/Peter Arnold, Inc.; 15.14b: © Frank Constantini, Kiran Chada, Jeanne Magram

Chapter 16

16.1b: © SECCHI-LEAGUE/Roussel-UCLAF/CNRI/ Science Photo Library/ Photo Researchers, Inc.; 16.4b: Chikashi Toyoshima and Nigel Unwin; 16.6d, e: National Multiple Sclerosis Society; 16.8: © CNRI/ Science Photo Researchers, Inc.; 16.10: © Paul Chesley/ Photographer's Aspen

Chapter 17

Page 340: Mallenckrodt Institute of Radiology © 1989 Discover Publications; 17.11a: © Chesher/ Photo Researchers, Inc.; 17.11b: © Dr. Jon W. Jacklet, Professor and Chairman Department of Biology, SUNY, Albany

Chapter 18

18.1 (both): © Thomas Eisner; 18.3b: © Omekron/ Science Source/ Photo Researchers, Inc.; 18.5: © Thomas Eisner; 18.8a: © Frank S. Werblin; page 355 (left): © Peter A Rora/ National Oceanic and Atmosphere Administration/ Woods Hole: Oceanographic Institute/ MIT, (right): © Steve Chamberlain, Syracuse University; 18.12: © Martin Dohrn/ Science Library/ Photo Researchers, Inc.; 18.15 (both), 18.18 (both): © Molly Webster © 1982 Discover Publications

Chapter 19

19.1: © Phillip A. Harrington/ Peter Arnold, Inc.; 19.9: Weidenfeld and Nicolson Ltd., Dept. of Medical Photography Westminister Hospital; 19.10 (all): Dept. of Illustrations, Washington University School of Medicine 20 (Jan. 1956) p. 133; 19.12 (all): Joseph Bagnara, Chromatophores and Color Change, J. T. Bagnara and M. E. Hadley, Prentice Hall, 1973; 19.14b: © Lester V. Bergman & Associates; 19.16: F. A. Davis Company, Philadelphia; and R. H. Kampmeier; 19.17b: © Edwin A. Reschke; page 380: © Martin Dohrn/ Photo Researchers, Inc.; page 382: © Tom McHugh/ Photo Researchers, Inc.; page 383: © G. Gransanti/ Sygma; 19.21a: © John Bova/ Photo Researchers, Inc.; 19.21b: © Dwight Kuhn; 19.21c: © Thomas Eisner

Chapter 20

20.1: © Bill Bachman/ Photo Researchers, Inc.; 20.3: © Bryan Hitchcock/ Photo Researchers, Inc.; page 392: © Gerald Lacz/ NNPA; 20.7: © Biophoto Associates/ Photo Researchers, Inc.; page 396: © Science Source Library/ Photo Researchers, Inc.; 20.10: © World Health Organization; 20.12: © Ken Rucas/ Biological Photo Services; 20.13: © Edward Lettau/ Peter Arnold, Inc.; 20.17: © Alexander Tsiaras/ Science Source/ Photo Researchers, Inc.

Chapter 21

21.1 (all): © Manfred Kage/ Peter Arnold, Inc.; 21.5 (both): © K. G. Murti/ Visuals Unlimited; 21.6 (both): © Toni Michaels; 21.12: © G. W. Willis, Ochsner Institution/ Biological Photo Service; 21.16b: © Biophoto Associates/ Photo Researchers, Inc.

Chapter 22

Page 423 (top): © Dr. Leland Clark, (bottom): Organogenesis Inc.; 22.8c: © Eila Kairinen/ Gilette Research Institute, Gaithersburg, MD; 22.9a: © The Royal College of Surgeons of England; 22.11: © Biophoto Associates/ Photo Researchers, Inc.; 22.15b: © SIU Biomedical Communications/ Photo Researchers, Inc.; 22.17a: Courtesy of Igaku Shoin, LTD; 22.23: E. K. Markell and M. Voge: Medical Parasitology, 6th ed. © W.B. Saunders Company, 1986; 22.24: © Dr. Carole Berger/ Peter Arnold, Inc.; page 437: © Science Photo Library/ Photo Researchers, Inc.

Chapter 23

23.1: © Douglas M. Munnecke/ Biological Photo Service; 23.2a: © Andrew J. Martinez/ Photo Researchers, Inc.; 23.2b: © R. Andrew Odum/ Peter Arnold, Inc.; 23.2c: © Tom McHugh/ Photo Researchers, Inc.; © Hans Pfletschinger/ Peter Arnold, Inc.; 23.2e: © Fritz Pokling GDT/ Peter Arnold, Inc.; 23.4: © F. Gohier/ Photo Researchers, Inc.; 23.8: © John Watney Photo Library; 23.10b: from TISSUES AND ORGANS: A TEXT-ATLAS OF SCANNING ELECTRON MICROSCOPY by R. G. Kessel and R. H. Kardon, © 1979 W.H. Freeman; page 454 (both): American Cancer Society; 23.12e, f: J. H. Comroe: PHYSIOLOGY OF RESPIRATION © 1974 Yearbook Medical Publishers, Inc.; 23.15: © Weinstein/ Custom Medical Stock Photo; 23.17 (both): © Martin Rocker/ Peter Arnold, Inc.; 23.18: The Bettmann Archive

Chapter 24

24.2a: © Jeff Lepore/ Photo Researchers, Inc.; 24.2b: © John R. MacGregor/ Peter Arnold, Inc.; page 466 (top): © Arthus Bertrand/ Photo Researchers, Inc., (bottom): © Tom McHugh/ Photo Researchers, Inc.; 24.5b, 24.7b: Courtesy of Utah Valley Hospital, Department of Radiology; 24.10: The Bettmann Archive; 24.11: © Martin M. Rocker/ Taurus Photos; 24.16a: © David Scharf/ Peter Arnold, Inc.; 24.16b: D. H. Alpers and B. Seetharan, New England Journal of Medicine 296 (1977) 1047; page 476 (left): © Susan Leavires/ Photo Researchers, Inc., (right): © Dr. Leonard Crowley/ INTRODUCTION TO HUMAN DISEASE, 2nd edition, fig. 23.22, p. 615 Jones and Bartlett, 1988; 24.21a: © Carroll Weiss/ RBP; 24.21b: © Sherril D. Burton; page 479: © Kenneth Murray/ Photo Researchers, Inc.

Chapter 25

25.5 (both): © G.W. Willis, Ochsner Medical Institution/ BPS; 25.6b: UNICEF; 25.7: © National Medical Slide Bank/ Custom Medical Stock Photo

Chapter 26

Page 498: © Fred Bavendam/ Peter Arnold, Inc.; 26.2: © Scott Camazine/ Photo Researchers, Inc.; 26.3: © Dr. R. P. Clark and M. Goff/ Photo Researchers, Inc.; 26.4: © Demi McIntyre/ Photo Researchers, Inc.; 26.9b, 26.11: © Biophoto Associates/ Science Source/ Photo Researchers, Inc.; 26.14: © J. & L. Weber/ Peter Arnold, Inc.

Chapter 27

27.2b: © NIBSC/ Science Photo Library/ Photo Researchers, Inc.; 27.3: © Manfred Kage/ Peter Arnold, Inc.; 27.9: Courtesy of Schering-Plough; 27.11: Courtesy of Blackwell Scientific, Reprinted from ESSENTIAL IMMUNOLOGY by Ivan Roitt, Fig. 8/7 P. 130; 27.12: © Zeva Oelbaum/ Peter Arnold, Inc.; 27.13a: © Professor Luc Montagnier/ Institute Pasteur/ CNRI/ Science Photo/ Photo Researchers, Inc.; 27.14: © Sygma; 27.15b: © Lennart Nilsson/ Boehringer Ingelhaim International Gmbh; 27.16a: © David Scharf/ Peter Arnold, Inc.; 27.16b: © Phil Harrington/ Peter Arnold, Inc.; page 530: Courtesy, National Library of Medicine; 27.17: © English, MD/ Custom Medical Stock Photo; 27.18: © Phillip Harrington/ Schering-Plough Corporation

Chapter 28

28.1a: © Scott Canazine/ Photo Researchers, Inc.; 28.1b: © W. H. Hodge/ Peter Arnold, Inc.; 28.2a: © Noron Thomas/ Photo Researchers, Inc.; 28.2b: © W. H. Hodge/ Peter Arnold, Inc.; 28.3a: © Charlie Oto/ Photo Researchers, Inc.; 28.3b: © Toni Michaels; 28.6: © Walter H. Hodge/ Peter Arnold, Inc.; 28.9: © Kellogg's and Kellogg's Corn Flakes Cereal are registered Trademarks of Kellogg Company. All rights reserved; 28.10: © W. H. Hodge/ Peter Arnold, Inc.; 28.11: © Douglas Kirkland/ Sygma; 28.12: © B & H Kunz/ Okapia/ Photo Reseachers, Inc.; 28.13 1,2: © Steven R. King/ Peter Arnold, Inc.; 28.14: © Gilbert Grant/ Photo Researchers, Inc.; 28.15a: © J. & L. Weber/ Peter Arnold, Inc.; 28.15b: U.S. Aid Photo; 28.15c: Courtesy of Dr. Daniel L. Klayman/ Science, Fig. 1, Vol. 228, Page 1051, 31 May 1985, "Quinghausu (artemyinin): Am Antimalarial Drug From China." © 1985 by the AAAS

Chapter 29

29.2: © D. E. Akin/ Visuals Unlimited; 29.3: © David M. Phillips/ Visuals Unlimited; 29.6 1,2: © P. Gates, University of Durham/ Biological Photo Service; 29.8: © Kjeil B. Sandved & Coleman; 29.11: © Michael Ederegger/ Peter Arnold, Inc.; 29.15: © P. Dayanander/ Photo Researchers, Inc.; 29.16a: © A. W. Ambler/ Photo Researchers, Inc.; 29.16b: © W. H. Hodge/ Peter Arnold, Inc.; 29.16c: © Walter Hodge/ Peter Arnold, Inc.

Chapter 30

30.1: © J. Alcock/ Visuals Unlimted; 30.2: William E. Ferguson; 30.3b: © Walter H. Hodge/ Peter Arnold, Inc.; 30.6a: © William E. Ferguson; 30.6b: © Francois Gohier/ Photo Researchers, Inc.; 30.7: © Thomas Eisner; 30.9a: © R. J. Erwin/ Photo Researchers Inc.; 30.9b: © Toni Michaels; 30.9c: © James Welgos/ Photo Researchers, Inc.; 30.10a: © W. H. Hodge/ Peter Arnold, Inc.; 30.10b: © Rod Planck/ Photo Researchers, Inc.; 30.10c: © William E. Ferguson; 30.10d: © Adam Hart-Davis/ Science Photo Library/ Photo Researchers, Inc.; 30.10e: ARS/USDA; 30.12b: © Dr. Jeremy Burgess/ Science Photo Library/ Photo Researchers, Inc.; 30.13a: © Runk/ Schoenberger/ Grant Heilman; 30.13b: © W. H. Hodge/ Peter Arnold, Inc.; 30.13c: © Runk/ Schoenberger/ Grant Heilman

Chapter 31

31.1: © David Whitcomb; 31.3: © David Newman/ Visuals Unlimited; 31.4: © R. Lyons/ Visuals Unlimited; 31.5: © Walter H. Hodge/ Peter Arnold, Inc.; 31.6: © Runk/ Schoenberger/ Grant Heilman; page 593 (both): © Dr. Randy Moore; 31.7: © John D. Cunningham/ Visuals Unlimited; 31.8: © William E. Ferguson; 31.9: © Adrian Davies/ Bruce Coleman, Inc.; 31.10: © Tom McHugh/ Photo Researchers, Inc.; 31.13: © Stephanie Ferguson/ William Ferguson; 31.14: © Runk/ Schoenberger/ Grant Heilman; 31.15: © Galen Rowell/ Peter Arnold, Inc.

Chapter 32

32.1: © Wilfred G. Oltis/ William E. Ferguson Photography; **32.2:** © Elliot Meyerowitz; **32.3:** © Dr. Jeremy Burgess/ Science Photo Library/ Photo Researchers, Inc.; **32.5a (all):** © Christian T. Harms; **32.7:** Courtesy, Calgene/ SCIENCE AND THE FUTURE YEARBOOK, 1986, p. 105 Encyclopedia Britannica; **32.8a, b, c, d:** © Runk/ Schoenberger/ Grant Heilman; **32.9a:** © Ted Spiegel/ Black Star; **32.9b:** DNA Plant Technology; **32.10 (both):** © Dan McCoy/ Rainbow; **32.11:** © Curt Maas/ Pioneer Hi-Bred International; **32.15:** Courtesy, Calgene; **32.16 (all):** © Dr. Paul Christou; **32.17:** Courtesy, Monsanto; **32.17b:** Courtesy, Calgene/ SCIENCE AND THE FUTURE YEARBOOK, 1986, p. 114 Encyclopedia Britannica; **page 615 (top):** Courtesy, DNA Plant Technology, **(bottom):** © Mike Greenlar/ The Image Works

Chapter 33

33.2: © William E. Ferguson; **33.3:** © Trans Lanting/ Photo Researchers, Inc.; **33.4:** © William E. Ferguson; **33.6a1:** © Lynn Rogers; **33.6a2:** © Michael Viard/ Peter Arnold, Inc.; **33.6b1:** © Ralph Eagle/ Science Source/ Photo Researchers, Inc.; **33.6b2:** © Jeff Rotman/ Peter Arnold, Inc.; **33.8:** © S. J. Krasemann/ Peter Arnold, Inc.; **33.9a:** © Tom McHugh/ Photo Researchers, Inc.; **33.9b:** © Tom McHugh/ Rapho/ Photo Researchers, Inc.; **33.9c:** © Robert and Linda Mitchell; **33.9d:** Field Museum of Natural History, Chicago, IL, Negative Number CKIT

Chapter 34

34.1: © Sandy Macys/ Gamma Liaison; **34.7:** © William E. Ferguson; **34.8:** © Porterfield/ Chickering/ Photo Researchers, Inc.; **page 639:** © Ray Pfortner/ Peter Arnold, Inc.; **34.9b:** Courtesy, W. Atlee Burpee and Company; **34.9d:** © Michael Viard/ Peter Arnold, Inc.; **34.10a:** © Jonathan Blair/ Woodfin Camp and Associates; **34.10b:** © Glenn Izett/ United States Dept. of Interior, Geological Survey; **34.12:** © Jonathan Blair/ Woodfin Camp & Associates; **page 644 (top right):** © Leonard Lee Rue III/ Animals Animals, **(bottom right):** © Barb Zurawski; **34.13:** © William E. Ferguson

Chapter 35

35.1a: © Jonathan Blair/ Woodfin Camp and Associates; **35.1b:** © Albert Copley/ Visuals Unlimited; **35.2a:** Courtesy Department Library Services/ American Museum of Natural History, Neg. No. 320496; **35.2b:** © George O. Poinar, Jr.; **35.6:** Zoological Society of London; **35.7a1:** © Ellan Young/ Photo Researchers, Inc.; **35.7a2:** © Lynn Rogers; **35.7a3:** © Steve Kaufman/ Peter Arnold, Inc.; **35.7a4:** © Tom McHugh/ Photo Researchers, Inc.; **35.11, 35.12a:** © William E. Ferguson; **35.15a:** Field Museum of Natural History; **35.15b:** © Martin Land/ Science Photo Library/ Photo Researchers, Inc.; **35.19a:** © Cabisco/ Visuals Unlimited; **35.19b:** © John Reader/ Science Photo Library/ Photo Researchers, Inc.

Chapter 36

36.1: J. A. L. Cooke; **page 668:** © Laura Riley; **36.3a:** © Doug Vargas/ The Image Works; **36.4:** © Roger Wilmshurst/ Bruce Coleman; **36.7:** © Marty Snyderman/ Visuals Unlimited; **36.9:** Nina Leen/ LIFE Magazine; **36.10:** Courtesy, Dr. Martin Ralph/ "CLOCKWORK IN THE BRAIN," Dr. Martin Ralph, BIO-SCIENCE, Vol. 39, No. 2, p. 76; **36.11:** © Gary Meszaros; **36.13a:** © Charles Walcott; **36.14:** © Lynn Rogers; **page 675a:** © Laura Dwight/ Peter Arnold, Inc.; **page 675b:** © Bill Bachman/ Photo Researchers, Inc.; **page 675c:** © Laura Dwight/ Peter Arnold, Inc.; **page 675d:** © Bob Busby/ Photo Researchers, Inc.

Chapter 37

37.1: © Runk/ Schoenberger/ Grant Heilman; **37.2:** © Stephan Dalton/ Photo Researchers, Inc.; **page 685 (bottom):** © Raymond A. Mendez; **37.3:** © Louis Quitt/ M.A.S./ Photo Researchers, Inc.; **37.4:** © Horst Schafer/ Peter Arnold, Inc.; **37.5:** © Laura Riley/ Bruce Coleman, Inc.; **37.6:** © Oxford Scientific 2 films/ Animals Animals; **37.7:** © J. P. Thomas/ Jacana/ Photo Researchers, Inc.; **37.8:** © 1990 Scott Canazine; **page 691 37.9a, b:** © Charles H. Janson; **page 691 (top):** © M. Marchaterre/ Cornell University; **37.11:** © Jonathan Scott/ Planet Earth Pictures; **37.12:** © Charles H. Jason/ NATURAL HISTORY, February, 1986, p. 444; **37.14:** © Professor Axel Michelsan; **37.15:** © G. Ziesler/ Peter Arnold, Inc.; **37.16:** © John Alcock; **37.17:** © V. Arthus-Bertrand/ Peter Arnold, Inc.; **37.18:** © Bildorchiv Okapia/ Photo Researchers, Inc.

Chapter 38

38.1: © Bob Thomas/ Gamma Liaison; **page 702 (left):** © C. Gable Ray; **page 702 (right):** Montana Department of Fish, Wildlife and Parks; **38.8a:** © Stephen J. Krasemann/ Peter Arnold, Inc.; **38.8b:** © Jonathan Scott/ Planet Earth Pictures; **38.10:** © Gregory G. Dimijian, M.D./ Photo Researchers, Inc.; **page 711:** © Alan Reininger/ Contact Press Images

Chapter 39

39.2a-f: Courtesy, Dr. Stuart Fisher, Department of Zoology, Arizona State University; **39.3a:** © Fritz Polking/ Peter Arnold, Inc.; **39.4:** © Charlie Ott/ Photo Researchers, Inc.; **39.6b:** © Steven C. Amstrup/ U.S. Fish and Wildlife; **page 727:** © Ken Spencer; **39.14a:** © Gordon Wiltsie/ Peter Arnold, Inc.; **39.14b:** © Jim Zippo/ Photo Researchers, Inc.; **39.14c:** © Luiz C. Marigo/ Peter Arnold, Inc.; **39.14d:** © L. West/ Photo Researchers, Inc.; **39.14e:** © Gregory G. Dimijian, M.D./ Photo Researchers, Inc.; **39.14f:** © Toni Michaels; **39.14g:** © John Bova/ Photo Researchers, Inc.; **39.14h:** © Stephen J. Krasemann/ Peter Arnold, Inc.; **page 732 (both):** © Space Biospheres Ventures; **39.16:** © G. Ziesler/ Peter Arnold, Inc.; **39.17a:** © David Hall/ Photo Researchers, Inc.; **39.17b:** © Peter Parks/ Oxford Scientific Films/ Animals Animals

Chapter 40

40.1a, b: © Al Grillo/ Picture Group; **40.2:** © TASS/ Sovofoto; **40.3:** © Ray Pfortner/ Peter Arnold, Inc.; **page 746:** © C. C. Lockwood/ Animals, Animals; **40.4:** © Joel Simon/ Society Expeditions; **40.5a:** © Ray Pfortner/ Peter Arnold, Inc.; **40.7:** © Michael Nichols/ Magnum Photos; **40.9a:** © George H. Harrison/ Grant Heilman; **40.9b:** © Imre De Pozsgay/ Alpine Color Lab; **40.11:** © George Antonelis, National Marine Fisheries Service

Appendix

Page A.2 (top): © Leonard Lessin/Peter Arnold, Inc.; **page A.6 (left):** USDA/ Science Source/Photo Researchers, Inc., **(right):** © William E. Ferguson; **page A.7 (left):** © Michel Viard/ Peter Arnold, Inc., **(middle):** © Martin Land/Science Library/ Photo Researchers, Inc., **(right):** © Tom Branch/Photo Researchers, Inc., **page A.8 (left):** © Fred Bavendam/Peter Arnold, Inc., **(middle):** © Andrew Martinez/Photo Researchers, Inc., **(right):** © Carl Purcell/ Photo Researchers, Inc.

Text/Line Art

Chapter 2

2.10c: From Eldon D. Enger, et al., *Concepts in Biology,* 5th ed. Copyright © 1988 Wm. C. Brown Publishers, Dubuque, Iowa. All Rights Reserved. Reprinted by permission.

Chapter 3

3.26: From E. Peter Volpe, *Understanding Evolution,* 5th ed. Copyright © 1985 Wm. C. Brown Publishers, Dubuque, Iowa. All Rights Reserved. Reprinted by permission.

Chapter 4

4.5: From Boston Medical Library in The Francis A. Countway Library of Medicine. Used with permission. **4.7:** Frederick C. Ross, *Introductory Microbiology,* 2nd ed. Reprinted by permission of the author.

Chapter 5

5.13, 5.14: From Bruce Alberts, et al., *Molecular Biology of the Cell.* Copyright © 1983 Garland Publishing, Inc., New York, NY. Reprinted with permission.

Chapter 7

7.2: From Stuart Ira Fox, *Human Physiology,* 3d ed. Copyright © 1990 Wm. C. Brown Publishers, Dubuque, Iowa. All Rights Reserved. Reprinted by permission. **7.7:** From Bruce Alberts, et al., *Molecular Biology of the Cell.* Copyright © 1983 Garland Publishing, Inc., New York, NY. Reprinted with permission. **7.12a-e:** Reprinted with permission from *Chem. Eng. News,* February 25, 1985, 63(8), p. 16. Copyright © 1985 American Chemical Society.

Chapter 8

8.8: From Linda R. Maxson and Charles H. Daugherty, *Genetics: A Human Perspective,* 2d ed. Copyright © 1989 Wm. C. Brown Publishers, Dubuque, Iowa. All Rights Reserved. Reprinted by permission.

Chapter 9

Page 178, fig. 3: Gilbert, *Developmental Biology,* Second Edition, 1988. Reprinted by permission of Sinauer Associates, Inc., Sunderland, MA. **9.4, 9.9 (text):** From Kent M. Van De Graaff, *Human Anatomy,* 2d ed. Copyright © 1988 Wm. C. Brown Publishers, Dubuque, Iowa. All Rights Reserved. Reprinted by permission. **9.9 (line art):** From Kent M. Van De Graaff and Stuart Ira Fox, *Concepts in Human Anatomy and Physiology,* 2d ed. Copyright © 1989 Wm. C. Brown Publishers, Dubuque, Iowa. All Rights Reserved. Reprinted by permission. **9.16:** From K. L. Moore, *Before We Are Born: Basic Embryology and Birth Defects,* 3d ed. Copyright © 1989 W.B. Saunders Company, Philadelphia, PA. Reprinted by permission of the publisher and author.

Chapter 10

10.8: Reprinted with permission of Macmillan Publishing Company from *July 20, 2019; Life in the 21st Century* by Arthur C. Clarke. Copyright © 1986 by Serendib, B. V. and OMNI Publications International, Ltd; and From *July 20, 2019: A Day in the Life of the Future,* edited by Arthur C. Clarke. Reprinted by permission of the author and the author's agents, Scott Meredith Literary Agency, Inc., 845 Third Avenue, New York, New York 10022.

Chapter 11

11.2: From E. Peter Volpe, *Biology and Human Concerns,* 3d ed. Copyright © 1983 Wm. C. Brown Publishers, Dubuque, Iowa. All Rights Reserved. Reprinted by permission. **11.4, 11.9:** Reproduced with permission from Nagle, James J.: *Heredity and human affairs,* ed. 3, St. Louis, 1984, Times Mirror/Mosby College Publishing.

Chapter 12

12.5b: From Linda R. Maxson and Charles H. Daugherty, *Genetics: A Human Perspective,* 2d ed. Copyright © 1989 Wm. C. Brown Publishers, Dubuque, Iowa. All Rights Reserved. Reprinted by permission.

Chapter 13

13.7, 13.8a: From *Genetics,* 2/e by Peter J. Russell. Copyright © 1990 by Peter J. Russell. Reprinted by permission of HarperCollins Publishers. **13.8b:** David Hogness, Department of Biochemistry, Stanford University School of Medicine, Stanford, California as in *Proceedings of the National Academy of Sciences,* U.S., Vol. 71 (1974), p. 135. **13.12:** From A. L. Lehninger, *Principles of Biochemistry,* Worth Publishers, New York, 1982. Reprinted by permission.

Chapter 14

14.4b: From *Human Genetics: An Introduction to the Principles of Heredity* 2/E. By Sam Singer. Copyright © 1978, 1985 by W.H. Freeman and Company. Reprinted by permission. **14.5:** From *Human Genetics* by Elof Carlson. Copyright © 1984 by D.C. Heath and Company. Reprinted by permission of the publisher. **14.9:** From Stuart Ira Fox, *Human Physiology,* 3d ed. Copyright © 1990 Wm. C. Brown Publishers, Dubuque, Iowa. All Rights Reserved. Reprinted by permission. **14.10:** Reprinted by permission of Macmillan Publishing Company from *Genetics* by Monroe W. Strickberger. Copyright © 1985, Monroe W. Strickberger. **14.13b:** Source: Terman and Merrill, *Measuring Intelligence.* Copyright © 1937 Houghton Mifflin Company, Boston, MA. **Table 14.2:** From Heredity, Evolution, and Society 2/E. By I. Michael Lerner and William J. Libby. Copyright © 1968, 1976 by W.H. Freeman and Company. Reprinted with permission.

Chapter 15
15.11: Source: Bob Conrad, *Newsweek,* March 5, 1984.

Chapter 17
17.8: From T. L. Peele, *Neuroanatomical Basis for Clinical Neurology,* 2d ed. Copyright © 1961 McGraw-Hill Book Company, New York, NY.

Chapter 22
22.15a: From Wallace, King, and Sanders, *Biosphere, 2d ed.* Copyright © 1986 Scott, Foresman and Company, Glenview, IL.

Chapter 23
23.2 (line art): From Wallace, King, and Sanders, *Biosphere, 2d ed.* Copyright © 1986 Scott, Foresman and Company, Glenview, IL.

Chapter 24
24.13: "Reprinted by permission from page 101 of *Understanding Nutrition,* Fourth Edition by Whitney and Hamilton. Copyright © 1987 by West Publishing Company. All rights reserved."

Chapter 25
25.2: From Y. H. Hui, *Principles and Issues in Nutrition.* Copyright © Wadsworth Publishing Company, Belmont, CA; **25.9:** From *Journal of the American Dietetic Association,* American Dietetic Association, Chicago, IL.

Chapter 27
27.6: From Linda R. Maxson and Charles H. Daugherty, *Genetics: A Human Perspective,* 2d ed. Copyright © 1989 Wm. C. Brown Publishers, Dubuque, Iowa. All Rights Reserved. Reprinted by permission; **27.8:** From Bruce Alberts, et al., *Molecular Biology of the Cell.* Copyright © 1983 Garland Publishing Company, New York, NY. Reprinted by permission.

Chapter 30
30.11a: From Street and Opik, *The Physiology of Flowering Plants.* Copyright © 1976 Elsevier Science Publishing Co., Inc., New York, NY; **30.11b:** From Devlin and Witham, *Plant Physiology,* 4th ed. Copyright c PWS-Kent Publishing Company, Boston, MA.

Chapter 31
31.12: From Raven, *Biology of Plants.* Copyright © Worth Publishing, New York, NY.

Chapter 35
35.13: As appeared in *Science News,* January 9, 1988, page 21.

Chapter 36
36.6: From Krebs and Davies, *An Introduction to Behavioural Ecology,* 2d ed. Copyright © 1987 Blackwell Scientific Publications, Ltd., Oxford, England.

Chapter 37
37.13a: Reproduced with permission from Goodenough, Judith, *Animal Communication;* Carolina Biology Reader Series, No. 143. Copyright © 1984, Carolina Biology Supply Co., Burlington, North Carolina, U.S.A. **37.13b:** From Keeton and Gould, *Biological Science,* 4th ed. Copyright © W. W. Norton & Co., Inc., New York, NY.

Chapter 38
38.2 (top): "Reprinted with permission from *The New England Journal of Medicine,* vol. 1321, page 1581"; **38.3:** From Arthur Boughey, *Ecology of Populations,* 2d ed. Copyright © 1973 Macmillan Publishing Company, New York, NY; **38.4:** From Barbara Boyle Torrey and W. Ward Kingkade, "Population Dynamics of the United States and the Soviet Union" in *Science,* page 1551, March 30, 1990. Copyright © 1990 by the American Association for the Advancement of Science, Washington, DC. Reprinted by permission of the publisher and authors; **38.5:** Population Reference Bureau, *1989 World Population Data Sheet* (Washington, D.C.: Population Reference Bureau, Inc., 1989). **38.9:** Adapted from *Natural History Magazine,* July 1989. Used with permission.

Chapter 39
39.6a: From "Stable Carbon Isotopes in the Study of Food Chains," by Stephen Hart, *Biology Digest,* February 1990. Used with permission; **39.8:** From Eldon D. Enger, et al., *Environmental Science,* 3d ed.

Copyright © 1989 Wm. C. Brown Publishers, Dubuque, Iowa. All Rights Reserved. Reprinted by permission; **39.12a, b:** From Eldon D. Enger, et al., *Concepts in Biology,* 6th ed. Copyright © 1991 Wm. C. Brown Publishers, Dubuque, Iowa. All Rights Reserved. Reprinted by permission; **39.13** and **39.14 (line art):** From McLaren, et al., *Health Biology.* Copyright © 1991 D. C. Heath and Company, Lexington, MA.

Illustrators
John Hagen: 4.13, 8.1, 8.2, 9.9 (after Diane Nelson), 9.13, 9.16, 9.18, 10.7a, 12.2, 15.7, Reading 11.1, figures 1, 2a,b, 34.3
Beck Visual Communication: 2.5, 2.11a, 2.12, 2.13, 2.18, 3.2, 3.25, 4.7a, 4.9a, 4.10, 4.11, 4.14, 4.16, 4.17, 5.10, 5.11, 5.15, 5.16b, 6.4, 6.8, 6.15, 6.21, 7.1a, 7.7, 7.9, 7.12, 9.2, 9.3, 9.4, 9.6, 9.7, 9.8, 9.10, 9.11, 9.12, 9.14, 9.15, 10.3, 10.10, 11.2, 11.3, 11.8, 11.13, 12.7, 15.8, 18.2, 18.3, 18.4, 18.6, 18.7, 18.8b, 18.11, 18.13, 18.14, 18.16, 18.19, 18.20, 18.21, 19.2, 19.3, 19.7, 19.8, 19.11, 19.13, 19.15, 19.17, 19.19, 19.20, 20.2, 20.4, 20.5, 20.6, 20.8, 20.9, 20.11, 20.14, 20.15, 20.16, 22.1, 22.5, 22.6, 22.7, 22.9b, c, 22.10, 22.12, 22.13, 22.14, 22.16, 22.17, 22.19, 22.20, 22.21, 22.22, 23.3, 23.5, 23.6. 23.7, 23.9, 23.10a, 23.12, 23.13, 23.14
Reading 4.1, figure 1
Reading 4.2, figure 1
Reading 9.2, figures 2, 3, 4
Reading 13.3, figure 1
Reading 20.3, figure 1
Reading 22.2, figure 1a-d
Reading 23.1, figure 1
Table 4.4
Table 10.4
Illustrious, Inc.: 1.1a, 1.3, 2.7, 3.7, 3.8, 3.10, 3.11, 3.12, 3.13, 3.14, 3.15, 3.16, 3.17, 3.18, 3.19, 3.20, 3.26, 4.6, 4.8, 5.4, 5.6, 5.7, 5.8, 5.12, 5.13, 5.14, 6.1, 6.2, 6.3, 6.6, 6.7, 6.9, 6.10, 6.12, 6.13, 6.16, 6.17, 6.18, 6.19, 6.20, 6.22, 7.2, 7.3, 7.4, 7.8, 7.14, 7.15, 8.3, 8.4, 8.5, 8.6, 8.7, 8.8, 8.9, 8.11, 9.19, 9.22, 10.5, 10.9, 11.4, 11.5, 11.9, 11.10, 11.16, 11.18a, 12.1, 12.3,

12.5, 13.2, 13.3, 13.4, 13.5, 13.6, 13.7, 13.9, 13.10, 13.11, 13.12, 13.14, 13.16, 13.17, 13.19, 13.20, 13.21, 13.24, 13.26, 14.2e, f, 14.3, 14.4, 14.5, 14.8, 14.9, 14.10, 14.12, 14.13, 15.1, 15.2, 15.9, 15.10, 15.11, 15.13, 16.3, 16.4a, 16.5, 16.7, 16.9, 17.12, 18.9, 18.10, 18.17, 19.4, 19.5, 19.6, 19.18, 21.4, 21.5, 21.8, 21.9, 21.11, 22.2, 22.3, 22.8a, b, 22.15a, 23.2, 23.11, 23.16, 24.1, 24.9, 24.13, 24.14, 24.19, 25.2, 25.3, 25.4, 25.9, 25.10, 25.11, 26.5, 26.7, 26.10, 26.13, 27.2a, 27.6, 27.7, 27.8, 28.2c, 28.4, 28.5, 28.7, 28.8, 30.11, 31.2, 31.11, 31.12, 33.4a, 33.5, 34.2, 34.4, 34.5, 34.6, 35.3, 35.7, 35.8, 35.9, 35.10, 35.17, 36.6a, 36.8, 36.12, 36.13b, 37.13, 38.2, 38.3, 38.4, 38.5, 38.6, 38.9, 39.5, 39.6a, 39.7, 39.11, 39.12, 39.13, 39.14, 40.8, 40.10
Reading 3.2, figure 1
Reading 17.2, figure 1
Reading 29.1, figure 1
Reading 36.3, figure 1
Reading 39.1, figure 1
Text art page 275
Todd Buck: 16.1, 16.2, 16.6, 16.8, 17.1, 17.2, 17.3, 17.4, 17.5, 17.6, 17.7, 17.8, 17.9, 17.10, 17.13
Carlyn Iverson: 17.14, 21.2, 21.3, 21.7, 21.10, 21.13, 21.14, 21.15, 21.16, 22.18, 25.1, 25.6a, 25.8, 29.1, 29.4, 29.5, 29.7, 29.9, 29.10, 29.12, 29.13, 29.14, 29.17, 30.2, 30.3, 30.4, 30.5, 30.8, 30.12a, 32.4, 32.6, 32.12, 32.13, 32.14, 40.5, 40.6
Reading 17.1, figure 1
Reading 21.1, figure 1
Reading 40.2, figure 1
Medical Art Services, Inc.: 24.3, 24.4, 24.5b, 24.6, 24.7a, 24.8, 24.12, 24.15, 24.17, 24.18, 24.20, 27.1, 27.4, 27.5, 27.10, 27.13b, 27.15, 27.18a
Reading 24.1, figure 2
Reading 35.1, figure 1
Molly Babich: 26.8, 26.9, 26.12, 35.4, 35.5, 35.12b
Phil Sims: 34.11, 35.14, 35.16, 35.18
Reading 35.2, figure 1
Laurie O'Keefe: 26.1, 33.1, 33.6c, 33.7, 36.2, 36.5, 37.10, 38.7, 39.1, 39.8, 39.9, 39.10, 39.15, 39.18
Reading 34.3, figure 1

Index